THE SUN AND THE SHADOW:

MY EXPERIMENT WITH LUCID DREAMING

KENNETH KELZER, M.S.W.

A.R.E.® PRESS • VIRGINIA BEACH • VIRGINIA

This book is dedicated to

> George Washington
> Thomas Jefferson
> John Adams
> John Jay
> Benjamin Franklin

... and to all the other founders of this great nation, who labored, some in relative obscurity, to establish a land where freedom of the spirit is truly possible.

... This book is dedicated to them all, as people of vision, and to all the visionaries yet to come ...

ISBN 87604-195-0

Printed in the U.S.A.

TABLE OF CONTENTS

Ackowledgments

The author gratefully wishes to acknowledge the contributions, support, and professional assistance of many people who have helped to make this book possible. To my colleagues, Frances Vaughan and Richard Gorringe, I am grateful for many hours of listening and responding to each other's dreams and for a great deal of clarity and insight about the inner life of the psyche. To Patricia Garfield I am grateful for personal communications on the subject of lucid dreaming and for her willingness to compare experiences as we explored this inner territory, ever new and ever fresh to both of us. To Nettie Hammond I feel extremely grateful for her capable and conscientious support as an author's assistant, for her many hours of labor at the word processor and for her faithful devotion to details, library research, bibliography, and the hundreds of items that can sometimes make or break a book. She has been what I suspect every author would wish for: a superb technician with a soul for the big picture. I also wish to acknowledge Polly Kettenhofen, a dear friend, for her generosity in making available her beach house as a writer's retreat, a special haven where many ideas for this book made their first appearance on paper. To Mark Thurston, editor of A.R.E. Press, I am grateful for a wonderful spirit of cooperation and many exciting interchanges as the book began to take its final form. To Scott Sparrow I am grateful in many ways: first as a mentor, then as a new-found friend and a soul brother who demonstrated a deep understanding of my work and who introduced me to the people at A.R.E. Press. I am grateful to Mary Ann Shaffer for sharing her vital knowledge of the world of publishing and for her beneficial guidance as I entered into that world for the first time. I am immensely grateful to Julia Poppy for her boundless enthusiasm and inspiration for my project from the very beginning. How well I remember the day when she looked me in the eye and said: "You have *got* to write this book!" To John Poppy I am grateful also; his nurturant nudgings, coming from the voice of an experienced writer, often replenished me and helped me to persevere. To Margaret Frings Keyes, Lorna Cutler, Jed Diamond, James Konwinski, Julia Poppy, Nicholas Pappas, Margy Pappas, and others I am grateful for reading my manuscript at various stages and for providing their candid critiques that were of great benefit to me. To George McLaird, Bob Trowbridge, Jeremy Taylor and Dody Donnelly I am grateful for personal support and technical assistance that also made the journey possible.

I also wish to acknowledge the many students and clients who have shared their dreams with me over the years in numerous workshops, classes, and group therapy settings. I feel a debt of gratitude to you all, for the breadth and depth of what you have taught me about human nature. Because of the need for professional confidentiality I cannot mention any of your names here. For the most part, however, you know who you are and many of your names are written in my heart.

I am particularly grateful to a special group of people, friends both old and new, family members, colleagues, and students, who graciously gave me permission to use their real names in the autobiographical portion of this book. Their generosity and openness have, I believe, added a dimension of genuineness to this work that would not have been present otherwise.

Above all, I am grateful to my wife, Charlene Kohl Kelzer, and to our son, Erik. They have lived my experiment with me from its inception, they have fostered its spirit of adventure throughout, and they continue to follow it into a future as unknown as the past had been in its day. I appreciate the many sacrifices that they made in response to my writing schedule. I appreciate their growing understanding of how to live under the same roof with someone who frequently has one ear attuned to the Muse. I appreciate their enduring support through a time of great intensity for us all.

Finally, I am grateful to the Almighty and to the Light, to the God and Goddess within and without, who has given us the dream: as a precious gift, a charism, a messenger, a revelator, a procreator of persons who seek to emerge and of worlds that wait to be born.

Introduction

Twenty years ago, hardly anyone would have recognized the term "lucid dream." Defined simply as the experience of becoming aware that one is dreaming during a dream, lucid dreaming went unnoticed by most early dream theorists and researchers. Today, however, we find numerous books mentioning the subject and several devoted entirely to it. And now, Ken Kelzer challenges us to consider the lucid dream as nothing less than a path to illumination and wholeness. One might ask how could we apparently have overlooked this phenomenon until now? If it *is* as important as Kelzer and others suggest, why do we find little or no mention of it in the writings of the great dream theorists or in the voluminous readings of psychic Edgar Cayce?

When surveyed, most people can remember having become lucid—if only momentarily—at the end of an otherwise ordinary dream. Even though the experience is rare and fleeting for most persons, the phenomenon is nonetheless universal. One reason lucid dreaming *seems* new is that the term itself has only recently been universally adopted. Although British psychiatrist Frederick Van Eeden used the term "lucid dream" in 1913 in his pioneering work on the subject,* the phenomenon went by many names until modern researchers like Celia Green** and Charles Tart†

---

* Van Eeden, Frederick. "A study of dreams." In *Proceedings of the Society for Psychical Research*, 1913, *26*, 431-461.

** Green, Celia. *Lucid Dreams*. London: Hamish Hamilton, 1968.

† Tart, Charles. *Altered States of Consciousness*. Garden City, New York: Anchor Books, Doubleday, 1969.

focused attention on Van Eeden's seminal work. In the late 1920s, Oliver Fox* called such experiences "dreams of knowledge," a succinct lable which nevertheless failed to convey what it was that set the lucid dream apart from ordinary dreams. One paper published in a psychological journal in 1936 was titled "Dreams in Which the Dreamer Knows He Is Asleep."** Even this explicit title, however, still did not attract much public attention. Unfortunately, our culture had no word, ready and available, to capture the essence of the experience. Consequently, the phenomenon of the lucid dream may *seem* new to many people, whereas it is only the establishment of the term that is new.

There are several reasons why psychologically oriented researchers have, until recently, ignored the phenomenon of the lucid dream to the point of allowing it to remain nameless. We must remember that modern dream research began around the turn of the century. Thus, when Freud and Jung began to apply their genius to psychological theory, the dream was as yet largely unexplored. Consequently, there was a need to understand dreams *in general* before speculating on anomalous or infrequent dream phenomena. While a few conventional dream researchers did mention lucid dreaming prior to 1960, they tended to dismiss it as a non-dream phenomenon, an "artifact" that appeared upon awakening from sleep.

Another reason for the neglect of lucid dreaming is that the ordinary dream, as a subjective experience occurring in the privacy of sleep, has until recently fallen outside the domain of empirical, scientific enquiry. Dreaming did not become a fully legitimate focus of science until the discovery in the 1950s of the *measurable* physiological aspects of dreaming. Add to that the rarity of the lucid dream and one can see why

---

* Fox, Oliver. *Astral Projections: A Record of Out-of-Body Experiences.* Secaucus, New Jersey: Citadel Press, 1962 (originally published around 1929).

** Brown, A.E. "Dreams in which the dreamer knows he is asleep." *Journal of the Abnormal and Social Psychology,* 1936, *31*, 59-66.

interest in lucid dreaming has not flourished in the mainstream until recently.

Above all, the lucid dream violates long-cherished assumptions about the healthy relationship between conscious and unconscious. For instance, Freud held such a dismal view of the contents of the unconscious that he believed the ego could ill afford to be fully aware of what dwells within the dream. Lucidity, from this standpoint, would appear to be a prelude to madness, since it seems to open the doors to free-ranging dialogue and interaction between the dreamer and everything he or she sees in the dream.

The fact that people do have lucid dreams strongly suggests that consciousness is less tethered to the body than some people would like to believe. Lucid dreamers report remaining fully "awake" while their bodies seem to slumber. They report observing an inner reality which is in no way inferior to that observed in the light of day, and they claim to have intensely meaningful spiritual and interpersonal experiences that are normally out of reach to them. Indeed, lucid dreaming has been, and to a lesser extent still is, a "can of worms" to prevailing psychological theories of the dream. Most traditional dream theories simply cannot explain lucid dreaming. In the face of so many intellectual challenges, then, it is not surprising that lucid dreaming was ignored for so long.

Students of the Edgar Cayce readings might be interested to know whether they contain anything about the phenomenon that we now call the "lucid dream." Besides recognizing that we must look for the mention of the phenomenon in the readings rather than the exact words "lucid dreaming," it is also important to clarify the context in which dreams in general were usually addressed by the readings. Except for a series of four general readings given by Cayce on sleep (5754-1 through 5754-4), he rarely made theoretical statements about dreams. Why? Because after Cayce became well known, he was besieged by requests for individual readings, leaving him relatively little time to give readings on general topics. Thus, to a large extent, the readings *responded* to individuals asking questions about their own experiences rather than *initiating* treatises on general topics. As a result, many topics of interest were never addressed theoretically by the readings. While the responses to individuals were, in many cases, universally applicable, the topics addressed tended to be defined by individuals seeking personal guidance.

What, if anything, did the readings say about the phenomenon of the lucid dream? At least on two occasions, Cayce was asked to interpret lucid dreams. In response to one (195-51), he interpreted the dream without commenting on the dreamer's lucid awareness in the dream. However, when he interpreted the other dream, which happened to be his own, he stated that the experience was a vision, "not one that might be termed the dream" (294-94). In that dream, Cayce found himself giving a reading for his grandmother. She was alive again, but in a mortuary with vines growing over and around her. He felt that the vines had to be removed before he could give the reading. After removing them, he then encountered some dogs which also had to be removed from the room. As he started running after the dogs, he said: "I realized it was all a dream, and I knew the interpretation of it. It meant that we . . . were letting our work go to the dogs . . ." In the reading about the dream, we find the added conclusion that this dream was *not* "one that was the working of the body-conscious mind [ego] with the mental body [subconscious] . . ." While this statement is intriguing, it is also ambiguous and leaves us considerable room to build a more complete theory.

Even so, the readings provide a more valuable contribution to the study of lucid dreams than a mere ackowledgment of their importance. The readings provide the necessary philosophical framework, or paradigm, through which one can appreciate that lucid dreaming is no less than an inner path to illumination and mystical union—a "yoga of the dream state," to use the terminology of the Tibetan Buddhists.* Although it is true that lucid dreaming has been lately recognized by some laboratory dream researchers as a significant and different type of dream, and by some psychotherapists as a therapeutic encounter with one's inner self, there is much more to the lucid dream than these frameworks recognize or, perhaps more accurately, *leave room for.*

But what *is* the philosophical framework offered by the Cayce readings which leaves room for the lucid dream to be viewed as a mystical experience? First, the readings say that the highest estate of the soul—the destiny to which we are all evolving—is *the awareness of oneness with God.* He stated this as a paradox in which individuality is preserved in this union:

And it is for that purpose that He came into the earth; that we, as soul-entities, might know ourselves to be ourselves, and yet one with Him ... 3003-1

In saying that union with God is the destiny of each soul, the readings depart from *traditional* Judeo-Christian thought (in contrast to some of the mystical sects within these religions). Typically, Christians and Jews alike have considered a harmonious relationship with a *separate* God to be the highest relationship to which we can aspire. This is exemplified by Moses receiving the Ten Commandments from God. Although we may aspire to having a *convenant* with God, the relationship stops there. God remains on the mountain, and only His commandments enter our lives.

In essence, the Cayce readings extend the path of the soul's evolution beyond the point where the traditional Judeo-Christian religions claim it ends. Transpersonal psychologist Ken Wilber** concurs with this idea by saying that Christianity as generally practiced has

---

* Evans-Wentz, W.Y., ed. *Tibetan Yoga and Secret Doctrines.* London: Oxford University Press, 1958.
** Wilber, Ken. *Up from Eden.* Boulder, Colorado: Shambhala, 1981.

been blocked and limited in its development. According to Wilber, it fails to accept the central teaching of Jesus, namely, that oneness with God is the ultimate promise for us all. While Jesus "thought it not robbery" to make Himself one with God and claimed that "I and the Father are One" (and died for saying it), we have persisted in thinking that the most *we* can expect in our relationship with God is to have a convenant with a caring, but ultimately separate, deity.

In contrast, some (but not all) of the Eastern teachings have made the awareness of oneness with God the pinnacle of human evolution. In the same spirit, the great Western mystics have understood that union, not merely convenant, is the promise for us all. But various sources, ranging from Tibetan Buddhism to the Cayce readings, concur that this oneness is a state in which the seeker maintains a sense of individuality. The seeker does *not* merely dissolve into unconscious union but retains a heightened sense of self-reflective awareness. In a similar fashion, lucid dreaming constitutes a heightened state of awareness in which individuality and responsibility are retained.

Besides providing a larger framework in which individual efforts toward mystical experience and eventual union with God are accepted and encouraged, the Cayce readings place a high premium on becoming aware of, and taking responsibility for, the enduring record we have created through our thoughts and actions. Among other things, this involves working through unfinished business stemming from past lives. It also means becoming aware of how our minds are perpetually creating our present realities so that we can participate more responsibly in the creative process here and now.

But we have a problem in that the record of our past mental creations remains largely unconscious. The readings stated on a few occasions that it is important for the conscious mind to become aware of the subconscious *so that* the superconscious (the readings' term for the awareness of our oneness with God) can come into expression.

Q-1. Explain and illustrate the difference in the faculties of mind, subconscious and superconscious. A-1. The superconscious mind being that of the spiritual entity, and in action only when the subconscious is become the conscious mind.   900-31

The reading could well have been talking here about the lucid dream. Indeed, lucid dreaming may be one of the *best* examples of what was alluded to here. After all, when the dreamer becomes "awake" and fully conscious in the dream, he or she can suddenly confront and integrate what has previously dwelled below the surface of waking awareness (i.e., in the subconscious) and which manifests through dream imagery. But where does the superconscious fit in? Recall that the highest state of consciousness is characterized by the awareness of *oneness*. In essence, lucidity inaugurates the birth of this awareness of oneness in the dream state, for the conclusion "I am dreaming" signifies no less than the realization that everything the dreamer sees is part of himself or herself. Lucidity, then, *is* superconsciousness beginning to emerge!*

When we begin awakening to what we have created on a subconscious level, we inevitably meet what Kelzer and others before him have called the "shadow." This concept provides a key word in the title of this book. We encounter the personification of forces within us which we have feared or neglected, and which need to be understood and integrated into consciousness. Kelzer's willingness to discuss the unsavory aspects of his own personality in conjunction with the mystical peaks in his life conveys what is perhaps the central message of his account: that what we consider unacceptable within ourselves and in others must be confronted lucidly,

---

* This does not mean that the images and symbols of the lucid dream are necessarily from the superconscious. Instead, it means that the self-reflectiveness which says, "I am dreaming and all I see is a part of me" is emergent superconsciousness.

modified through dialogue and interaction, and wedded to our conscious selves. Kelzer not only willingly exposes his own ordeal with his shadow side, but he shows how this confrontation serves as an initiation which, if met properly, ushers the dreamer into experiences of ecstasy and Light.

Most of us, in theory, can accept this approach. But when Kelzer speaks, for instance, of turning his previously repressed power into "creative aggression," it is easy to balk. After all, various spiritual teachings have urged the seeker to avoid anger as a destructive element in our lives. Under what circumstances, then, can we justify attitudes and actions which might offend others?

Interestingly, the Cayce readings stated on numerous occasions, ". . . anyone without a temper is worth little; but one who does not control same is worth less." (2284-1)

So even though the readings emphasized the need to control one's temper, they considered anger valuable. On another the occasion the readings stated:

What is more real, the love manifested in the Son, the Savior, for His brethren, or the essence of love that may be seen even in the vilest of passion? They are one.
254-68

This statement resonates with the words of the poet Rilke when he said, "Perhaps everything which is terrible is, in the deepest sense, something that wants our love." Of all the principles Kelzer introduces in his narrative, this may be the most difficult for readers to accept. But I have found in my work as a counselor that accepting the shadow is the most important step toward healing and transformation.

Another key word in the title of this book is "experiment." Students of the Edgar Cayce readings are sometimes surprised to find how much emphasis the readings placed upon research and how they insisted that the word itself become part of the name of the organization Cayce founded—the Association for Research and Enlightenment. It is easy to interpret this emphasis as support for conventional research. But when one looks at the passages referring to the value of research, one can see that the readings place great value on *individual* application and experimentation, not laboratories and quantitative analyses.

Ken Kelzer's description of his inner work as an "experiment" is in keeping with the readings' concept of research. His subtitle, "My Experiment with Lucid Dreaming," reflects the philosophy that one can bring an objective, experimental attitude to bear on one's inner experiences, and that the results of such experiments can be meaningful to others. While modern science tends to favor experimentation in which the researcher removes himself from the experimental context, individual experimentation has nonetheless played a crucial role in the growth of knowledge and often leads to pivotal discoveries. Jean Piaget's experiments with his own children would hardly rank as "controlled" experiments. But his work stands as one of the most important contributions in developmental psychology. As a record of one man's quest for wholeness, Ken Kelzer's experiment, too, represents research in its most fundamental and meaningful form.

While *The Sun and the Shadow: My Experiment with Lucid Dreaming* is ostensibly about lucid dreaming, Kelzer frequently suggests that "lucid dreaming" is simply a metaphor for how all of life could, and perhaps should, be lived in order to enter into a co-creative relationship with God. Thus, whether or not the reader has ever had a lucid dream, this account may nonetheless help to instill an attitude toward all of life which will bring forth new meaning and a much greater sense of "co-creatorship."

Without a doubt, this book will become a classic in the field of dreaming. Even more important, it will endure as a major treatise on the mystical path.

Scott Sparrow, Ed.D.
Lucid Dream Researcher

Author's Preface

When I first began to speak about lucid dreaming at professional conferences and workshops several years ago, I often referred to the lucid dream as a "frontier of consciousness." I thought this metaphor was accurate and fitting then, and I still think so now. A frontier indicates the growing edge of a culture or civilization. Frontiers are, by their very nature, relative and changing. Today's frontier may well become the stabilized mainstream of tomorrow's society. In America, we have a special appreciation for this process, because we are such a young civilization that the memories of frontier towns along our riverbanks and in remote wilderness areas are still fresh in our collective mind. These memories are kept alive and romanticized in our contemporary novels, movies, and television serials. America, in many ways, is still a "frontier culture."

But what is a frontier of *consciousness?* The phrase itself implies that human consciousness could be viewed spatially, that it could be compared to a territory. It implies that consciousness can be studied objectively, and that a body of knowledge can be built up around it. These are professional assumptions that I hold in my work as a psychotherapist and as a serious student of the dream state. However, I am quick to add that these terms are analogies, and only analogies. In psychological circles the term "inner space" has become increasingly popular in speaking about mental processes or highly subjective experiences.

This is a book about human consciousness. Properly speaking, it belongs in such categories as parapsychology, consciousness studies, metaphysics or mysticism. I might also classify it under humanistic psychology or transpersonal psychology. As such, the book is offered as a contribution to a growing body of knowledge about the human mind. It is an attempt to become conscious about consciousness; it is an endeavor to use the human mind to study the human mind. The eighteenth-century poet Alexander Pope wrote that "the proper study of mankind is man." I believe, that in our quietest moments, most of us know that this assertion is true. But many people, throughout history, have lacked the leisure time, the method, and the motivation to put this principle into daily practice. With the advancement of culture, a civilization becomes conscious of many wide-ranging areas of study, such as medicine, physics, chemistry, and astronomy, to name just a few. But only in recent decades have we seen a growing number of people in our society seeking to become conscious about consciousness per se. The publication of Dr. Charles Tart's book *Altered States of Consciousness* in 1969 had an important galvanizing effect on this steady evolution. The book's title, as well as its contents, alerted many of us to the wide range of human consciousness and the many varieties of consciousness experiences that people might have.

I would not hesitate to regard the lucid dream as an altered state of consciousness. In addition, I regard it as a unique altered state, in that it occurs within the normal dream. Insofar as the normal dream itself is an altered state of consciousness, I have now come to the point of saying that the lucid dream is an "altered state within an altered state."

In chapter ten of this book, I offer a lengthy *descriptive* definition of the lucid dream, an attempt that I have not seen anywhere on this subject in the material published to date. I offer this descriptive definition because of the frequent looks of confusion I have encountered on people's faces as I attempted to speak about the lucid dream state, a subject that can be rather difficult to address. A lucid dream is a subjective experience and, like many subjective experiences, it cannot be fully communicated in language. These inherent difficulties in communication, though burdensome to me in the beginning, have stimulated and challenged me to refine my own understanding of the phenomenon of lucid dreaming on progressively deeper levels over a period of time. In writing this book, barriers have become challenges and difficulties have become opportunities.

I would like to offer here an introductory working definition of the lucid dream in order to orient the reader and provide some initial understanding of this complex phenomenon. According to the definition that is generally accepted by dream theorists and researchers today, *a lucid dream is a dream in which the dreamer is aware that he is dreaming while he is dreaming.* This process is distinct from an ordinary dream in which the dreamer is often thoroughly confined in the dream experience, so much so that he or she often believes the dream to be fully "real" as it is occurring. By contrast, the lucid dream contains a second level of awareness which emerges from and runs concurrently with the first level, that is, the ongoing content and process of the dreamscape. On this second level of awareness the dreamer, when fully lucid, knows with absolute certainty that what is seen and experienced around him or her is a dream, and this unusual certitude affords a level of freedom and personal power that is impossible to attain in an ordinary dream. This experience of simultaneous dual consciousness in the lucid state has many important implications for life in the waking state, and I discuss these implications at length throughout this book.

In many lucid dreams the dreamer experiences a distinct transition point in which he feels his consciousness shift from the normal dream to the lucid state, a point that lucid dream researchers now refer to as the onset of lucidity. This shift of consciousness is sometimes felt very distinctly, like bursting out of the clouds in an airplane flight and feeling dazzled by the clear sunlight. Or sometimes it occurs so slowly and gradually as to be almost imperceptible to the dreamer. The lucid dream state is also frequently characterized by highly refined energies that move about through the dreamer's body and mind, leaving a pleasant, tingling sensation that is often accompanied by gorgeous, vivid colors, intense and ecstatic feelings or celestial, rapturous music that seems to come from another world. In short, the lucid dream can lead the dreamer into a whole new realm of human possibilities.

For those readers who would like a fuller theoretical orientation to lucid dreaming at this point, I would suggest that you read chapters ten and eleven in this book before reading the account of my experiment in Part I. For those who prefer to read the account of my experiment before formulating concepts, I recommend that you read the book from front to back in the customary manner. We are at somewhat of a crossroads here: Shall we first speak of something that is almost indefinable, or shall we first attempt to define something that is almost unspeakable? My only suggestion is to encourage each reader to take his or her own path here, knowing that either fork in the road will eventually lead to the same destination.

This is not a general or introductory book about dreaming or dream interpretation. Having worked as a psychotherapist and educator in this area for many years, I am content with several fine introductory books on dreams that have already appeared, and I did not want to repeat or duplicate these earlier works.* Instead it is my intention in this book to explore in depth, in a

---

* For readers seeking introductory books on dreams, I would recommend *Creative Dreaming* by Patricia Garfield and *Dream Power* and *The Dream Game* by Ann Faraday.

personal, subjective and autobiographical account, one of the most interesting and promising aspects of the dream world: the lucid dream state. As far as I know, only one similar, autobiographical book of this type has been written, *Pathway to Ecstasy: The Way of the Dream Mandala* by Patricia Garfield. I am strongly indebted to Dr. Garfield for her work and for personal communication that we have had in the past few years on the subject of lucid dreaming. Basically, my book and my experience will corroborate many of her experiences, as well as outline certain personal differences that are inevitable among lucid dreamers, simply because no two dreamers can be carbon copies of each other.

Throughout this book, I have used the word *experiment* in a personal and symbolic sense, and not in a strict scientific sense. The word *experience* could easily be substituted in my particular case, for this book is a personal account of how I conducted my experiment, of the extraordinary dreams that resulted from it, and of my reflections and commentary upon these dreams. It is also an account of the numerous emotional responses that I had to these lucid dreams, depicting certain psychological barriers that I discovered within myself and their corresponding stepping-stones to growth as well.

In selecting the title for this book, *The Sun and the Shadow,* I have chosen to emphasize the interplay between the light and the darkness within my own psyche and, by implication, within the psyche of everyone. This interplay emerged and developed in many ways as my experiment with lucid dreaming unfolded. I see now that it was inevitable that as I opened up to and contacted the Light in the lucid dream state, that I would also become more aware of the unresolved emotional conflicts of my own past, and the negative personality traits and patterns that still persisted within me. In working through the intimate details of my experiment, I have come to appreciate the meaning of the Jungian adage, "The brighter the sun, the darker the shadow." Seeing how true this adage was for me constituted a realization that was frightening at certain times, sobering at others, and yet, somehow, reassuring in the long run. In the end I have felt a certain peaceful satisfaction that has emerged from my own willingness to examine and understand this internal interplay.

Certainly, from re-examining my own dream journal over the past ten years, I have come to see that my dreams had been speaking of this interplay all along. It was only a matter of time and willingness before I realized a much broader and more penetrating picture of this internal and universal state of affairs. In my own mind I believe that I have clarified, for myself at least, some wider spiritual and psychic principle, namely, that as a person advances into an altered state or a "higher" state of consciousness, he or she will also probably discover some heretofore hidden aspects of the dark side of his own psyche. Or at the very least, the voyager will rediscover these hidden, dark aspects on deeper levels than ever before or with a greater intensity of feelings than ever before. "The brighter the sun, the darker the shadow." If this really is one of the laws of psychic growth, I believe it would be beneficial to study this axiom in depth.

It will be important for my readers, in examining this kind of autobiographical account, to ask two basic questions continuously as they move through the text: What aspects of the author's experiment are essential to lucid dreaming per se and would, therefore, be common to the experiences of other lucid dreamers? What aspects of the author's experiment are unique and would probably not occur to most other lucid dreamers? Throughout the text I have endeavored to assist the reader with this issue by distinguishing, to the best of my ability, those ingredients from my lucid dream experiments that originated from my own personal history.

At this point in the evolution of consciousness studies, a growing number of psychologists and researchers in Western societies are beginning to pay particular attention to lucid dreaming. Most of them seem very enthusiastic and excited about this new form of energy. At the same time, most sound a bit uncertain about its specific benefits and uses. I have addressed that issue at length in chapter eleven. Personally, I am inclined to agree with Stephen LaBerge's analogy, that our present understanding of lucid dream power is comparable to the general understanding that people had about electricity in the time of Benjamin Franklin. In the mid-eighteenth century, many people knew that electricity existed, and some even knew how to tap into its power with simple experiments. But most people at that time were still unaware of how electricity would be used in practice, even if its energy could somehow be harnessed. Uncertainty, however, does not stop the adventuresome spirit of humankind; on the contrary, it spurs us on to seek new discoveries. Benjamin Franklin was somehow searching for all of us when he went out into a thunderstorm with his kite and his key to develop his own understanding of the relationship between lightning and that new phenomenon called "electricity."

I am particularly proud to dedicate a book such as this to the founders of our country. I do not ordinarily think of statesmen and parapsychology in the same context. Yet, as I was finishing the initial draft of the text, I felt welling up inside of me a tremendous debt of gratitude to these people from our national past. I strongly realized my own good fortune, to have had the leisure time, the education, the professional background, and all the cultural resources that supported me in writing a book such as this, a book that may seem esoteric or farfetched to some. I realized with deep appreciation that a field of endeavor such as lucid dreaming could only come to fruition in a culture where intellectual, social, and academic freedom have been highly valued and jealously guarded for centuries. The expanded psychological *freedom* of the lucid dream state is an outgrowth of the *freedom* of our American social and political matrix. Freedom: this one word, perhaps more than any other, conveys the essence of the American dream as well as the essence of the lucid dream.

As I finished my manuscript, I saw it as one more contribution to that contemporary cultural stream, now widely known as the human potential movement. I saw that movement, or stream, flowing beside many others that have emerged in my own lifetime with tremendous force and evolutionizing potential. I saw the civil rights movement, the anti-war movement, the women's liberation movement, the environmentalist movement, the anti-nuclear movement, and the world peace movement all arising like so many streams from the earth, flowing down the mountainsides and merging into a giant, thundering torrent, a Niagara Falls of human energy that will effect sweeping changes upon our nation and eventually upon the world. All these streams of thought are connected to each other somehow. Though a single book may be but a drop in the torrent, the torrent itself derives its power and sense of purpose from *vision*. In writing a book about *vision*, I felt the need to re-acknowledge the vision contained within the Bill of Rights and the Constitution of the United States, because I believe the original vision of our founding fathers still inspires the contemporary torrent of human freedom and creativity that is called America, a nation state unparalleled in human history. I felt strongly compelled to acknowledge my personal gratitude to those individuals of the past who risked all for the expansion of their vision, who expressed it to a tired and skeptical world, and who worked and fought to establish it in concrete forms.

I am particularly pleased to witness in the 1980s a renewed awareness of the social dimension to the field of psychology. As more professionals in this field speak out at conferences and workshops on the tremendous economic and social problems of the globe, the more we can begin to bridge the gap between "inner world" and "outer world," between "inner reality" and outer reality." This gap has grown too wide in recent decades. The drive toward specialization and subspecialization in professional life can so easily create a kind of cubicle thinking. I think it comes as a great relief to many of us to see this trend being reversed, and to see more professionals participating actively in processes for social and political change.

Let me include here a few words about the mechanics of this text. Throughout the book I have consistently used indentations and smaller print for all accounts of actual dream material. This will assist readers to distinguish dream material from commentary, especially where some of the dreams are rather lengthy. The title of a dream is usually one that I have ascribed myself, following my own intuition. The dates mentioned in the text are the dates on which the dreams occurred. I would also like to ask my readers to bear with me in the traditional use of masculine pronouns to designate both sexes. Though I have used "he or she" and "his or her" sentence structure in various places, I found this to be somewhat cumbersome and chose to use it sparingly for considerations of literary style. The grammatical challenge of creating for the English language a single pronoun that could refer to both men and women remains, still, unanswered in our culture.

The experience of lucid dreaming, I believe, offers people a concrete avenue to expand their psychological and intellectual freedom into a realm that many have never known. That realm, though still generally unknown, indeed does exist, and its potential and possibilities are limitless. Part I of this book offers a detailed, in-depth narration of my own personal journey into this "altered reality," without the assistance of psychedelic chemicals or substances of any kind. I trust that my account will serve to assist others who have an interest in the world of lucid dreams and who wish to know more about this frontier of the mind. This frontier is only now beginning to open into the fields of parapsychology and consciousness studies. I believe that I have learned enough at this point to share my initial explorations in writing, and I believe I still have a great deal yet to learn. I am pleased and willing to invite others who are interested to explore this new inner world. Perhaps together we can stand at yet another "gateway to the West," and if we become sufficiently strong in numbers and patient in the quality of our adventure, I am convinced that the gateway will open wide.

PART I

My Experiment with Lucid Dreaming:

A Personal Odyssey

CHAPTER ONE

Confronting
the Wildebeest

*"Expect nothing.
Be ready for anything."*
—George Leonard

CONFRONTING THE WILDEBEEST
June 8, 1983

I am walking alone in a mountainous country area. I begin to climb upward on several huge slabs of solid granite. Leaning forward as I climb, I patiently work my way up these massive, steep, grayish-white monoliths. At last I reach the summit, a high plateau, and see a broad, vast plain ahead of me. The plain extends for a great distance, as far as the eye can see, and is covered with grass and occasional clumps of trees. At some distance on the plain, I see a large, goat-like beast, similar to an African wildebeest, with long, shaggy, black hair. A primitive man, a naked aborigine, looking like an American Indian, is riding the wildebeest. Suddenly, the beast turns directly toward me and begins to charge. I realize that the aborigine has no control over the beast at all; in fact, the beast is controlling him! I feel alarmed. I clearly see that the beast has two, short, curved horns with sharp points, exactly like those of an American buffalo.

Suddenly, I realize I am dreaming, and I feel a great surge of energy shoot through my whole body and settle in my forehead. I tell myself I have absolutely nothing to fear because I *know* that what I see is a dream. I stand ready to meet the wildebeest's attack and feel tremendous energy bristling out of my arms. My arms feel much more muscled and stronger than usual, each one surrounded by a powerful energy field, shaped like a cylinder about eight inches in diameter, completely encompassing each arm, and extending from my shoulders all the way down to the fingertips of both hands. I feel incredibly powerful. I think to myself that, at just the right moment, with perfect timing and balance, I will grab the charging wildebeest by the horns and bulldog it to the ground as if I were a rodeo cowboy. I wait with full confidence as the wildebeest and the naked aborigine charge directly toward me, headlong, at full speed.

At the very last moment, just as I expect to feel their impact, the wildebeest and the naked aborigine come to an abrupt halt, directly in front of me. For several minutes, I confront the wildebeest, powerfully, looking straight into one of its bloodshot eyes, as it nervously paws the earth, stirring up a small cloud of dust only a few feet from where I stand. I think to myself with great satisfaction, "I don't have to bulldog it after all." The naked aborigine sits calm and immobile on top of the shaggy beast and has an empty and faraway look in his eye as I glare at him powerfully. Then I look back at the wildebeest, and for several long moments we continue to stare directly into each other's eyes as it repeatedly paws the earth, restlessly. I feel totally balanced and poised, mentally clear, and very satisfied. Slowly the dream fades out and I return to a normal sleep.

The above narrative is an account of one of my more memorable lucid dreams. The dream was a gift that I have cherished and reflected upon at length many times because it had many of the special features and qualities that make lucid dreams unique and distinct from ordinary dreaming.

In its opening scene, "Confronting the Wildebeest" portrayed me on a solitary journey, climbing up huge, granite rocks that seemed almost like walls or sheer cliffs. When I reached the summit and stood on an inspiring plateau, I had an incredible view that extended in all directions. This scenario was an accurate and typical reflection of how I often felt in many of my lucid dreams which are frequently marked with unbelievable and indescribable clarity. In a clear dream,* one can see forever, to paraphrase the popular song.

Throughout my experiment, I was working mostly alone, and this dream clearly portrayed that aspect of my commitment. Though I had discussed the experiment and shared it often with colleagues and students, I felt alone with it so often because of the highly introspective nature of the work. I had certainly reached "plateaus" numerous times in the work, as will be described at length in the chapters that follow. This dream, however, portrayed an interesting and crucial dynamic: just as I reached the plateau, I was confronted with an overwhelming force of primitive, negative energy bearing down on me. What did the dark, shaggy wildebeest and the naked aborigine symbolize? Their primitive, negative energy, as I soon discovered, was fear.

There is a kind of magic in many lucid dreams. This one had the potential to become a nightmare, but in the moment that I became lucid I experienced total inner transformation. All my fear vanished in an instant, and inside of myself I felt full of courage. Complete clarity of vision, in this dream, yielded instant transformation. This became one of the important principles that I learned from this particular lucid dream. To see *fully* is to have courage. To see *fully* is to have no fear. But, as is so evident when we examine our world, we human beings seldom see anything fully in our normal state of consciousness. More often than not, as the apostle Paul wrote: "We see now through a glass, darkly, but then we shall see face to face."** His intriguing word "then" has been a source of debate for philosophers and spiritual teachers for many centuries. Does clear vision or enlightenment come only after death, when a direct union with God or some universal

---

* A contemporary German researcher, Paul Tholey, refers to the lucid dream as "der Klartraum," literally, "the clear dream."
** I Corinthians 13:12.

consciousness is achieved? Or is it possible to have a taste of illumined vision now, to experience moments when we see fully, now, in this life, while we still inhabit a mortal body? This question, perennial to the evolution of our Judeo-Christian culture, will be addressed throughout this book as one important aspect of the lucid dream state.

At the point where I knew with absolute certainty that what I saw before me was a dream, I had a strange mixture of emotions, a full energized presence combined with relaxed detachment. It was the magic combination that one often wishes for when confronted by the extreme press of circumstances, feeling fully present and fully detached at the same time. After reaching lucidity, I felt full confidence in my ability to create a positive outcome from this attack. The magician is the master of the elements that lie before him. The lucid dreamer is the master of all the elements of the dream, no matter what they may be.

One of the purposes of lucid dreaming, I am now convinced, is to give people the experience, however fleeting or temporary, of spiritual and psychological mastery. These tastes of mastery and moments of transformation spur us on to continue the inward journey.

As the charging wildebeest and the naked aborigine bore down upon me, pressing closer and closer, I felt not the slightest twinge of fear after I had entered the lucid state. Upon my becoming lucid, the outcome of victory was certain in my mind. Only the exact, last-moment details of my victory were unknown to me. The surge of power bristling out of my arms, as if they were giant hams, was more than enough to bulldog the wildebeest to the ground. Waiting, watching, and standing my ground as the wildebeest charged was experienced as a single, relaxed, and even timeless moment. As I stood there in the dream, fully clear and outside of time, nothing within me changed or wavered as the dark beast and its naked rider eventually came upon me to

6

the exact place where I was standing. Suddenly the attack was ended. The sudden halt of this primitive duo brought about a transformation that was completely unexpected. "Expect nothing; be ready for anything." Thus reads the motto of the dojo,* the martial arts studio where I once studied and practiced the Japanese martial art of Aikido. This part of the dream taught me a lesson I will never forget: sometimes the projection of one's inner power based on complete, inner clarity is sufficient to stop the attack of an aggressor. In this lucid dream, my power was a vibration, like an energy field, that extended all around me, inside and out. This vibration of power with its corresponding confidence and mental clarity were enough to halt the wildebeest's attack. To be ready for anything, in this dream, included the willingness to adapt instantly to any sudden turn of events and to move with any unexpected variations, allowing the dream to end in its own way, establishing peace in its own manner.

Eventually, after some reflection, I realized that this lucid dream taught me a lot about fear. Fear is perhaps the most primitive human emotion of all, and we all have a great deal of it inside ourselves. We all need to learn how to confront the objects and sources of our fear in order to thrive and prosper in this world. I realized, too, that the dream was bearing a personal message, telling me that I still have a lot of powerful fears inside myself, which at times threaten to overwhelm my conscious mind. I did not associate the wildebeest to any particular fear, but more to fear in general. The dream remined me of Franklin D. Roosevelt's famous statement, "The only thing we have to fear is fear itself." Now I am wondering if this lucid dream was suggesting that I might surrender one step further and give up the fear of fear. To be unafraid of fear itself implies a willingness to face all of my fears, whatever they are, regardless of what plateaus I may already

---

* "Dojo" is a generic term meaning a training hall or a place of the way.

have reached in my personal growth.

The threatening images in this dream were a strange blend of American and African. The African wildebeest had the horns of an American buffalo, and the naked wild man had the appearance of an American Indian. I have often wondered about this intriguing combination of images coming from America, my home continent, and from Africa, the so-called "dark continent." My reflections on this bizarre blend of imagery lead me to a number of realizations. All true spiritual and psychological work leads a person into a deeper appreciation of the dark and primitive side of his or her own human nature. This primitive psyche in all humanity is really one and the same, all over the world. Spiritual work, when it is true and genuine, is expansive of awareness and not "displace-ive" of awareness. It leads us to see and appreciate the whole of our humanity, and does not lead us to reflect upon our higher natures only. While we need to dwell upon our higher nature in order to grow in a positive direction, we must not do it by rejecting our dark and primitive side. A whole person, then, is someone who has walked with God *and* wrestled with the devil.

One of my favorite stories is that of the famous nineteenth-century French priest, Jean Vianney (1786-1859) who became widely known as the Curé of Ars. In his day Ars was a small, rural town. Over the years of his tenure there as the local curé, or pastor, Father Vianney acquired a widespread reputation as a man of wisdom, courage, and personal integrity. Many people traveled great distances from all over France to seek his personal counsel and guidance in troublesome matters. The town of Ars itself was generally viewed as a God-forsaken place, not exactly a plum of an assignment for a parish priest. There was also a prison in Ars and, as was the custom in those days, on the day of execution the condemned men were led through the streets to the gallows where they would be publicly executed. The curé made a special practice of standing on his front porch as the prisoners went by, to give his final blessing to each one. After blessing the prisoners, the priest's houseguests often overheard him say in his quiet, reflective way: "There, but for the grace of God, go I." For many years, through my teens and young adult years, I had never seriously accepted this statement and other similar statements attributed to great people of the past. I had always suspected such words were some sort of official display of humility, some sort of party line for creating an admirable public image. It was only after I had been working with my own dreams for many years and had come face to face with many of the dark elements of my own primitive psyche, and had actually seen my own deepest potential for evil, destructiveness, aggression or hate, that I began to realize that the Curé of Ars was telling the literal truth about the psyche, his own and everyone else's. The man whom many regarded as a saint had apparently searched deeply enough within his own soul, to see without a doubt his own capacity for evil. His humility, I suspect now, was real and literal, and based upon a depth of self-knowledge that I find admirable.

My lucid dream in the confronting of the wildebeest has deepened this realization within me. Through experience, it taught me on a far deeper level than I ever could have learned from a book or from hearsay. The wildebeest is now one of my companions, a constant reminder of the dark side of my own psyche. Such a reminder is needed, because this dark side will always be present, no matter how many "plateaus" I may reach in my personal journey in this lifetime. We are all like the Curé of Ars. As the curé needed to look upon the condemned criminal and see in him a reminder of his own shadow side, so do we all need some similar frequent reminder in our own lives. This is one of the prime psychospiritual purposes of the dream: to serve as the bearer of the shadow into the conscious mind. In this function the dream has the potential to reawaken our humility and self-honesty. It reminds the dreamer, inexorably, that his or her dark primitive side is perpetually present in the psyche and will remain so, forever, throughout one's lifetime.

The most primitive of human instincts are universal: fear, self-preservation, survival, power, lust, possessiveness, etc. These basic "animal" drives can be found in every man, woman, and child and in every culture throughout history. It is only in a momentary aberration of the mind that anyone can actually say that the "other person" suffers from these primitive urges and that "I" do not. Such an aberration is the essence of the "holier-than-thou" game, and, in moments in which a person plays this game, it is a safe bet that the game is motivated by fear, usually the fear of feeling inferior to another person in some way. One of the most comical examples of this projection of one's own darkness onto another is the legendary blame game that occurs over venereal disease: The Russians call it the German disease, the Germans call it the French disease, the French call it the English disease, etc. . . .

The blending of the Afro-American images in this lucid dream suggested to me a strange interplay between "civilized man" and "primitive man." It suggested that these traditional distinctions are quite arbitrary and depend totally on one's point of view. Not only do Americans and Europeans sometimes speak of Africa as the "dark continent," but Africans in turn have created their own equivalent formulation in saying "The white man is a devil" or "The white man has a devil." There is also a similar, popular saying among the Chinese who sometimes refer to Caucasians as "those white devils."

I reflected here on Carl Jung's theory about the collective dimension of the dark side of the human psyche which he termed "the shadow." He said, in essence, that not only does each human individual tend to project his or her own darkness onto other individuals, but that each ethnic group or racial group tends to project it

10

collectively upon other ethnic groups which are then viewed as alien and foreign, or radically different from and inferior to one's own group. These collective projections from within the psyche allow us to hate collectively, kill in times of war, and generally regard other cultures as primitive, barbaric, or somehow less human and less noble than our own. Without a thorough understanding of this mental mechanism (called "projection" by depth psychologists) there may be little chance of establishing true peace in one-to-one relationships or true and lasting peace between nations. With such understanding, however, and with conscious ownership of the dark side of the psyche, both individually and collectively, we reach into a whole new realm of human growth in which genuine peace becomes a practical possibility.

Today, in the 1980s, our white, American-European civilization has reached the absolute end of the line in this process of the public denial of our own dark side. As we look at our stockpile of nuclear weapons and the mammoth armies that glare at each other now from East to West and West to East, we realize our own self-destructive potential as we have never realized it before. We realize also that it cannot go on forever. The continued amassing of arms, combined with official public statements that place the blame on the "other side," can only lead to destruction of our civilization, or even worse, annihilation of the entire planet. We must ask ourselves if we really are as civilized as we had once imagined and as enlightened as we would like to believe. The depth psychologies of Freud and Jung have as many important contributions to make to the field of international relations as they have to our understanding of interpersonal relations. The heart of darkness resides as much in the soul of the white man as in the soul of the black man. It resides as much in the soul of the American as in the soul of the Russian.

After spending a good deal of time and energy in understanding the dark and threatening images of this lucid dream, I opened myself to its enlightening and enlivening potential as well. I asked myself a number of penetrating questions: Am I ready to live a life that is permeated with joy? Am I ready to feel the potential for ecstasy conveyed through the lucid dream? Am I ready to approach the experiences of psychic awareness in the lucid dream, knowing full well that they will some day be transferred from the lucid dream state into the waking state? It is only a matter of time and openness before the transfer takes place. Once a person has had a taste of ecstasy, he or she will soon desire it on a regular basis. These questions and many more will be addressed in this book, through the unfolding of my own experiment as I lived it.

The lucid dream is a doorway to mystical experience. Toward the end of her book, describing her own experiences with lucid dreaming, author-psychologist Patricia Garfield concludes: "I understand! I understand at last! My lucid dreams have the same content as my meditation periods because both are part of the mystic process: *lucid dreams are microcosms of the mystic experience.*"* My personal findings concur with hers. The lucid dream is indeed a doorway to the mystic state, a "pathway to ecstasy" as the title of her book suggests.

In "Confronting the Wildebeest" I experienced once again a tremendous expansion of consciousness and an upsurge of energy within myself. Although the incredible clarity of vision that occurred was indescribable in words, I am committed to putting this lucid dream and its attendant feelings into words as best I can. The ending of the dream provided me with an experience of myself and a positive self-image that I shall never forget. I now often remember that image of myself, fully lucid, alert, and mentally clear, with my arms bristling with power, ready to grab that charging wildebeest by the horns and throw it to the ground. Through repeated meditations and moments of quiet

---

* Patricia Garfield, *Pathway to Ecstasy*, p. 213.

reflection I have deliberately focused on this highly confident image. Using self-hypnosis, I have planted it and re-planted it deep within my mind. I have chosen to carry it with me, through the months and years that have passed since I originally had this dream. And now, when I encounter any problem or fearful situation in the waking state, I often re-picture myself as I was in the final scene of that dream: fully alert, energized, confident and powerful, prepared to face my adversary as I faced the wildebeest and the aborigine. When I reflect on this image of myself and allow it to fill my mind once again, I can feel a boost to my courage and self-confidence, and feel encouraged to act bravely in the moment. In a moment of crisis I can tell myself: *"This* is who I am. *This* is how I act."

"In my Father's house there are many mansions..."*
The finale of this lucid dream has given me another mansion, another dwelling place for my thoughts. Every person needs a place for his noble symbols, a place in which his higher self can dwell, because whatever we dwell upon is that which we shall ultimately become.

Let me go now to the beginning of my story. How did I become interested in lucid dreaming? Where and from whom did I first hear about this unique type of dream experience? To answer these questions I must retrace my steps and turn back the calendar some two-and-a-half years to the autumn of 1980. In that year, filled with the exuberant air of the beginning of the new decade and sensing in my own way some collective, spiritual rebirth emerging in our culture, my journey began.

---

* John 14:2.

CHAPTER TWO

The Experiment Begins

*"The only tyrant I accept in this world is
the 'still, small voice' within."*
—Mahatma Gandhi

Sometime during the early autumn of 1980 I began to feel a quiet yet profound change developing within myself in my attitude toward my dreams. Slowly and gradually, I began to feel receptive toward cultivating lucid dreaming in my own life. By this time I had been faithfully keeping a dream journal for about eight years and had collected several volumes of dreams. As a psychotherapist and dream educator, I had also been paying a good deal of attention to my students' and clients' dreams for many years. Prior to this growing sense of inner readiness, the lucid dreams that I occasionally had, about once a year on the average, occurred spontaneously and unpredictably, without any particular desire or intention on my part. There was a special beauty and intensity in these extraordinary eruptions of the psyche, and I placed a high value on them whenever they occurred. Their lasting effect lingered on in my mind long after ordinary dreams and ordinary waking memories had faded. Although I knew that these dreams were a special gift, for some years I was not sure how to respond to them.

The first contact that I had had with lucid dreaming in the literature came from Carlos Castaneda's book,

Journey to Ixtlan. * While I was intrigued with the aura of mystery that surrounds most of Castaneda's works, I also felt a certain amount of criticism and suspicion toward an author who seemed to be tantalizing his readers from some remote hiding place. I had never seen Castaneda's name listed on any public speaking forum, nor had I ever heard of anyone who had spoken with him in person. I was quite uncertain as to whether his Yaqui sorcerer-teacher, Don Juan, was real person, a fictional character, or an imaginary composite of several real or fictional persons. With such lack of resolution in my mind, I had for several years been reluctant to attempt to induce lucid dreaming using Don Juan's method of looking at one's hands in a dream.

However, at the time that I began to feel this growing inner commitment to induce lucid dreaming for myself, I also began to resolve my doubt and inner debate about Don Juan's authenticity. I realized that, for me, Don Juan's historicity was less important than his psychological astuteness. I realized that his method for inducing lucid dreams could be completely effective *for me,* regardless of whether or not he ever existed in the flesh. The power of this realization, coupled with my own sense of readiness, launched me into my experiment.

On approximately October 25, 1980, sitting in a quiet place in my own home, I practiced my first induction of the lucid dream, using the following method as described by Castaneda. I sat in a relaxed, quiet frame of mind for several minutes until I felt very peaceful and my mind was clear of all other thoughts. Then, I held up both of my hands in front of me at arms length and focused my gaze upon them, intently yet with relaxation at the same time. Using my eye as if it were a camera, I took a clear, distinct, visual impression of my hands and I said to myself in a solemn, serious tone of

* Carlos Castaneda, *Journey to Ixtlan,* pp. 88-155. Author's note: After a careful study of these pages I concluded that Carlos' teacher, Don Juan, uses the term "setting up *dreaming*" to mean inducing the lucid dream.

15

voice: "I see my hands in my dream; I *know* I am dreaming." I repeated this statement to myself, out loud, several times while gazing steadily at my hands. Then, I looked away at the wall at the far end of the room and neutralized my gaze for several moments by simply focusing on the wall. Then I returned my gaze to my hands again, focused on them steadily and comfortably, and repeated the suggestion to myself as before, saying several times, "I see my hands in my dream; I *know* I am dreaming".... "I see my hands in my dream; I *know* I am dreaming." Then I looked at the blank wall again, neutralizing my gaze. I repeated this process about five or six times, focusing and neutralizing, focusing and neutralizing, and then sat quietly for a few moments. After this, I arose and proceeded with the ordinary activities of my day. The whole process of relaxing, inducing, and focusing took about five minutes.

I repeated this entire procedure step by step about four or five times per day, every day, faithfully for the next two weeks. I felt excited to spend my time and energy this way because I continued to feel that gentle, vague, semidefinable sense that something beautiful was about to happen, that the lucid dream was imminent for me. Whenever I had a few extra minutes during the day I would practice this induction, sometimes by actually looking at my hands with my physical eyes, and sometimes by vividly picturing my hands in my imagination. I almost always repeated the induction just after getting into bed for the night.

Then on November 7, 1980, after two weeks of steadily practicing this self-hypnosis method, I had the first of a series of beautiful and inspiring lucid dreams. The first dream went as follows:

THE LUCID DREAM RETURNS
November 7, 1980

I have been dreaming for a short time and now I

become aware that I am dreaming. I begin to feel a very pleasant, light-headed sensation. I say to myself, very deliberately, "This is a lucid dream," as I look at the dream scenario depicting some houses and buildings along an ordinary city street. Now my left hand suddenly appears before me and I say to myself, "Oh, yes, I see my hands in my dream. The Castaneda technique really does work." Now I mentally command my right hand to appear also, and it does. I decide to practice directing the actual content of the dream. I focus on a tree in the dream scene, and I mentally command it to turn into a house. Slowly, the tree dematerializes and disappears and a small white house appears in its place. I feel pleased with my power and progress, and the thought comes that my practice of self-hypnosis and visualization of the past two weeks has definitely paid off.

I wake up feeling excited, and I realize that if I continue this practice, I can develop my psychic and intuitive awareness in the dream state. This is exactly what I would like to do and exactly what I intend to do.

This dream had some interesting elements in it that I find worthy of comment. First, I actually became lucid *before* my left hand appeared in the dreamscape. The appearance of the left hand served more as a confirmation of lucidity than as the stimulator of it. Secondly, upon becoming lucid I began immediately to practice different forms of mental creativity in the dream, by taking charge and commanding, mentally, the future direction of the dream. I commanded the right hand to appear and it did. Then, I commanded a tree to turn into a house, and that too was accomplished.

As I write now, over four years after the dream, I see that this type of experience in which one influences the actual content of the dream is a prelude to a certain type of psychic and intuitive power. This creative power can be exercised both in the dream state *and in the waking state* through the channeling of telepathic communication and visualization. The following recent example is intriguing and is the type of experience that seems to be occurring more and more frequently in my waking world.

17

Recently, I was conducting a dream group therapy session and I noticed that one of the group members had placed a used, squeezed tea bag upon one of the pillows next to where she was sitting. I felt a bit annoyed that the moist tea bag might stain the pillow. Still, I chose to say nothing. I wondered whether or not I was being too fussy about "small stuff" and whether I could just relax and let the situation be. Clearly, I wished that this lady would, of her own accord, pick up the bag and put it in the wastepaper receptacle nearby. I began to visualize her doing that very act, spending part of my conscious attention on this visualization, while devoting the rest of my attention to listening to another group member who was speaking at the time. I kept visualizing this woman removing the tea bag and, within one minute, she picked it up and dropped it into the receptacle. A positive surge of energy moved through me at once! The woman seemed to appear totally relaxed and poised as she disposed of the tea bag. How marvelous, I thought, if our simple requests could be communicated telepathically, in complete silence, and if these kinds of needs could be met with only the slightest expenditure of energy! Also, the more human beings are able to rely on intuitive and telepathic communication, the more energy they would have available for other more important things! From the onset, then, my work with lucid dreaming began leading me in that direction, inch by inch, nudge by nudge, and sometimes push by shove.

Nine days after "The Lucid Dream Returns" I had a second lucid dream which I entitled "The Magical Rabbit."

THE MAGICAL RABBIT
November 16, 1980

I have been dreaming for some time and suddenly I realize that I am dreaming. As soon as I become lucid, I feel a flow of tingling energy rising up into my head and settling in my forehead. The dream images shift suddenly and now I see an amazingly beautiful evergreen tree in front of me. Its branches are covered with snow, each one carefully and delicately poised, sagging under the weight of the beautiful, clear, brilliant, white powder. The scene is absolutely marvelous in its beauty and clarity.

I decide to take charge in the dream and I mentally command the tree to turn into a . . . (pause) . . . rabbit! After this short pause the thought comes to me, "A rabbit! Why not? A rabbit will do quite nicely." Instantly the tree vanishes and I see only a blank, brown screen in my field of vision. I feel disappointed and I choose to keep visualizing a rabbit. Soon I see the white outline of a rabbit on the brown screen. First I see it from a side view and then from its backside, as it begins to hop about with movements similar to an animated cartoon.

Suddenly the scene changes. I arch my head back and look straight up into the air. I see a beautiful eagle, or perhaps a hawk, floating in the air above me, hovering in place with poised, widespread wings. The sky is absolutely clear blue and the rays of the sun filter slowly and gloriously down through the outstretched feathers of the bird. Sparkles of sunlight slowly fall down toward me, like a soft, gentle shower. I feel impressed and joyous at the marvelous beauty of this scene which I savor, fully and deliberately, in every detail.

Suddenly I awaken, and I lie in bed with my eyes closed, my mind fully alert, basking in the afterglow of the vision.

It is impossible to convey in words the beautiful scenery that I saw in this dream. The scene of the snow gently sagging on the branches of that evergreen tree was absolutely exquisite, and the glorious rays of the sun, filtering down through the feathers of the eagle, were incredibly vivid. These images have left an indelible impression on my memory which I can clearly recall even now as I write, years after the dream occurred. With this dream, and with a number of subsequent lucid dreams, I became increasingly convinced of the unlimited ecstatic potential that is available to us through the lucid dream state. I saw the unspeakable beauty of these visions, as described by Patricia Garfield in her book,* and I began to learn, based on my own experiences, that these kinds of visions are indeed available.

This lucid dream also was marked by the conscious choice of the dreamer to take charge in the dreamscape and to re-create and rearrange the raw material presented in the dream. The tree was dematerialized and eventually rematerialized in the form of a rabbit. When I have recounted this dream in various classes and workshops students have often asked me, "Why a rabbit?" In this dream a rabbit was simply the first playful image that came into my mind. My unconscious mind, I believe, chose the rabbit out of its own spontaneity. Any image would have sufficed because the principal purpose of this scene, I believe, was for the dreamer to experience himself as the conscious creator of his dream. There was a definite tone of playfulness and whimsy in this dream scene, reminding me of the essential link between creation and play. With the coming of "The Magical Rabbit" I felt even more confirmed in my experiment. It was wonderful to receive such a dream response to my consciously chosen intentions.

At this time, I was also strongly influenced by Scott Sparrow's book, *Lucid Dreaming: Dawning of the Clear Light.* Earlier on that morning of November 16th I had experimented with one of his suggested techniques for inducing the lucid dream. I had actually awakened around 5:00 a.m. and, since I was unable to fall back to sleep, I arose and meditated from 5:30 to 6:30 a.m. At the end of the meditation, following Sparrow's instructions, I planted a suggestion in my mind that I would have a lucid dream when I returned to sleep. I then went back to bed around 6:30 and awakened at 7:30 with this lucid dream. I felt very pleased to have received instant results and such gratifying results at that!

* Garfield, *op. cit.*

Since the dream of "The Magical Rabbit" I have on a number of occasions meditated in the early hours of the morning and have often obtained good results in using meditation to assist in the inducing of a lucid dream. Of course, the outcome was not automatic or achieved every time. One needs to approach this type of project with a spirit of adventure and detachment, and with what Sparrow calls an attitude of "the surrendering of acquisitive desire."* The psyche does not yield up her secrets through force, demands, or tenacity, but more through the process of gentle coaxing and ongoing faith.

One of the more challenging questions that arose for me at this point was: How can I prolong or sustain lucidity once it occurs? From reading Sparrow and Garfield, I knew that this challenge arises because the onset of lucidity often injects a powerful jolt of energy into the dreamer. Sometimes this jolt will shock the dreamer into awakening. So far, this had not been my experience. Sometimes the lucid consciousness pushes the dreamer back into the normal dreamscape, and sometimes the dreamer helplessly feels his lucidity fade away in gradual degrees like watching a sunset fade at the end of the day. For me thus far, it appeared that lucid dreams simply ended of their own accord and that I awakened when it was time to awaken. Another related issue, according to Sparrow and Garfield, was that sometimes powerful forces within the dreamscape itself could pull the dreamer out of the lucid state and thrust him back into the ordinary dream. As I continued my experiment, I soon acquired firsthand knowledge of all these possibilities. Consequently, I now began to focus on staying lucid in the dream and attempting to prolong, and abide in, that delicate balance that arises from this altered state.

The following lucid dream, the third in this series, occurred ten days after "The Magical Rabbit." It

* Scott Sparrow, *Lucid Dreaming: Dawning of the Clear Light*, pp. 36 ff.

provided a good example of how lucidity can be interrupted by negative forces operating within the dream.

THE BEASTLY INTERRUPTION
November 26, 1980

I am dreaming and I see myself sleeping in my bed at home, alone. I feel a strange state of consciousness coming on, and I half wonder whether I am dreaming or awake. I am aware of my hands and arms; they possess an unusual yet delightful energy moving through them. To test out whether I am dreaming or not, I gently rub together the thumb and fingers of my right hand. A delicate, refined energy quickly flows from my fingertips and rushes all through my upper body. The feeling is so unique that now I realize I am dreaming. I feel delighted to be lucid, and I begin by exploring the sensations of my hands, arms, face and chest. I feel pleasure in my body—gentle and delicate.

I decide that since I am lucid, I will write a poem. Immediately a Source, that seems to come from somewhere deep within me, creates these lines:

"O God, you have created man,
And from the beginning knew,
All that he must suffer and endure,
You, nonetheless . . ."

Now I hear a loud knocking on the front door and my wife, Charlene, goes to answer it. As she opens the door, I see a man standing there with the hairy, dark face of a beast. He is very neatly attired in a dark blue suit, dressed like a typical businessman. He stands just outside the door and speaks with a deep, rumbling, gravelly voice, garbling and mumbling his message in a very guttural yet urgent way. I do not recognize any of his utterances, though I clearly perceive the tone qualities of urgency and beastliness in his voice. His voice becomes so loud and distracting to me that I begin to lose my lucid awareness as I listen to him, growling on and on in this guttural and gravelly way. Suddenly I awaken. I realize I have just had a lucid dream and I feel excited.

22

This dream demonstrated how the advent of some negative or "beastly" force within the lucid dream was powerful enough to interrupt the creative process. The interruption happened in two ways: the creative flow of the poem was interrupted, and soon thereafter the state of lucidity was lost altogether and I awakened. The disruptive, forceful image clearly reminded me of the proverbial "wolf in sheep's clothing." The primitive, inarticulate beast, impeccably dressed in the blue suit of a modern civilized man, suggested to me that I needed to resolve some negative elements within myself before my creative process could advance. The feeling tone that I felt coming from the beast was one of urgency mixed with gentleness and neutrality, certainly not one of hostility or aggression in this instance. I was reminded of the relationship between Beauty and the Beast in the classic fairy tale, in which the Beast was an ally and friend to Beauty from the beginning, although a demanding friend at that. These well-dressed beasts from dreams and folk tales convey the notion that even the dark side of our personality can be of benefit to us, if we will take it in and hear its urgent messages. They demonstrate Jung's basic concept that the "shadow" is ultimately an ally and source of strength to the dreamer.

Unfortunately, in this dream, I did not maintain the continuity of lucid consciousness long enough to confront and decipher the message delivered by the beast. The undeciphered utterances here may well indicate that I was not ready to face and understand certain negative forces that were currently "knocking on my door" and interrupting my creativity at this juncture. Such is the dilemma of human existence: Ready or not, here comes the "shadow"! Ready or not, our human tranquility and creative ventures can be disrupted at any time.

No doubt, in this lucid dream I was about to learn something about the nature of suffering, since that was the explicit content of the dream poem. But, at that moment, the beastly part of myself was not ready to articulate its message clearly enough, and so its lesson and the lesson of the poem both remained unintelligible. Whatever the lessons were, they would no doubt be kept in reserve and presented again at some later time. The unconscious is a perfectly patient teacher and will continue to approach us with what we need to learn, until we have mastered its messages.

Another interesting element exemplified in this dream was the three-step transition of consciousness from ordinary dreaming to pre-lucid dreaming to full lucid dreaming. As I "felt" a strange state of consciousness coming on and "half wondered" whether I was dreaming or awake, I was entering the pre-lucid state. From this dream I learned that in the pre-lucid state the dreamer often wonders, guesses, questions or doubts whether or not he is dreaming. The dreamer may ask himself, "I wonder if this is a dream?" Or, he may flatly assert to himself, "No, this couldn't possibly be a dream." In either case he has posed the valuable question, but has not yet reached full, affirmative resolution of it in his own consciousness. If the dreamer moves through this kind of confusion, doubt, and guesswork, and enters into full clarity ("I *know* this is a dream"), then he or she has advanced into the fully lucid state. From this dream, and other subsequent dreams, I learned that there are degrees of lucidity, and I began to think of the fully lucid state as one in which the dreamer possesses *full conviction in the moment* that he or she is dreaming. Anything less than full conviction and full clarity I have chosen to view as a pre-lucid dream. I also discovered that not all pre-lucid dreams lead to lucidity in its fullness. However, they are still valuable and exciting signposts along the way, because they provide some sense of progress in the overall cultivation of lucid dreaming.

I made an entry in my dream journal at this time that "The Beastly Interruption" was also preceded by an early morning meditation, which took place between

5:00 and 6:00 a.m. At the end of this meditation I again had given myself the suggestion that I would have a lucid dream upon returning to sleep. When I awoke from the dream around 7:00 a.m., I felt pleased with another success in the use of this new method.

The fourth lucid dream in this series took place about two-and-a-half weeks after "The Beastly Interruption." It too indicated an interesting step forward in my experiment in that, this time, I was able to stay balanced and remain in the lucid state, even though I was accused unfairly by a demanding authority figure in the dream.

RELAXATION UNDER PRESSURE
December 14, 1980

I am standing in a small rustic building, an outdoor bathroom at a summer camp for young men. It is a beautiful summer day in the mountains, and the crisp, clear air is filled with the scent of pines. I remember that someone in our particular group has been unjustly accused of being gay and I am concerned about the general atmosphere of suspicion and excessive interrogation in the camp. I look in the mirror and see that my beard is gone. In surprise I ask myself, "Now when did I shave off my beard?" I think that I must be dreaming because I don't remember having shaved my beard. Immediately, I hold my hands up before me and I gaze at them steadily. Feeling the pleasant and familiar rush of energy in my body, I now realize beyond any doubt that I am dreaming and I become fully lucid. I gaze steadily at both hands and watch as they slowly become ethereal, beautiful and sparkling with light. Soon they become translucent and they appear to be malleable because they are basically made of light.

Now, Father George S. enters the bathroom. He is the director of the camp and he wants to know, demandingly, what I'm doing in here. Standing with my back to him, I tell him that I am simply urinating as I unzip my fly and prepare to urinate into a strange-looking urinal. I can tell he feels relieved, and I feel confident that I can act "normal" and convince him that I'm not gay and I haven't done anything wrong. With a certain amount of effort to stay relaxed, I manage to urinate and Father George walks out, apparently satisfied that everything is okay. I feel relieved now that the unjust and excessive interrogation is over.

This dream scenario is very amusing to me for many reasons. In this dream, the interruptive, intrusive force was symbolized by Father George, a Catholic priest who was the dean of discipline at the high school seminary which I attended many years ago. I remember many humorous incidents of his catching me and other seminarians innocently fooling around in the hallways or washrooms when we were supposed to be getting ready for bed at night. In the dream I felt the power of his forceful interrogations all over again. However, in contrast to the previous dream, this time I remained balanced and poised under pressure. I continued to act appropriately in the dream *and* retained the lucidity throughout the rest of the dream.

This dream also exemplified another common method that can be used to trigger lucidity, the presence of an incongruity in the dream. This occurred when I looked into the mirror and noticed that my beard was gone. The incongruity shocked me into questioning my experience and eventually led me to think that I must be dreaming. At this point I obtained the full confirmation of lucidity for myself by holding up my hands before me and gazing at them steadily. When I saw my hands, I became fully lucid and felt great pleasure and joy in seeing the luminous, ethereal rays of light, sparkling all around and emanating from my hands. Once again, a familiar, lightheaded, intoxicating feeling swept through me in the lucid dream as I absorbed and soaked up with my eyes the glowing luminescence, this time coming from my hands. The lucid state was beginning to feel familiar to me now, and I knew that I had returned there again to a state of mind that is alluring in its magnetism, inspiring me and calling me to remain there longer if I could.

At this point in my experiment I asked myself: How can a dreamer maintain and prolong his lucid balance in the lucid dream state? My best response was to compare the process to my childhood experience of learning to ride a bicycle. I remember as a child how shaky and wobbly I felt as I first attempted to pedal around the track of the high school football field in my home town. Many times I lost my balance, fell and scraped my knees. Once I ran directly into a tree. With persistence, however, I was eventually able to extend the distance that I was able to pedal before I toppled over. Finally, I was able to ride around and around the track and sustain my balance indefinitely.

However, a second aspect of learning to stay balanced in the lucid dream seemed quite different from riding a bicycle. It felt more like a state of inactivity, quite distinct from bicycling or any other kind of action or "doing." This aspect seemed more like the fullest cultivation of a feeling state, a feeling of deep receptivity, openness and allowance for these lucid energies to emerge and run their course. Perhaps *allowance* is a good word for describing this second aspect of balancing. Sparrow uses the word "surrender." Other writers speak of "letting go" or "transcending the ego." In lucid dreams where I have felt this fullest state of allowance, I felt as if the lucid dream images and the refined, subtle energies that moved throughout my whole body seemed to *seep* into my awareness. The images did not occur because I created them, but because I had, in these rare and precious moments, allowed them to emerge. To increase my lucidity was to increase my allowance of this unique state of mind; to maintain it was to maintain it through this attitude of allowance; and to prolong lucidity was to allow it to be prolonged.

This degree of allowance is relatively rare for me and for most people in our society. The reason, I think, will be obvious to most readers. We Americans live in a culture that emphasizes all the opposite human traits. Action, power, control, manipulation, hoarding, hanging on, striving, pushing, and struggle are very common character traits that have been instilled into the American people as a whole. Those traits were once needed to forge a pioneer society out of the vast and oftentimes harsh wilderness to which our ancestors came. Today, we are considering the possibility of relaxing from these traits and opening up our collective psyche to enjoy a different set of values. My own personal evolution in lucid dreamwork has appeared to parallel our societal evolution. In my experiment I began to explore the possibility of opening myself up to deeper feelings and sensitivities, to the deeper joys and ecstasies that can be experienced in the lucid state.

The next lucid dream in the series demonstrated this shifting of mental balance quite clearly. In the dream I went back and forth between the pre-lucid state and the lucid state several times. The dream went as follows:

AM I DREAMING OR NOT?
December 20, 1980

I am dreaming and I have a dim awareness that I might be dreaming. I am aware of myself lying in my bed, face down, and I hear my son Erik* come running into the bedroom. He says, "Dad . . . Dad," and shakes me slightly. I decide to remain motionless so as not to disturb myself and soon Erik leaves. His voice and touch seem so real to me that I think I must not be dreaming after all.

Now the scene changes. I am looking at a beautiful country scene in springtime. It seems that some time has passed and I think I am dreaming again. I see a bright red flower of extraordinary, radiant beauty and at once I realize I am dreaming. I begin to feel the familiar flow of refined energy coursing through my chest and rising upward into my head. I say to myself that the flower is so absolutely beautiful that I am convinced I am lucid. Now I see a beautiful, tall, pink tree covered with thousands of gorgeous, brilliant, red bottle-brush flowers growing on the end of each branch. My body

---

* Erik was four-and-a-half years old at this time.

28

gently lifts off the ground and floats patiently and deliberately through the air until I reach the tree. I examine it very closely and carefully, absorbing into my consciousness in an extremely receptive way, every detail of the brilliant red flowers. I feel such joy in their beauty. Now by a conscious act of my will I levitate slowly upward into the air and I continue to examine the tree, very deliberately and consciously, all the way to the top, about sixty feet from the ground.

Suddenly, the scene changes. Now a handsome young man, with a meticulously, neatly trimmed, reddish-brown beard stands before me. His face is radiant and he wears gray slacks and a neat-looking, dark-green, pullover sweater. Now he disappears, and I wish he had stayed longer.

Again, I hear Erik running into my bedroom and he touches me gently on the arm and says, "Time to get up, Dad," as he tries to awaken me. Again, I choose to remain motionless and he promptly leaves. Now I am not sure if I am dreaming or not. As a test, I blink my eyes very deliberately and forcibly. The physical sensation in my eyes is so vivid and realistic that I conclude I must not be dreaming after all. I feel some disappointment.

The scene changes again. Now I am standing in the executive suite of an elegantly furnished, high-rise hotel with a well-dressed man in his fifties. I hear a radio playing. I think it is an FM station because the pace is slow and the words and music are very clear. I hear a catchy tune and a mellow, male voice giving a commercial for coffee beans. I think to myself that I am a well-paid, high-level advertising executive and, therefore, I feel quite sure that I am dreaming. I feel fine as an advertising executive though I am clearly aware that this is not my line of work at all. I realize I have not the slightest interest in this line of work and so I conclude decisively that I must be dreaming.

Now I choose to awaken from all these scenes and, still lucid, by a deliberate act of the will, I awaken.

Upon awakening I realized that the whole experience was, indeed, a dream and that I had been lucid and pre-lucid several different times. I felt overwhelmed. The dream was quite long and I could not possibly remember it all. However, I shall always remember the radiant beauty of the thousands of bottle-brush flowers swarming all over that tall pink tree. I felt incredible joy in being able to examine them so closely and fully immerse myself in them, and levitate my dream body at will anywhere and everywhere in that scene. The process of levitation and subsequent freedom of movement in the dream allowed me to see those exquisite flowers from any angle I desired and with as much closeness as I desired, even to the point of being stunned by their beauty. As I shifted back and forth between the pre-lucid state and the lucid state, I acquired valuable experience toward learning to maintain my balance in the dream, just as I acquired balancing skills in learning to ride my bicycle when I was a boy. This practice and its repetitions gave me a sense of progression as my experiment continued its initial unfolding.

In this dream my consciousness shifted back and forth several times from the normal dream to the pre-lucid state to the lucid state. This shifting nature of consciousness posed some challenging questions for me. After awakening I spoke with Charlene and Erik, who both assured me that Erik had not entered the bedroom during the past hour. In fact, the bedroom door had been closed the whole time and he could not have opened it because we had, at that time, a special plastic device placed over the doorknob, which made it impossible for a small child to turn the knob. Therefore, from the waking state I had to conclude that Erik had not actually and physically entered the bedroom, and that I had *dreamt* that he had entered the bedroom. This posed an interesting dilemma, because that part of the dream was so literal and vivid that I was convinced (while in the dream state) that he had entered the room and tried to wake me up. The test that I had constructed for myself (that is, blinking my eyes forcibly while in the dream) also had failed to answer the question, "Am I dreaming or not?" Again, I had simply *dreamt* that I had blinked my eyes! In my dream body, it felt exactly the same as if I had blinked my eyes with my physical body. This little experiment added credence to Scott Sparrow's suggestion that the lucid dreamer "try not to test the lucid dream by waking standards."* This experience showed me how easily the dreamer can fool himself if he tries to determine whether or not he is dreaming by pinching himself, blinking his eyes, or engaging in any other simple act in the dream state, because all of these acts could be performed, vividly and "realistically," by the dream body in the dream state.

Upon rereading my dream journal at the time of this writing, I found that I had meditated on this particular morning from 5:30 to 6:30 a.m. Once again, I had ended this early morning meditation by giving myself the suggestion to have a lucid dream upon returning to sleep. I realized now that this particular tool was proving to be quite effective for me, as I awoke with the dream around 7:30 a.m.

I had no desire to anaylze this lucid dream or do therapeutic work with it in any way. It had a sense of completion that is common to many lucid dreams, almost as if the dream were a work of art in itself. This sense of completeness and wholeness is one of the features that clearly distinguishes many lucid dreams from ordinary dreams. Most schools of psychotherapy generally follow or build upon Freud's basic idea that the dream expresses the content of the unconscious mind and usually presents the dreamer with some kind of problem to be solved. Many lucid dreams, however, are simply nonproblematic; they seem to emerge from a different category or realm of the mind. As such, they serve many important purposes other than assisting the dreamer toward the confrontation of personality problems, although such confrontations can certainly be one of their functions.

Fritz Perls, the father of Gestalt therapy, often spoke of dreams as depicting the "unfinished business"** of

---

* Sparrow, *ibid.*, p. 47.
** Frederick S. Perls, *Gestalt Therapy Verbatim*, p. 69.

the dreamer's past, thereby offering him or her the opportunity to complete some unresolved psychological issue. Speaking as a psychotherapist, I do not see any inherent contradictions between the works of Freud, Jung, Perls and other psychotherapists and the ramifications of lucid dreaming. I do believe, however, that one of the biggest challenges that psychotherapists may have in approaching the lucid dream will be to step aside from their traditional problem-oriented point of view in order to appreciate that the lucid dream is more likely to serve the dreamer on another level. A lucid dream is more likely to be instructional about the nature of consciousness *per se* than to reveal the dreamer's particular disturbances of consciousness. It is more likely to depict something about the general evolution of consciousness than reveal something about the individual dreamer's particular "arrestment of development." As its first function, the lucid dream is more likely to reveal the dreamer's inner joy and creativity, while addressing his or her emotional problems as a secondary function. In short, the lucid dream is more likely to be the bearer of good news than the bearer of bad news.

Along this same vein, I suspect that the layperson with an interest in dreams may have to make a corresponding mental shift in viewing the lucid dream. He or she may have to surrender the urge to ask the common question, "But what does the dream mean?" The urge to *interpret* a dream is at this point so deeply ingrained in our culture that some people may have difficulty in approaching a dream in any other way. For thousands of years we have been so culturally conditioned toward searching for the meaning of a dream that some students of the lucid dream may have to make a major attitudinal change in order to approach it creatively. Simply to appreciate and enjoy the lucid dream and to bask in its light, its vivid images and colors may well be the primary creative response that we can make to most lucid dreams. Not that lucid dreams do not offer us messages or insight. They often do, though these messages are often of a much higher or much more subtle nature than the meanings of ordinary dreams. The lucid dream is a subtle teacher. As my experiment progressed I began to grasp this concept in many ways.

I have often wondered and speculated about the tremendous creative potential of the lucid dream state. How many brilliant discoveries, insights, and creations could be made if the lucid dreamer could maintain his delicate, inner balance for an extended period of time? If the dreamer could prolong his lucid state long enough to write a poem or an original song from beginning to end, or perhaps to analyze and solve a business problem and create a solution that could be viable in his waking world, he or she would be operating on a very advanced level vis-à-vis the dream world. Anyone who could command his inner resources to such an extent would be filled with feelings of high self-esteem, self-confidence and assurance. Before making any major life decisions, such a person might say, "I'll sleep on it; give me a few days to turn it over to the unconscious." Such a person would know whereof he spoke. His inner psychic consultant would be waiting in the lucid dream.

So at this point in my experiment I began to ask: Would it be possible to sustain a creative flow of images, words and ideas while I was in the lucid state? Could I actually create something in a lucid dream? The next lucid dream in my series began to address this question.

LUCID AGAIN
December 23, 1980

I am dreaming and I know that I am dreaming. To test out my lucidity I deliberately think that my hands will appear before my eyes and immediately they both appear. My mind races with excitement as I think, "Aha! There are my hands again . . . . This Castaneda technique really works . . . . This is the second lucid dream in the past few days."

Now I look carefully at my left hand and I notice my wedding ring is gone. In its exact place I can see two parallel pink lines going around my ring finger as if the ring had left its impression there. With my right index finger I carefully and gently rub the spot where the lines are, and I am surprised that I can feel my ring with my fingertip. I can feel the form and shape of the ring quite realistically but I cannot see it at all.

Now I think that since I am lucid I will create something from this dream. As I mentally search about for an idea or image to command, I feel myself being pulled out of the lucid state and falling back into ordinary dream consciousness. I feel the delicate balance of the energies shifting; I realize I have no control over it now. I wake up with a keen appreciation of just how poised and balanced the mind has to be in order to maintain the lucid state for a prolonged period of time. In order to create from that tender position, I realize I will have to learn much more about sustaining the inner balance indefinitely.

In recalling this dream, as I write, I remember the definite feeling of the shifting of my inner energies. I remember wanting to prevent the shift from taking place in the dream and that I had no control over it then. I somehow "fell" back into the state of normal dreaming, and I was clearly aware of this falling sensation as it occurred. In this dream I was not able to stay lucid. At this point I began to believe that one who aspires to be a regular lucid dreamer would probably have to undergo numerous similar experiences of "falling" or of "losing it" in order to learn the process of remaining lucid for as long as one wishes. Just as I had to fall off my bicycle as a child numerous times before I fully learned that sense of balance, so, too, I began to suspect, I would have to go through these inner experiences of falling from the lucid dream any number of times.

Another interesting item which I found worthy of reflection in my "Lucid Again" dream was the missing wedding ring. Though it was present to my fingertips (tangible) in the dream, it was missing to my eyes (invisible). One of my five senses could perceive it whereas the other could not. How fickle the senses are, I thought, and how easily we can be deceived by any one of them! My wedding ring is the symbol of my connection to a female in the world and, correspondingly, a symbol of my connection to my inner female (feminine consciousness) in my inner life. The dream, I realized, was giving me a significant message here in saying that my connection to my feminine or feeling side was still not solid enough. I could touch it, though I could not see it. It was half-present, yet half-absent. My own self-analysis was that for the present my approach to lucid dreaming still contained too much of my *willing* it to happen and not yet enough of my *allowing* it to happen. The "masculine" attitudes of willpower, order, goal setting, intentionality and control are very strong in my personality and always have been since childhood. Correspondingly, the "feminine" attitudes of trust, patience, relaxation about goals and allowing it all to happen have been my less-developed traits. These feminine mental qualities, I realized, would need to be increased within myself if the fullest psychic cross-fertilization was to take place.

The symbol of the missing feminine element has occurred several times throughout my experiment with lucid dreaming.* Its recurrence had led me to see that I cannot escape its message or importance. A series of recurrent dreams, recurrent images or recurrent themes is one of the surest ways in which the unconscious mind, patiently and perseveringly, reminds the dreamer of ways in which he or she needs to grow to become a more complete person. So, at this point, I began to focus my conscious mind on trusting the process more and relaxing about it in order to allow the experiment to unfold in its own natural way. This recurrent theme of deepening my sense of trust in the creative process is one that I would be reflecting upon for some time, certainly throughout the rest of my experiment and probably throughout the rest of my life.

* See my dreams entitled "Amputation" in chapter five, "The Arrival of the Serpent Power" in chapter six, and others throughout this book as an example of a recurrent theme in dreams.

CHAPTER THREE

The Gift of the Magi

"For me there is only the traveling on paths that have heart, on any path that may have heart. There I travel, and the only worthwhile challenge is to traverse its full length. And there I travel, looking, looking breathlessly."

—Carlos Castaneda
The Teachings of Don Juan

My exploration of lucid dreaming came to a tremendously satisfying and overwhelming peak on January 2, 1981. Early that morning, about 6:00 a.m., I awakened from sleep and realized that I had just received three lucid dreams in a row. The third dream of this series was totally incredible to me, and remains to this day the most exceptional, powerful and astounding lucid dream I have ever had or heard. I entitled it "The Gift of the Magi."

I had spent much of the preceding day, New Year's Day, rereading sections of *Creative Dreaming* by Patricia Garfield, particularly immersing myself in her chapter on lucid dreaming. I was also at that time busily outlining the content for a course on lucid dreaming that I was planning to offer soon. By the end of the day I was very excited and energized by all this stimulation which was racing through me.

Arriving some time early in the morning, these three companionate dreams occurred one after the other, with some normal sleeping time occurring between each one.

PRIME TIME FOR LUCID DREAMS
January 2, 1981

I am dreaming and I become aware that I am dreaming. As a confirmation to myself, I mentally call up my hands into my field of vision and they appear instantly. My hands have an ethereal, luminous quality to them and I am convinced that I am lucid, as I feel that refined, lucid energy moving through my hands, face and head once again.

I see my surroundings. I am in a small jail cell, lying on my back, sleeping on a simple cot. Retaining my face-up position, I consciously and deliberately levitate my body up into the air and then roll over a couple of times.

Now I hear my son, Erik, walking into the bedroom in his usual manner. I hear the shuffle of his feet on the carpet and feel the waterbed shake as he plops onto the far side of the bed next to Charlene. I hear them speaking and soon Charlene tells him to go back to his own bed, which he does reluctantly. I continue to focus on my lucidity in the dream state. I keep full concentration on my body floating in the air and feel quite pleased with myself. I am fully convinced that this conversation between Charlene and Erik is occurring *on the physical plane completely outside the dream.* I am able to overhear it all and still maintain the continuity of this lucid dream. I determine to stay balanced, and I do so. I realize clearly that I wish there was some way that I could set limits against Erik coming into the bedroom in the early morning because I remember what I read yesterday in *Creative Dreaming:* that the hours of the early morning are prime time for lucid dreams. I feel good in getting clear about this particular desire. After a few moments the lucidity begins to fade and then the dreamscape also fades as I fall back into a sound sleep.

LUCID BALANCING
January 2, 1981

I am dreaming and I become aware that I am dreaming. I am, again, in the same small jail cell which I recognize from the previous lucid dream. I am lying, again, face up on the same, simple cot in the cell, and after a while with a distinct act of the will I deliberately levitate my body up into the air and float there above the cot. Again, I hear Erik's footsteps as he shuffles into our bedroom and crawls into bed on Charlene's side. Again, I overhear their conversation in which Charlene tells him to return to his own bed. He resists and whines at first, and then eventually complies with her request. As he walks out of the bedroom, I feel convinced that this time also I am overhearing their conversation occurring *on the physical plane outside of the dream* while I remain aware of the dream scenario and my lucid consciousness. Again, I enjoy maintaining my balance, as I realize that I am not being pulled out of the lucid dream state into the waking state. Soon my lucidity fades and the dream also fades. I fall asleep again.

THE GIFT OF THE MAGI
January 2, 1981

I am dreaming and I become aware that I am dreaming. I feel the strong, tingling sensation come over me as the lucid energy rises up into my head again. I see that I am in the same small jail cell, which I clearly remember from both of the previous dreams. I decide to fly, and I easily and effortlessly sail through the air out of the cell. I burst into a whole new scene and soon I am floating gracefully over a beautiful, bustling college campus. It is a brisk, early morning and I see many students with books under their arms heading for their classes.

I see an old friend, Jacques Jimenez, and I decide to tell him about my experiments with lucid dreaming. I know he will be amazed. I invite him to fly with me, assuring him that I have the power to levitate his body at will. He is incredulous yet willing to take a risk at the same time. I raise him up, and together we fly, belly down, across the campus. Jacques is very impressed, but tells me he has an important class to catch and says he has to go. I say good-bye and I fly off, away from the campus.

Again, I hear Erik coming into our bedroom and repeating with Charlene almost the exact same dialogue as occurred before, as I was dreaming the two previous dreams. He shuffles in and crawls into bed next to her. Soon she asks him to return to his own bed. Again, I am convinced that I am hearing this conversation *on the physical plane,* while still maintaining my delicate balance of remaining lucid in the dream state.

The scene changes. Still lucid, I am now one of the three magi, traveling alone by camel across northern Africa in search of the Christ child. I feel a tremendous pull in my chest to complete this journey, though at times I do not know for sure which direction to take. I know I must go eastward, and occasionally I see the star, glimmering faintly on the eastern horizon, calling me onward. The journey is long and arduous, and yet I gladly continue, day after day, night after night, and week after week for a very long time. At times the passage of these countless days and nights seems like one long moment of measureless time. At other times, each distinct moment of the entire journey is very clearly etched in my awareness. Clothed in long, flowing robes, sitting alone on top of my camel, I feel fully immersed in its deep, steady, rhythmic motions as I sway widely from side to side with every step that it takes. Upon its back I feel in total harmony with this gentle and faithful beast, at one with the complete cycle of its movements, leaning out on each sideward swing and riding each corresponding return swing back to the camel's center with full, conscious deliberation. As I travel now, I enter a state of deep meditation and see so clearly that my ability to see the star at all is based on my *inner attunement.* Without this fine, delicate, inner tuning of consciousness I would not even see the star nor care that the Christ had been born, much less find him.

At one point, as I travel by night, I overhear two highwaymen lying under a tree near the roadside. One is boasting loudly and crudely about his plans to rob some traveler soon. I focus my energy inward at once, feeling a most unusual kind of strength as I ride my camel and feeling fully confident in this method of protecting myself from their kind. I also feel fire coming out of my eyes and know that if I chose, I could with a powerful glare, send two burning beams of light in their direction and fry them both to a crisp. With a sense of measureless power and poise, and keenly aware of my journey's ultimate purpose, I pass on.

Through this whole drama, I am continuously aware that I am dreaming. My inner self is flooded with a rarified and highly refined "light-energy" that circulates gently and continuously inside my whole body. I feel extremely uplifted.

Now I am approaching the gates of Jerusalem and the star grows brighter and larger on the horizon. At times the star disappears behind the taller buildings of the city. I am pleased at the size, modernity and prosperity of Jerusalem. I enjoy entering the city.

I enter the palace of Herod the king and am given a most gracious, hospitable and royal welcome. Everyone is most interested in my story as I tell of following the star, my long journey, and as I ask them for help in finding the new king. Herod seems so warm and friendly, I assume that he would be as eager as I to find the new babe. Herod is a handsome young man, about twenty-five years old, with dark hair and bright, flashing eyes. He wears a gorgeous, full-length robe, deep burgundy in color, and the entire chamber floor before his throne is covered with a plush, pale blue carpet, absolutely dazzling in its beauty. However, I sense that Herod does not believe my story. I tell him that I am an expert astrologer and am well versed in esoteric matters. He scoffs, and at once I realize that he is not conscious enough to understand and appreciate what I am saying. I quickly look about me and feel out the inner vibrations of the astrologers of his court. With full clarity about their inner life I can see they are all mediocre. I plead with Herod: "But surely you must believe in ESP?" Again, he scoffs. Instantly, I decide to continue my journey without his help.

As soon as I leave Herod's court I see the star again, looming large and bright on the northeastern horizon. With great joy and anticipation I quickly arrive at a small, modest home where I behold a marvelous scene. I see the small Christ child, probably a year old, lying in his crib with Mary and Joseph sitting beside him. Several shepherds and two other magi who have arrived before me are kneeling before the child in humble worship. A beautiful, bright light radiates from the child continuously. I hurriedly dismount from my camel and take my place, kneeling beside the others.

Suddenly I feel a tremendous rush of emotion within me, welling up from my stomach and chest so strongly that I burst into uncontrollable sobbing. I sob and sob and sob, heaving my chest for a long time as all of the feelings of the journey pour through me: extreme joy, relief, sadness over Herod, courage, determination and many other feelings. With my eyes brimming with tears I look at Mary and Joseph and then back to Mary. In a flash, many deep and tender feelings are communicated back and forth between us, all telepathically, each message clearly sent and clearly received with the fullest speed of thought. Not a word is spoken and none needs to be spoken. I feel so relieved; she understands me totally.

I reach into my bag to offer my gift to the child. With tentativeness, and sobbing continuously, with a flood of tears streaming down my cheeks I ask, "Will you accept pure gold?" The child with a delicate little smile simply radiates in silence. Several times more I ask, "Will you accept pure gold? . . . . Pure gold? . . . . Pure gold? . . . . Will you accept pure gold?" Still sobbing profoundly with my whole body, my thoughts now begin to race. I realize that pure gold is the best that the world can offer, and yet the babe and the Light are priceless beyond compare. I am completely overwhelmed.

For a long time I kneel quietly beside the other magi gazing earnestly at the infant. I am totally entranced by the dazzling, beautiful light that emanates continuously from his whole body and especially from his loving eyes, that simply look back at me, so calm and steady. I feel as if I could kneel here forever.

Now I feel Charlene moving on the waterbed and putting her arms around my physical body. She is extending a sexual invitation to me and I am completely clear that she is touching my *physical body* and is hoping to arouse me from sleep. Still lucid, I gaze with total absorption at the infant Jesus, appreciating so much the beautiful, glowing light that radiates from him continuously. I feel so solidly established in the lucid state and so transfixed by this vision that I know that Charlene's touching my physical body cannot pull me out of lucidity or out of the dream. I feel fully concentrated and centered in the light. As Charlene continues with her sexual advances, there is no doubt or hesitation in my mind as to which I would choose in this moment. I realize I would never abandon this experience of immersion in the Light for sexual pleasure or any other pleasure that I have ever known. I realize that it is rare for me to decline a sexual offer, and yet I do so without hesitation. I prefer with one single-minded focus to concentrate all my attention on the glowing Christ child. I realize that compared to this Light, all the other pleasures of life that I have ever known are absolutely pale. I feel completely content and yet enraptured, totally at peace and enlivened at the same time.

After a time, the light that surrounds the child slowly begins to fade. Still lucid, and still aware of Charlene persistently caressing my physical body, I now plan my exit from the dream, for I sense that this marvelous scene is coming to its own natural conclusion. For a few moments longer I watch as the light slowly fades from the Christ child until the dream has almost vanished completely. And then, with a conscious act of the will and with a deep feeling of reluctance, I choose to leave the lucid dream. Instantly I awaken, and as I return to the physical world I feel a tremendous amount of energy and emotion rushing all through me, body and mind. I feel *totally ecstatic,* in a way that I have never felt before.

At first I simply lay there in my bed for a few moments, basking in the afterglow of the three dreams, feeling stunned and amazed. In a flash, I intuitively entitled the third dream "The Gift of the Magi" and made a silent, mental note to myself to that effect. I then told Charlene that I had just had the most incredible lucid dream and proceeded to tell her the third dream in its entirety. As soon as I completed the telling, she also felt overwhelmed by it and said with full conviction in her voice: "The title of this dream is 'The Gift of the Magi.' " This piece of telepathic communication added even more intensity to my experience because she gave the dream the exact same title as I had only a few minutes earlier, in my silent, unspoken reflection.

I got out of bed, went downstairs to my office, and entered all three lucid dreams in my journal. This time, however, I encountered a problem I had never met before. As I wrote, I occasionally felt paralyzed and overwhelmed as the power and vividness of these three dreams continued to surge through me. These feelings often made it impossible to continue writing, and so I got up from my desk several times and walked briskly back and forth for five or ten minutes at a time. This brisk-pacing technique helped to settle down the potent energies that were surging through me. Then, as soon as I felt balanced and grounded again, I returned to my desk and continued writing. It took me about two hours to write out all three dreams and when I had completed the task I felt both exhausted and exhilarated. I went upstairs for breakfast about 8:00 a.m. and the incredible glow and the uplifting energy from the third dream stayed with me all day. In fact, for several weeks afterward it often returned with tremendous vividness. The image of the light frequently came into my mind during the initial adjustment period after the dream. Whenever I thought of it I always felt inspired and uplifted all over again, especially when sharing it with students and friends, months or even years afterward. Even now, at the time of this writing, over five years after its arrival, it still brings back the most amazing and positive feelings for me. The dream constituted what some writers have called a "peak experience." I believe it will nourish me for the rest of my life.

At breakfast I felt the need to verify, from Charlene's testimony, whether or not Erik had come into our bedroom that morning. In the lucid dream state I was completely clear that Erik had, indeed, entered our bedroom several times on the physical plane and had carried on his dialogue with Charlene on the physical plane. But now, in the waking state, I had some uncertainties about what had actually happened. So I asked Charlene several open-ended questions (so as not to bias her answers) about what had occurred. She informed me that Erik had, in fact, entered the bedroom several times, had crawled into bed next to her, and had tried to persuade her to allow him to stay there. Each time she told him to return to his own bed and each time he eventually complied.

This added confirmation was important to me and it allowed me to see that I had experienced another breakthrough in the lucid dreaming process. For the first time in the lucid state I became conscious on three levels *simultaneously*. I was conscious of the dreamscape (the dream content and imagery), conscious of the fact that I was dreaming (lucidity), and conscious of certain events occurring simultaneously around me on the physical plane. However, it was, above all, the exceptional degree of clarity (lucidity) experienced especially in the third dream, that enabled me to distinguish these three levels of awareness and to maintain the lucid state until the natural completion of the dream. This high degree of lucidity provided something like a mental platform upon which I could stand very solidly within the dream. From this platform I could easily distinguish the three levels of consciousness, while being fully in charge of my experience in the dreamscape and fully able to sustain lucidity for an indefinite period. From this experience I have concluded that when a lucid dreamer's level of lucidity is high enough, he or she is able to experience all of these processes simultaneously and even effortlessly. In addition, in such a lucid state, the whole experience is permeated with overwhelming feelings of joy, ecstasy, loving power, and the overriding desire for one thing only: to be one with the Light!

My experiences with Charlene in this particular dream added still another interesting dimension to my growing perspective on the lucid dream as an energy field. Unbeknownst to me, at the time that "The Gift of the Magi" arrived, her conscious energies were strongly aligned with my own and working in harmony with mine in a special way. I found out later that day, when discussing the whole experience with her at length, that she had on the previous day felt very pleased with my excitement about lucid dreams. Upon retiring to bed, she had done extensive visualization on my behalf, visualizing that I would have special dreams that very night. Since she had not verbally communicated this to me, I did not know consciously that she was visualizing for me. Little did she realize that her wishes would be fulfilled so abundantly! This added, for me, an extra delight over the silent intuition that we shared in giving the dream the same title. It also demonstrated the power that is possible in a dream experiment when two people, who are close to each other, have their energy fields united and pointed in the same direction.

This dream was a marked step forward in my experiment. In contrast to my previous experiences, in "The Gift of the Magi" neither forces from the dreamscape nor from the waking world were able to throw me off balance and disrupt the lucidity. In my earlier dream, "The Beastly Interruption," the interruptive force from within the dream pulled me out of the lucid state. On another occasion, several years before my experiment began, as I was once in the midst of a lucid dream during an afternoon nap, I was jolted back to the waking state when my next-door neighbor turned on his radio. "The Gift of the Magi," however, gave me a clear demonstration that if the dreamer's lucidity is strong enough and clear enough, the dreamer can remain lucid for a much longer period of time, can consciously choose to remain in the lucid state for an extended period of time, and from the lucid state can clearly distinguish the dream scenario from certain physical events that may be occurring around him at the same time.

Here I began to speculate that if the dreamer, firmly grounded in the lucid dream state, can be conscious on three levels at once, then he or she could also possibly become conscious on four, five, six or more levels at once. If the human mind is capable of holding distinct conscious "awarenesses" on multiple levels simultaneously, then it must also have the potential to develop these capacities through special training. I further began to wonder if lucid dreaming could become a special tool for teaching people to expand their awareness in such a fashion.

Unlike some of my lucid dreams, these three seemed to be filled with messages. They all began by presenting me as a prisoner in a small jail cell. This theme reminded me that I still have work to do in order to liberate myself psychologically and spiritually.

Though I think that I have grown substantially as a person throughout my life, there still remain many higher levels of freedom to attain and many imprisoning thoughts and habits to break. The jail cell did not suggest to me any particular type of imprisonment. Rather, I saw it as a generic metaphor, symbolizing the basic inner duality that I have (and that everyone has) about the personal struggle between confinement and ultimate freedom. Until the "The Gift of the Magi" it was difficult for me to imagine what full human liberation might feel like. But as a human possibility full liberation seemed far more real to me now after I experienced the sustained lucidity of this dream and my single-pointed desire to seek only the Light. This taste of lucid liberation was somehow both sobering and intoxicating at the same time.

Most of us have had selected moments in our lives when we have felt totally free and totally in harmony with the universe. Sometimes people have such experiences when walking by the ocean or standing alone on a mountaintop. We have come to refer to these feeling states as "oceanic" feelings or "peak experiences." They can sometimes be overwhelming, beautiful and powerful. For most of us, these experiences do not last very long. They are brief and momentary, and after their passing we usually tell ourselves that, unfortunately, we have to return to the "real" world. In reflecting upon this lucid dream in particular, I have come to believe that we are all invited to touch upon these high places within ourselves more and more frequently, and to build up, gradually, our conscious awareness of how to live in these heights. I have come to see, too, that until a person possesses the full conscious awareness of how to tolerate these exhilarating energies, he would not be strong enough, internally, to sustain them. All he could do would be to touch upon them from time to time, promptly lose them, and then look back upon them, wistfully, as "peak experiences." These peak experiences, however, even if they are fleeting and fragile, are no small contribution to the spiritual evolution of the person who receives them. Without them life could easily become drab and dull. In reflecting on my experiment, I have come to see that the ultimate purpose of the peak experience is to provide us with a taste of ecstasy now, because a taste is better than nothing at all and because a taste is all that most of us can bear *now*. In addition, we need to understand that if we were to receive the full impact of ecstasy without adequate preparation, most of us would probably die, because we are simply not yet strong enough internally to bear the fullness of the Light.

In terms of meaning, the symbol of the jail cell in these three dreams provided me with an essential reminder that I am still a prisoner, still working to attain to that fullness of mental freedom to which I aspire. I did not feel badly about this image or even view it as negative. Rather, in assessing my own present state of growth, I viewed it as a simple and direct statement of what is so. Interestingly enough, this imprisonment theme appeared for me again some ten months later in still another powerful lucid dream entitled "The Arrival of the Serpent Power."*

Through private reflection and from sharing this dream with students in my classes and dream groups I received many other instructional benefits from "The Gift of the Magi." The dream reminded me of a number of spiritual principles which I had heard before and which I now relearned. One principle is that true desire to see the light comes from the heart. In the dream I felt the tremendous pulling in my heart and chest area while riding the camel. True fulfillment of this desire is also felt in the heart. In the dream I felt the intense heaving in my chest as I came into the presence of the Light manifested through the Christ child. In the dream I felt a great opening of my heart center, and through the full and uncontrollable sobbing, a great outpouring of desire and love for the child. The spiritual path is, primarily, a path of love and not an intellectual inquiry. Its initial motivation and final culmination are

* I have discussed this dream in detail in chapter six in this book.

a matter of the heart. It is a journey of love from beginning to end. Though the intellectual understanding of the journey is of value, the love for the journey is of the highest value. On any true spiritual path the intellect serves not as the master of the heart, but as the servant of the heart.

I have also reflected considerably on the notion of spiritual "attunement" as I experienced it in this dream. In the dream I felt this attunement in the heart center of consciousness and felt how delicate and refined it was. It reminded me of moments when I have stood in front of my FM radio receiver and fingered the fine-tuning knob very slowly, listening to the quality of the music coming out of the speakers. There is a gentle peace of mind and clarity that comes from matching the wavelengths or vibrations of my own mind with those of the stereo system. So too, as I was traveling across the desert of northern Africa in this dream, astride my camel, I could feel that attunement to the object of my desire, the Christ child, although the child was hundreds of miles away. I saw, ever so clearly, that the inner attunement was a prerequisite for the journey, and that without it I would not even feel the desire to undertake the journey. Moreover, I learned that *with* this attunement I was somehow filled with a great pleasure and felt an immediate joy and satisfaction that already made the long, arduous journey totally worthwhile. There was no delay of gratification. In *this dream* and with *this level* of lucidity every step of the journey was already providing me with an instant reward. When one's life is completely "on course" every moment carries an undertone of joy.

The long journey of seeking in this dream was a good illustration of a person living and acting in harmony with the Tao,* the flow of the universe. This experience of inner harmony, with my inner attunement fully

---

* The Tao, or Dao, is the "Way" of the ancient Chinese religion called Taoism. The essence of Taoist teachings is that the spiritual life consists essentially of creating inner harmony, balance and poise so that the individual can live in harmony with the flowing and changing movements of the world around him. Flowing with the Tao

connected to the final goal of the Light, provided such joy that I was able to transcend all the negative forces experienced within the dream. In that marvelous lucid state I easily rose above the discomforts and hardships of the journey because I was totally concentrated upon the Light and the joy that comes from seeking it.

After receiving numerous lucid dreams over the past six years, I realize now that I learned a great deal about the levels of lucidity from "The Gift of the Magi." I realized, for one thing, that there are many different levels of lucidity. Perhaps the number of these levels ranges all the way to infinity, so that no one could really number them all or create any psychological blueprint to map them out. Any such endeavor would seem to be meaningless and impossible to achieve.

"The Gift of the Magi" was an extremely bountiful event in many respects. Not only did I receive an amazing and lengthy dream scenario with an abundance of rich and meaningful images, but above all, the quality of lucid consciousness in this dream was higher and more pure than any state of mind that I have ever experienced before or since. It was, in itself, clear beyond all possible description and multiplex in its capacities. In that state, for example, I experienced simultaneously two types of time, *chronos* and *kairos,* as I made the long journey through the desert. These terms, borrowed from the ancient Greeks, speak of their awareness of two dimensions to time. *Chronos* was, for them, the experience of time as duration, the linear, chronological sequence of events that we ordinarily refer to when we speak of the "passage of time." *Kairos,* however, was their word for the experience of "timeless time," the fullest awareness of the present moment which somehow contains all within itself. In traditional Christian terms this dimension of time has been referred to as "the holy instant" or "the eternal now."

One of the surprising realizations that came to me in the altered state of "The Gift of the Magi" was the

is analogous to the traditional Christian concept of acceptance of the will of God.

discovery that one can experience both of these dimensions of time *simultaneously*. Previously, I had held an "either-or" consciousness about this duality and had usually been able to experience only one type of time at a time. In this highly lucid state I experienced a fusion of this mental duality for the first time in my life that I can consciously remember. If this lucid, light-filled consciousness is anything akin to what spiritual masters refer to as *satori, samadhi,* or enlightenment, then I can now appreciate the desire that they must feel to dwell in those states at all times. Bliss is incomparable. Its pull is fully engaging and even addictive in a certain sense.

It seems mandatory to me now to rethink and expand upon our present paradigm for dream studies in which we customarily distinguish ordinary dreams from pre-lucid dreams and lucid dreams. I firmly believe that these three categories of distinction are incomplete and insufficient, since in this dream I experienced a lucidity that was so vastly different and beyond the range of anything I had previously encountered. At this point I prefer to apply the concept of the spectrum of consciousness to the lucid dream and assert that within the lucid state a person may have access to a spectrum or range of psychic energy that is so vast, so broad and so unique as to defy classification and to transcend what we ordinarily speak of as "consciousness" from the perspective of the waking state.

Let me return now to further commentary on the dream itself. The two highwaymen in "The Gift of the Magi" symbolized for me the ever-present possibility of violence in the world. I took them as a reminder that violent forces could come upon me at any time and pose their challenges as part of the spiritual journey. In fact, I had begun to feel somewhat vulnerable at this time from the practice of cultivating lucid dreaming. One of my specific fears was that I might become "too sensitive," so sensitive to feeling and to the subtle realms of the mind that I might not be able to relate to ordinary situations or survive the ordinary stresses of

50

everyday life. Apparently, I needed to be reminded that I was not above and beyond the threat of direct assault, physical or emotional. The dream gave me that clear reminder and some excellent instruction on how to respond when I am potentially threatened. It demonstrated a way to concentrate my attention inward, to become balanced and centered with full power, and to feel the self-confidence that is possible from that position. In the dream I felt totally safe from the highwaymen, with an almost inexplicable feeling of inner strength. From that solid, inner position I was wrapped in the grace of God. The feeling of fire that came out of my eyes was a wonderful bonus. I felt as if I could send two burning laser beams of light out of my eyes, as if I had some special, incredible weapons that I could use if necessary. However, I felt a deeper joy in the dream in knowing that I would not have to use such force, and peace of mind in feeling myself above the urge to punish the highwaymen or strike them first. I felt no urge to attack them in that lucid state though I possessed the full awareness of my power to do so. I only felt completely and totally safe from whatever they might do. The dream gave me a clear message: Peace is created from the fullness of inner strength. My own peace of mind does not depend on whatever actions others may take or propose to take. When I am fully strong and fully conscious (lucid), then I am at peace.

At this point the question arose in my mind: "What type of aggression did the highwaymen in the dream symbolize?" Did they refer to any individuals in my world who were threatening me in some way, or did they symbolize my own inner aggression, my aggressive feelings and instincts?

In working with dreams over many years I have eventually opted to replace this "either/or" framework with a "both/and" framework. I have found that it is more valuable to view a dream as if it were poetry rather than prose, and therefore to assume that it speaks to us on multiple levels of meaning at the same time. At some point in my evolution I came to see that we can gain the maximum benefit from a dream if we ask, "What *all* can it say to me?" rather than "What does it mean?" As we give up the assumption that a dream has only a single meaning, we open ourselves to the fullest abundance that the dream world has to offer.

Accordingly, I came to view the two highwaymen in the dream on both levels, as symbols of external aggression and of my own internal aggression as well. Either way, the basic principle that the dream was teaching was the same: If I remain centered and balanced with a strong inward focus, I will not be assaulted or overwhelmed by aggressive forces. To be sure, the acknowledgment and resolution of my own inner aggression proved to be the most challenging task of all. This was amply illustrated with a very difficult situation that was occurring in my life at the time.

About a year before I had begun my experiment, the teenage neighbor boy who lived next door made a frequent practice of playing very loud punk rock music on his stereo set. The volume was extremely high most of the time and would come crashing in on me and my family at all hours, sometimes in the wee hours of the morning. We were quite vulnerable at the time since our bedroom window was very close to his house. For months I had made repeated efforts to elicit his cooperation and asked that he keep the volume down, but to no avail. Eventually he became quite sullen and would promise me whatever I asked whenever I approached him, just so I would leave him alone and not make any further requests. When I took my complaint to the boy's mother I began to see a fuller picture of the family situation. With his stepfather recently gone from the home and the boy feeling very upset, I soon realized that he was beyond parental control. For many months the ordeal dragged on. Frequently we were blasted by extremely loud music several times a week, sometimes in the middle of the night. Sometimes these assaults would last for five to ten minutes; sometimes they would last for two or three hours.

After about a year and half of this emotional assault I began to be filled with feelings of frustration, intense anger and rage at the teenager. Eventually, I became so enraged that I even felt like killing him for his violence and on several occasions I had thoughts of taking a baseball bat, going next door and smashing everything I could in a flurry of blind rage. Of course I had to check these impulses and checking them made them even more intense and explosive. I was shocked to discover that I had become filled with murderous rage. For the first time in my life, I actually contemplated killing another human being. I was shocked to realize that now *I knew* from the inside, from my own inner feelings, how one human being could be driven to kill another. Now *I knew* that the highwaymen inside of me could indeed take over my personality if certain negative conditions persisted long enough.

Charlene and I had already begun to call the police whenever the boy and his teenage friends would set their bedlam in motion. But repeated visits by the police to his doorstep made no difference either, except to aggravate a situation that was already quite tense. The boy and his friends began to play a cat-and-mouse game with the police, turning their stereo off as soon as the police car arrived, feigning cooperation, and then turning the volume up full blast again as soon as the police drove away. Not at all intimidated by the police nor respectful of what they stood for, they proceeded disrupting our family life, our sleep, and, of course, disrupting the quality of my dreamlife. Eventually, not able to stand it any longer, Charlene and I made a hasty, pressured decision to rent out our house and move. We had been planning this move for some time anyway, but in this context I actually felt prematurely driven from my own home. The total frustration of this experience made it one of the most painful I have ever had in my whole life. Still more painful was the admission that I was helpless in the situation and had not been able to create the clarity of mind and inner strength that I needed to protect myself from the "highwaymen" who were living right next door to me.

I had received "The Gift of the Magi" about one year before our pressurized decision to move out of our old neighborhood. I soon saw that this lucid dream posed many lessons about life, about darkness as well as the light. The lessons of the dream came at me fast and furious then, so fast and furious that I was not able to learn them all at that time. I simply did not have enough time and energy to assimiliate and digest such a rapid influx of ideas, events and emotions. Perhaps the hardest lesson of all was the need for me to acknowledge the "inner highwayman," that is, my own capacity for violence in a violent situation. This part of my own dark side, my "shadow" as Jung has termed it, had become strongly projected onto the teenage boy and his "hoodlum" friends next door. The intensity of my projection made me extra vulnerable to their conduct, extra hurt and offended by their aggressive behavior. Though I had always been careful to keep my negative view of the teenage boy to myself and to be outwardly friendly toward him in the years that we were neighbors, inside myself I had often felt critical and rejecting toward him. Unfortunately for me, at this time I did not withdraw my negative projection toward the teenager, and the inner dimension of my conflict with him became increasingly intense.

Equally unfortunate at this time was the fact that I was unprepared to protect myself on the external dimension of the conflict as well, completely baffled and frustrated in my attempts to stop the stereophonic assault coming from next door. I eventually realized all this in hindsight, and hindsight is, of course, easier than foresight. I was unprepared, I realized, because I had not completely broken out of my early childhood conditioning to be a "nice guy." My parents had always taught me "not to fight," and somewhere in my development I had thoroughly bought their message. I had also spent eleven years of my life in the Roman Catholic seminary system studying for the priesthood. Between the ages of fourteen to twenty-five, I was repeatedly trained to "turn the other cheek" and to practice "tolerance" and "infinite patience." Priests, above all, are trained to be nice, and seldom encouraged to be aggressive, even in self-defense.

But even more important than familial or social conditioning, I have, for a male, an extremely sensitive temperament and personality. I hate fighting. Aggression, noise, and chaos have always been repulsive to me ever since I was a child. Consequently, my own aggression has been buried, relatively unavailable to me, living in my unconscious since early childhood. Specific ideas on how to fight back against this teenage adversary *in any effective way* did not really occur to me at the time of battle. I finally learned this particular lesson with crystal clarity from another dream that I received and understood almost two years after Charlene and I moved out of the old neighborhood.* However, at the time that I was totally embroiled in the conflict, both inside myself and in the relationship with the teenage boy, the possibility of my being effectively aggressive was the farthest real option from my mind.

After the appearance of the highwaymen, the symbol of Herod the king was the next prominent image that appeared in the dream. Herod reminded me of myself in a couple of ways, with his dark hair and bright, flashing eyes, and with the gorgeous, burgundy-colored robe that he was wearing. The robe in the dream was the exact same color as the long, specially made, burgundy-colored robe that I had worn on my wedding day, and which I have carefully kept over the years as a special memento. The similarity of the color between Herod's robe and my own special wedding robe provided an extraordinary twist to this dream, making it abundant-

---

* I have included this dream and my reflections on it in chapter nine. It is entitled "The Sweet Horn of Genevieve."

ly clear that the Herod figure was truly a part of myself. So strongly did the unconscious want me to view Herod in this way that it created this unique dream symbol, one that could be easily overlooked by an outsider's analysis, but one that I as the dreamer grasped immediately and with a good deal of emotional intensity. This type of dream nuance is a good example of the creative and compelling way in which the unconscious mind can speak to us through a special dream image.

Herod also symbolized that part of me that appears outwardly to embrace intuitive, lucid consciousness for its own sake but inwardly is not really attuned to it. His external trappings were elegant in the dream but his inner attunement was lacking. His repeated scoffing reminded me of my own occasional feelings of skepticism and cynicism about pursuing my work with lucid dreams, meditation, visualization and other related psychospiritual work. Although I have pursued this work for many years, I have at times been assailed by inner doubts and skepticism about its real value and effectiveness. Though my doubts have been strong at times, I have always managed to rise above them and to receive sufficient rewards and confirmation through the years that working with dreams is a viable and beneficial psychotherapeutic tool. The Herod figure in my dream was that polished, sophisticated, urbane, skeptic part of me who is not in touch with the efficacy of psychological healing, though he overtly pretends to be. Like a typical scoffer, Herod surrounded himself with a circle of pseudo sages, the mediocre astrologers, who unwittingly reinforced his own level of mediocrity.

Yet in the dream, the wise man, the magus, was the stronger part of myself and it prevailed over the Herod image, seeing through his scoffing and all his superficial trappings. From the extraordinary quality of this lucid moment, I quickly saw again that so much of what one sees and creates in this world depends on the inner quality of consciousness that one carries. With his inner attunement lacking, Herod was simply not able to appreciate the quest of the wise man, nor could he value the star, the Christ child and ultimately the Light itself. As a man of darkness and accustomed to darkness, he could only resist the coming of the Light. The dream offered a strong note of encouragement here in that my higher self, symbolized by the wise man, easily overcame the skeptic and the scoffer. In the dream, as soon as I saw that Herod lacked the inner attunement I made an instant decision: to continue my journey without his help. This instant choice reinforced the concept that the attunement of one's consciousness to one's "heart center" is *the essential prerequisite* for the psychospiritual journey. Without it, all else fails. The king's gorgeous robe, his beautiful carpet, his coterie of astrologers count but little; they are not essential to the quest. Material trappings, no matter how tasteful, elegant or beautiful, are all incidental to the journey. The Christ as a bearer of the Light has come to make us conscious about consciousness itself. He has come to proclaim that nothing else in this world is as valuable as the quality of our consciousness.*

As soon as I left Herod's court in the dream, I saw the star again, "looming large and bright on the northeastern horizon." This part of the dream provided me with a wonderful example of how good a person feels, in life, when he returns to his essential path after a major distraction. I was impressed to notice how quickly my inner attunement allowed me to relocate the star and to follow it after taking the corrective action of leaving Herod's court. In this instance the rewards of such corrective action were instantaneous. At this point in the dream, I finally arrived at my long-sought destination, and felt a great joy and had a wonderful sense of anticipation. This scene from the dream has so much to teach me; I doubt that I shall ever exhaust it in a lifetime. In its outward appearance the scene was one

* "I have come that they may have life, and have it abundantly." (John 10:10)

of full serenity and simplicity, in contrast to the sumptuous sophistication of Herod's court. The spirit of humility and silence were there in abundance, the important signs of true greatness. And above all—there was the Light! At long last, the traveling wise man had arrived at the source of the Light! It radiated continuously, outward from the child's body, and illuminated the entire house and everyone in it. The child had a simple and loving smile on his face . . . beaming and beaming, steadily and constantly. Just like the sun itself, his sole purpose was to send forth his beautiful rays into the world.

I have often reflected here that the essence of this scene was the Light and not the Christ child. The child was the vehicle, the bearer of the Light. The Light itself, however, was the essence of the quest. It is the Light that the lucid dreamer approaches and with which I had been seeking to unite throughout my experiment. With my strong Roman Catholic background and upbringing, and living in a Christian culture, it is not surprising that the lucid dream would offer me the Christ child as the bearer of the Light in my particular case. Nor is it surprising that in order to convey the Light, the dream would offer me a re-enactment of one of the major stories of the New Testament and offer me a position in the drama. Both were very familiar and deeply gratifying to me. However, I am also convinced that the Light of the lucid dream world could be conveyed through any other appropriate symbol, whether it is considered to be explicitly religious or not. I am convinced that the Buddha, the Mahatma or Moses could easily be such a vehicle in a lucid dream, according to the cultural and educational background of the dreamer. The Light could also be conveyed through images, generally regarded as nonreligious, as has occurred in certain other lucid dreams that I have had, such as the eagle with outstretched wings, trees, flowers, crystals, objects of art or other beautiful images. Ultimately, it matters less how the Light is conveyed. It is the contact with the Light itself that is the most valuable and important benefit in the cultivation of lucid dreaming, and the light itself is always more important than the vehicle that conveys it.

In further reflections I realized that a dream such as "The Gift of the Magi" would probably be highly regarded in the eyes of many people. Yet the arrival of such a treasure can never be predicted or guaranteed. One needs to approach the lucid state with a combined sense of "seeking" and "letting go" at the same time. It may be timely to invite the Light, but certainly futile to demand that it appear. This type of "non-acquisitive desire"* that is appropriate for this quest is a tender and delicate state of mind. It is a state that is full of expectancy, yet empty of all expectations. It is a state that cultivates a deep mutuality between the self and the cosmos. It is a state that is willing to cultivate a strange yet vital inner balance and remain with that balance for an indefinite period of time. If and when a great "gift dream" arrives, it will be expected and unexpected at the same time, a gift of the Spirit, a pearl of great price that arrives in its own fortuitous moment.

As "The Gift of the Magi" approached its climax, I felt a tremendous rush of emotion surging through me, a rush that was so overwhelming that it broke through my customary ego defenses and self-control. In the dream I sobbed and sobbed for what seemed like a long time, completely out of control. My entire body convulsed with this flood of emotion which actually felt very good. For me, it was the epitome of relief, relaxation and coming to completion. In this scene of the dream I was home at last; there was no further need to travel, search or brave the hazards of the long, arduous quest. The sense of completion-at-last was firmly and emphatically punctuated by two specific psychic phenomena in the dream: the flashback of the entire journey and the telepathic communication with Mary.

In the flashback the entire journey, in every single

---

* Sparrow, op. cit., pp. 36-37.

detail flashed through my memory in an instant. All of its history was recapitulated in a single moment. The absolute pregnancy and fullness of this moment were clear and unmistakable. This complete flashback reminded me of certain descriptive accounts that have been given by people who survived near-death experiences and who reported that at the moment in which they realized they were about to die, they saw their entire lifetime rush before them in a single instant. In the past I had usually been skeptical of such reports, wondering how so much material could pass through anyone's mind in only an instant of time. But after having this experience in this lucid dream, I became fully convinced that in an altered state of consciousness, such as a lucid dream or a near-death experience, such possibilities are quite real. In this incredible dream moment thousands or perhaps millions of thoughts and memories flooded through my mind as one giant torrent, with each individual image flowing in its proper sequence. It was as William Blake has said that in such a moment the soul can hold "eternity in an hour."*

The telepathic communication with Mary, the mother of the Christ child, appeared as yet another amazing highlight to this lucid dream. In the dream it was a wonderful experience to look into her eyes and to know that her understanding of me was total. This mutual, simultaneous, telepathic communication, like all genuine telepathic experiences, was completely beyond the framework of words. The relief and joy that I felt in this experience of oneness were indescribable.

Telepathic communication brings many wonderful and exciting possibilities into our lives. Perhaps some day, when human beings as a whole are more psychically attuned, people will be able to communi-

---

* William Blake, "Auguries of Innocence," *The Portable Blake*, p. 150: "To see a World in a Grain of Sand
And a Heaven in a Wild Flower,
Hold Infinity in the palm of your hand
and Eternity in an hour."

cate with each other telepathically, to the extent where words are hardly necessary to all. The telepathy in this dream inspired me to speculate about the potential that awaits us at some future state of our evolution. In the dream I understood Mary totally just as she understood me totally. In that moment dozens of messages and thoughts flashed back and forth between us, again and again, each with the speed of light and with full accuracy. Every message was clearly sent and fully received. Every message was clearly transmitted in its proper order and sequence. There was no distortion or need for explanation on either side. It all happened effortlessly and in a matter of moments.

According to the New Testament account,* the three wise men brought three special gifts to the newborn Jesus, gifts of gold, frankincense and myrrh. The traditional interpretation of these gifts that I received in my Roman Catholic upbringing was that each gift had its own special meaning, each gift conveying a prophetic message about the life of the newborn babe. According to this oral tradition Jesus was given gold because he would one day be proclaimed a king, frankincense because he would one day be proclaimed divine, and myrrh, a special medicinal ointment, because he would one day suffer and die.

As I reflected upon my offering of the gift of gold to the Christ child in my dream I was reminded of many things. Every person has an existential need to make his or her contribution to the world. I regard this need as "existential" in that it springs from the bare fact of one's existence. Everyone has a gift to offer. Our journey, the pilgrimage of life, cannot seem complete to the pilgrim until he has offered his gift. Each person is compelled from within to offer his gift. To withhold it leads to an eventual withering of the personality and the gradual turning of the self from joy into bitterness. Therefore, the giving of one's gift and the release of personal creativity go hand in hand.

* Matthew 2:11.

Not only is each person existentially impelled to give his gifts and make his contributions, but I also believe that each person has a special gift, his "gift of gifts," that surpasses all his other contributions. Some of us seem to struggle and search in life for a long time to find this special gift in ourselves, to become fully conscious of some particular talent. Others seem to discover it easily and rather early in life. Upon discovering it, however, we have an important decision to make: Will we allow ourselves to release this gift into the world? This release calls for a type of surrender and for passing through the internal ego-chatter and feelings of vulnerability that people often have about exhibiting their special offerings. We often need to work through fears and anxieties about failure or success, acceptance or rejection, appreciation or depreciation, having our gift compared to someone else's, receiving fame or notoriety through the gift, and so forth. As we work through any barriers we may have, we eventually align ourselves with that larger force that helps us find our truest place in the world and take it with peace of mind.

In my lucid dream, as I offered my gift of "pure gold" to the Christ child, I had full clarity that I was offering my very best gift. There was no thought of withholding in the dream. I was offering my very best because I had, at long last, come into the presence of the Pure Light itself. This ultimate gift was given with full release, instant abandon, and total loss of control (the uncontrollable sobbing). The surrender was total; it occurred on every level of my being in the dream. I felt as if every cell in my body was sobbing. In no way, however, was this surrender experienced as a "loss." On the contrary, I experienced it in the dream as an immeasurable gain, as an exchange with the universe through which I felt fabulously enriched. I gladly surrendered my pure gold, my sobbing body and my loss of composure in order to receive the greatest gift of all: the loving, peaceful embrace of the Pure Light. In no way was this surrender perceived as a "defeat." On the contrary, I experienced it as culminating in the greatest victory I have ever felt in a dream or anywhere else in my whole life. In this lucid dream scenario, I was confronted with the essential paradox* of spiritual transformation: It is in surrendering that we are victorious; it is in giving that we receive; it is in letting go that we gain the finest gift that the universe has to offer: the pure Light itself.

The closing moments of this dream reminded me of a Christmas tableau. All the figures were motionless, standing, sitting or kneeling in their appropriate places as the light was emanating from the central figure, commanding my full attention. At the end of the dream I was still totally lucid and totally concentrated on the Christ child, allowing the precious light that emanated from him to enter my heart and soul. I desired only to allow that light to enter into every part of me, every pore of my skin, to absorb it totally.

In many ways, the ending of this lucid dream experience proved to be stranger than fiction and carried a humorous note that seems anticlimatic. It is amazing that Charlene was making a sexual invitation to me (to my physical body) as my dream was approaching its final moments. Such incredible timing! After a certain amount of reflection, I have come to see that her overtures were also an important part of the total teaching power of this particular dream. For many years I had heard of teachings from Eastern spiritual masters that certain heightened states of consciousness are more pleasurable and more ecstatic than sexual intercourse and orgasm. Now, from personal experience acquired in this lucid dream, I can attest that these theories are valid. At the end of the dream, as I was conscious on three levels at once and as I clearly knew what my choices were, I did not feel the slightest hesitation or doubt about which I would choose. I would never have given up the spiritual ecstasy of this lucid

---

* The best definition I have ever heard for the term *paradox* is: "A paradox is an *apparent* contradiction in terms, which is somehow, nevertheless, true."

dream for sexual pleasure in the physical body. Even now as I write, the qualitative difference between the two levels of pleasure is unmistakably clear in my mind. In discussing this point, I do not in any way devalue or minimize the appeal and value of sexual pleasure. I am only attempting to say that from this experience I have become convinced that higher levels of ecstasy do indeed exist, and that the pleasure and fulfillment that people can receive from them surpass our wildest imaginings. The lucid dream state offers us an access to these altered or higher levels of consciousness, with their many attendant surprises, pleasures and ecstasies that are unexpected and beyond ordinary human experience.

Coming to this new insight about sexual pleasure has placed sexuality in a new perspective for me. This new perspective did not change my sex life in any way, either in the frequency or quality of sexual activities. In fact, the added awareness that came from this lucid dream has served as an enhancement and addition to my sexual life and not as a revolution against it. Neither did this new experience serve as a demolition of any of my old beliefs. Rather, it basically served as a clarification of certain teachings of Hindu and Buddhist masters that I had already been vaguely familiar with for some time.

From my present perspective "The Gift of the Magi" is the crowning point in my experiment with lucid dreaming. If I picture myself as a traveler, hiking through the highest mountain range in the world, this dream at present remains as the highest peak on which I have been privileged to stand. However, one does not simply stand on a mountaintop forever; the journey of life goes on, and there are other parts of my story that are intricate, complex and challenging. To come down from the peak means to descend into the valley where one meets whatever obstacles one must face in the pursuit of a far-reaching vision. I soon realized that I would have to "integrate" this peak experience. For me, this meant that I had to do more inner work to become strong enough and willing enough to open myself to these channels of power and light on a regular basis.

At this point in my experiment it now became clear to me that in my explorations of lucid dreaming I had tapped into a most unusual energy source within the dream state, far more beautiful than I had anticipated and far more powerful than I had ever personally experienced before. With this turn of events I began to reconsider every important aspect of my experiment, realizing that I needed to cultivate a far greater inner strength to allow this amount of energy to move through me. In addition, I also realized that I had to dedicate myself anew to the creative rather than the destructive use of this energy. Above all, I was now filled with an overriding sense of awe and wonder. After all this, I wondered: where will the world of the lucid dream lead me next?

CHAPTER FOUR

Down from the Mountain

"The brighter the sun,
the darker the shadow."
—Attributed to C.G. Jung

From "The Gift of the Magi" my experiment with lucid dreaming led me onward through many successive valleys and peaks. Soon after this dream, the frequency of my lucid dreaming dropped considerably, from an average of one per week to approximately one every three weeks. Then, after several months, I had a "dry period," in which no lucid dreams appeared. This dry period was the first of several that were to occur from time to time. It lasted approximately four months and ended with a burst of three lucid dreams in one night, coming one after the other. In this interim period I had three pre-lucid dreams in which I came very close to entering the lucid state. At this point I began to wonder: Why did the frequency of my lucid dreams drop off so dramatically? Why did I have a totally "dry" period?

These questions led me to examine my resistance to lucid dreaming. Soon after the Magi dream, I suddenly began to feel a large number of doubts, fears and internal rumblings (resistances) about the whole project of deliberately inducing lucid dreaming. My mind went awash with concerns like: What am I getting into? Am I really ready for this? Do I need a spiritual guide or some special expert to assist me? Can I tolerate the high levels of power that are now starting to move through me? Will I burn myself out if I am not careful? Do I need to pace myself to prevent burn-out? Am I really worthy enough to receive direct contact with the Light? Should I pay more attention to the cautionary remarks of other writers in this field, like Patricia Garfield,* and Gopi Krishna,** who suffered certain amounts of mental distress as a result of their experiments. Had I actually tapped into the powerful kundalini energy without realizing it? Am I sufficiently free of ego concerns to pursue this path properly and creatively?

In short, with so many questions and concerns suddenly arising within me, it was not surprising that the quality and quantity of my lucid dreams diminished. As my experiment progressed, however, every one of these questions turned out to be of the greatest import, and I soon realized that every one of them would be answered and resolved in due time. In fact, all of these questions soon became the nuts and bolts, so to speak, of my experiment, providing many of the lessons that arose from it. These concerns launched me into a period of internal probing that was to become the next phase of my journey. The need to examine myself deeply and to proceed carefully began to become more important at this time and proved to be crucial to the long-range success of the experiment. There is no doubt in my mind now that my ego and my conscious mind had been overwhelmed with new and powerful energies and images, and that I would need plenty of time and reflection to integrate all this material in order to see it, eventually, in a clear and meaningful perspective.

About three-and-a-half weeks after "The Gift of the Magi" I had an ordinary dream that gave me some comfort and reassurance about my whole project. I

* Garfield, *Pathway to Ecstasy, passim.*
** Gopi Krishna, *Kundalini: The Evolutionary Energy in Man, passim.*

entitled this dream:

MY TURTLE IS A WINNER
January 26, 1981

I am completely under water standing in an upright position. As I look up toward the surface, the water appears clear and bright because of the sunlight. The rays of the sun are slowly filtering down through the water.

Now I see a turtle swimming past me overhead. It is brown and green, about ten inches long, and it paddles its legs at a brisk, steady pace. Instantly I know the meaning of the dream as I also remember a television program I had recently seen in which a man raced his pet turtle against a rabbit and the turtle won the race. The turtle means I will be a winner if I continue to persevere steadily in my work with dreams and not be seduced into quick, flashy approaches, symbolized by the rabbit.

I wake up and I feel calm and reassured by the turtle. I feel good when I realize that the interpretation to the dream came within the dream itself.

This dream clearly reminded me of the well-known folk tale of the hare and the tortoise and the couplet that sums up the tale's message:

Slow and steady sets the pace,
Slow and steady wins the race.

The messages from the turtle symbol seemed to be rather straightforward. I saw that the attitudes of perseverance and steady commitment were very important at this stage of my experiment in order to ensure its ultimate success. I also began at this time to think about writing a book about my lucid dream experiences, sensing that writing would be an excellent method to resolve inner doubts and to gain the fuller understanding of this portion of the dream world that I had now begun to explore. The more I reflected on the turtle, the more I saw it as a healthy antidote to the hare. This seemed particularly important to me, precisely because the image of the rabbit had appeared in my earlier lucid dream "The Magical Rabbit." This turtle dream now added a new dimension to my understanding of that rabbit image that had appeared in my previous dream two months before.

In "My Turtle Is a Winner" I was completely under water. I asked myself: was I possibly in over my head? Was I in a dangerous situation? The emotional tone of the dream did not seem to convey a sense of danger. Rather, it conveyed a more straightforward message. Yes, I had certainly gone into deep waters and, no doubt, needed to look up from time to time to see the light and keep a sound orientation.

Shortly after the turtle dream appeared, the value of slow and deliberate reflection in approaching the unconscious became even more deeply instilled in my mind as I was currently rereading Carl Jung's autobiography, *Memories, Dreams, Reflections.* In several places in this book, Jung described how he was frequently baffled and mystified by some of his dreams throughout his life. He also spoke of the deep respect he held for these dreams nonetheless, and of his deep, intuitive trust that some of them were very important to his personal growth and development. Those dreams that were unforgettable and that held the strongest emotional charge, he eventually deduced, were those to which his unconscious mind most urgently wished him to attend. So he made a practice of reflecting on these dreams through the years, turning them over and over in his mind, and allowing his conscious mind to examine them from every conceivable angle. Some of them, he states, he was never able to understand, and some of them became clear and meaningful to him only after years of contemplation. At this time, with the benefit of Jung's reflections, I became clear that *deliberation,* not time or speed, was of the essence in the examination of the lucid state and its attendant phenomena. I realized also that it may take me many years to integrate all these gifts and their corresponding resistances into my conscious understanding, and that, if such were the case, I could be content with it. I took a good deal of comfort in appreciating Jung's well-paced deliberations, realizing that I needed to allow for the same process of eventual unfolding in my own life and work.

Five days later, on January 31, 1981, I had my next lucid dream.

LUCID WITH KARL
January 31, 1981

I am dreaming and I wonder if I can become lucid. I think about seeing my hands, and at once they come up into my field of vision. Now *I know I am dreaming for sure,* and I feel a light, refined energy coming up into my head. I enjoy this feeling very much as I gaze steadily at my shimmering hands, glowing in the light. My friend Karl* is present. His face looks round and very happy as we talk about lucid dreaming. He says that he is lucid too as he looks at his hands. I feel wonderful having both of us lucid together at the same time.

The scene changes. Now Karl and I are walking through an almond orchard at harvest time in my home town of Sutter, California. I enjoy telling him about my experiences knocking and harvesting almonds here in this orchard many years ago when I was in my late teens. As I talk I occasionally check back with myself to see if I am still lucid, and I discover that I am. Now the dream fades out and I return to sleep.

My friend Karl is a psychologist colleague who has given me a great deal of support and encouragement in my work with dreams in recent years. I felt delighted to have him appear in this dream. I felt a comfortable and easy familiarity this time in calling up my hands into my field of vision in order to stimulate or confirm lucidity. My shimmering hands! What a beautiful image they were, and now they were becoming an appropriate symbol for my whole experiment!

There was a new element in this dream which

---

* A fictitious name.

appeared for the first time. Someone else in my dream told me that he too was lucid, and therefore we participated together in this altered state of consciousness. Soon after the dream, I began to wonder what an LSD trip would be like when two good friends are taking the trip together, an experience I have never had in waking life. The dream with the simultaneous lucidity of two characters was delightful.

The comparison to LSD is appropriate here because of certain parallels between lucid dreaming and psychedelic experiences. At this point I began to see these parallels, illustrating both similarities and differences between the two states. I soon began to refer to my experiment humorously as "L.S.D.," that is, "lucid, spiritual dreaming." I began to see that the altered state of lucid dreaming offers some of the same types of inner experiences as reported by people who have taken LSD and other psychedelics. Some of the more obvious similarities are: (1) intense sensual delights, vivid colors, more beautiful than anything one usually experiences in ordinary dreams or in the waking state; (2) religious, mystical experiences, such as direct contact with the Light, seeking contact with God; (3) synesthesia, the blending of sense perceptions, so that sights and sounds are synchronized into one consensual experience (in synesthesia one can often see the pulsations of the sound waves, so that one perceives sound simultaneously with one's eyes as well as with one's ears); and (4) the experience of ecstasy, religious ecstasy or ecstasy over the beauty of nature and the universe. The similarities between psychedelic experiences and lucid dreaming reminded me that lucidity is an important option for people who seek to expand their consciousness through a path that is free of the liabilities of injecting chemicals and questionable substances into their bodies.

In addition, I began to learn that heightened sexual ecstasy was another possible benefit or gift that could come from the lucid dream state. Though I had not experienced this myself, one of my students at this time reported an orgasm in a lucid dream, which, she stated, was absolutely indescribable. She assured all of us in the class that she had never before felt such intense and pervasive sexual pleasure in her entire life, either in the waking state or in any other dream. From the reading I had done I was aware of numerous ecstatic-orgasmic lucid dreams reported by Patricia Garfield in *Pathway to Ecstasy*. Is it any wonder, I soon began to ask, that some of the greatest of the Christian mystics have spoken of their relationship with God in explicit, sexual imagery. I recalled some of the writings of St. John of the Cross, the sixteenth-century Spanish mystic and poet, who spoke of the union between the human soul and God as one of ecstatic, sexual union. In time I began to realize how appropriate and accurate his metaphor really was. Ordinary orgasm, I began to speculate, was perhaps a preparation for and a small foretaste of the ultimate orgasm (or bliss) for which every human soul is longing.

The next lucid dream in my series provided a good deal of comic relief and relaxation for my whole experiment. This dream helped me to appreciate that the unconscious mind indeed has an excellent sense of humor and can offer important strategies for the total balancing of the psyche. At this point, I was beginning to feel the weightiness of my experiment, and I definitely needed to lighten myself up a bit. In its wisdom, my unconscious now gave me a view of lucidity from another perspective.

LUCID AND LOOSE
February 19, 1981

I am walking uphill, along a dirt road that appears like a typical Marin County fire trail. The road is winding and hilly, and I know intuitively that I am going to encounter some Vietnamese soldiers soon. I feel completely calm. I round a bend and I see the small band of soldiers approaching now, dressed in olive-green uniforms and carrying rifles. They are all women, rather short and petite in size and stature. I feel especially attracted to one woman and she is also strongly attracted to me. Suddenly, I realize I am dreaming, and I feel the familiar yet delightful feeling of lightness and delicate inner balance, primarily in my head and forehead area. I say to myself, "I am lucid and I see my hands in my dream" as a confirmation for myself. My hands do not appear in my field of vision. I repeat the statement two more times and still my hands do not appear. Now I dismiss that idea and think, "Oh, what the heck! What matters is that I am lucid" and I move on with the dream.

The Vietnamese woman now appears more beautiful than ever. She walks directly up to me and we embrace tenderly. I pick her up into my arms; she is so light. I feel her powerful sensual-sexual magnetism. She is drawing me to her with an unusual power that is strong and gentle at the same time. Eagerly and lovingly, I caress her genitals and I kiss her repeatedly on her face as I say several times, "You are so beautiful,. . . You are so beautiful." Her face has a soft luminous quality as if bathed in moonlight and I eagerly soak it up. I am highly aware of her "seduction," her magnetic energy. However, it all feels so good to me that I am most willing to be with her.

Suddenly, the scene changes. I am still lucid, and I am standing now on Butte House Road, a back country road near my home town of Sutter. The area is quiet, peaceful and deserted at the moment. It is a beautiful spring day; the pastures along the roadside are thick and green and I notice a number of cows grazing peacefully nearby in the lush, green grass. Suddenly the road is jammed with vehicles and traffic has stopped completely. A long line of cars is waiting on the road, bumper to bumper, and my van is one of them. I enter my van and sit for a while as traffic remains stalled. After a while I get out of my van and stretch my legs, waiting for the first sign of any movement in the traffic.

Now I notice that the line of traffic is moving again and that my van is moving right along with it. I see it up ahead, inching slowly forward, without a driver! Quickly I run forward, and as soon as I catch up with it I climb inside into the driver's seat. I discover my psychologist friend Karl riding in the passenger's seat and we chat with excitement as we drive along.

The scene changes again. Still lucid, I am now sitting around a table right alongside the Colusa highway, the major highway leading to my home town. The table is covered with many platters of delicious food. Karl and three student hitchhikers are with me having a very exciting discussion about psychology. Two of the students are young Oriental women and one is a young Chinese-American male. They all have cigarettes in their lips and are about to light up. I do not have a cigarette and am protesting strongly, while joking and laughing loudly at the same time. I say to Karl, "Oh, no! Even *you* are going to pollute us all." One woman now walks around the table and playfully puts a cigarette in my lips. We all laugh uproariously as I take it out. I realize I am being extremely "loose" about a matter I regard as very serious.

Now the same young Oriental woman returns to the table and picks up a large platter of luscious, juicy, sliced pineapple. Holding it up to me in a very playful and vivacious manner, she smiles broadly and says, "Would you like to have a piece?" Quickly I respond with a very suggestive tone in my voice: "Oh, I would *love* to have a piece from you ... And I would *love* to give you a piece." Everyone gets the joke and we all laugh outrageously again. I wake up feeling very lighthearted and playful.

I thoroughly enjoyed reading this dream again as I came to write out this part of my story. It was full of sensuality, playfulness and pleasure. I especially enjoyed remembering the uproarious laughter at the end of the dream and was able to experience it all over again upon rereading it. The outrageous sexual teasing, the obvious sexual symbolism of the cigarettes and the round, juicy pineapple slices (with holes in their middles) could not be overlooked. There was something very healthy and wholesome in this dream, because the laughter was so deep and wholehearted. I felt a strong validation for sexual humor in mixed company that goes beyond the normal boundaries of "propriety." The dream was a unifying experience for me, showing me how it might be possible for men and women to tease and joke together in this fashion. Above all, it reminded me to laugh and laugh, and then laugh some more over

74

certain matters that I was starting to regard as totally serious. For over ten years I have been an active supporter of environmentalist groups working to place restrictions on indoor cigarette smoking. I actually take this issue quite seriously and for many years have been looking forward to the recent changing of public attitudes and laws on this issue. The cigarettes in the dream, then, had a double or even triple meaning for me, telling me to relax with my concerns about cigarette pollution, with my lucid dream experiment and with sexual joking and teasing as well. The unconscious turned out to be uproarious at this phase of my journey.

The beauty and the alluring magnetism of the Vietnamese woman soldier were another highpoint in the dream. She represented to me the "feminine energy" within me in a very powerful and provocative way. My embracing her in the dream reminded me of my process of embracing the lucid dream state itself. I asked myself: Isn't she a lot like the lucid state? Isn't she rather foreign? Isn't she tender, petite and delicate? Isn't she magnificent and utterly attractive with her face bathed in all that soft, luminous moonlight? I found myself answering "yes" to all these questions. Our embracing of each other in the lucid state was so loving and so totally sensual-sexual. Yet, just as we were embracing, the dreamscape suddenly shifted and somehow my mind jumped away from her. This sudden shift within the dream, beyond my control, took me back to the countryside near my home town and plunged me into the familiar scenes of my childhood. The traffic jam and the forward movement of my driverless van, I suspected, had something important to tell me here.

Perhaps something from my past, my childhood and adolescent beliefs and experiences, had interrupted my full embrace of the lucid state, symbolized by the beautiful woman soldier. This type of sudden and unexpected "bounce to the past" is exactly the way in which the mind works, whenever it is confronted with something new, mysterious and perhaps overwhelming. Eventually, I began to realize from this dream that my embracing of the lucid state would inevitably push my consciousness in many directions, both forward and backward in time. It would invariably compel me to examine the oldest parts of my psyche as well as its newest growth, the past as well as the future. I realized that any unresolved blocks (traffic jams) from my past would of necessity be brought into my conscious mind now, from the mere experience of entering the lucid state. After reflecting on these images, I had to conclude that there are still times in my life when I am not in the driver's seat, and my energy (my van) is moving without me. I saw that there still are times when I feel stuck and jammed, and these old mental habits, orginating in childhood, could prevent me from remaining in the full embrace of the lucid state.

This dream also provided me with a good deal of comfort in giving me an exciting companion in my friend Karl. Over the years we have shared many stimulating discussions and many good laughs in the waking world. Now, he and I were sharing more good times and more good laughs in my lucid dream world as well.

This dream "Lucid and Loose" contained one particularly interesting note of progress in my experiment. In this dream I tried several times to call up my hands into my field of vision and they did not appear. After several unfruitful attempts, I let go of that method and moved on with the dream. I saw an important message here, namely that certain psycho-spiritual methods are time-limited in their value. Methods that initially assist the student may eventually ensnare the student. At some point in one's growth, it may be important to let go of an old method and take up a new one. At this point the "familiar yet delightful feeling of lightness and delicate inner balance" which I felt primarily in my head and forehead, became my new, confirmatory signal that I had become lucid again in a dream. In many lucid dreams subsequent to this one, I began to use these sensations of light-headedness and tingling pulsations in my forehead to confirm lucidity, and consequently began to abandon the method of seeing my hands in the dreamscape as my confirmation. In all forms of spiritual work, it is important, I think, to recognize the point at which one needs to abandon an old method for a new one. The hands technique was only a vehicle. Although this vehicle was important at the beginning of my project, it now appeared that I was about to abandon it and move into another stage of my journey.

I wrote a short commentary on this dream in my journal. The entry stated that for two weeks prior to this lucid dream, I had been using self-hypnosis regularly to give myself the suggestion, "I am lucid and loose in my dream," meaning that I would be lucid and relaxed at the same time. I had felt a consistent desire to add some relaxation to the whole experiment because I was beginning to feel weighted down by the seriousness of it. Most of all, I was continuing to feel overwhelmed by the three powerful lucid dreams I had received on January 2. My mind was racing in many directions, sensing the importance of this subjective research and yet not knowing where it would lead. I wondered if I would be having more dreams of the same level of intensity as "The Gift of the Magi."

At about this time, I developed a recurring fantasy about the experiment. I began thinking that lucid dreaming would assist me and other serious students to cultivate psychic and intuitive powers that could be extraordinary. In my fantasy, I thought that perhaps these psychic powers would eventually go far beyond what the average psychic reader now can mobilize at this stage in our societal evolution, and lead us to whole new levels of consciousness and mental clarity. I began to envision a society in which more and more people were practiced in lucid dreaming and were reaping untold and unimagined benefits from this evolution. I pictured a society that would eventually be free of military secrecy and political manipulation because lucidity in the dream state would make heretofore hidden knowledge readily available to everyone. I began to imagine that growing numbers of people would some day be able to enter the lucid state and easily retrieve any kind of vital knowledge or information that they needed. In such a society, I imagined, premeditated crime would eventually cease to exist and political intrigue and conspiracy of all kinds would be outmoded methods of operation, because large numbers of lucid dreamers would be able to read the thoughts and dreams of potential conspirators and expose or rechannel these negative energies in creative ways.

Soon afterward, as I reacted to this fantasy, I saw that it was in itself quite grandiose. I began to think that either it was pure megalomania or it was a doorway to some quantum leap in psychological and social transformation. In the former case, I would have to work through my own megalomania and deflate my ego back down to healthy proportions. In the latter case, there would still be many problems and questions, ethical and professional, that would have to be settled along the way. In retrospect, I think the fantasy was a combination of megalomania and futuristic thinking, which was for me a natural consequence of the infusion of these new and powerful dreams into my life.

Eventually, I even developed an appreciation for my megalomania and for various other dark qualities of my psyche as well. At some point, I saw that *for me* the megalomania was not only natural, it was probably inevitable, necessary, and ultimately a good consequence of my lucid dream experiment. Its eruption was one particular ego outgrowth that I needed to face and resolve if I planned to continue the journey. Although my megalomania, if left unchecked, might have limited or even destroyed my project, it could also be faced and pruned away in some appropriate manner.

This long dream "Lucid and Loose" was actually a favorable response to my practice of self-hypnosis intending to influence the content of my lucid dreams. My desire to be lucid *with* relaxation manifested tenfold in this dream. Laughter at oneself and laughter at the world are nature's time-honored methods for the deflation of the ego and for the tempering of megalomania. Several years after I began my experiment, I saw that it was inevitable that the dark forces of my psyche would soon emerge if I were to succeed in becoming a lucid dreamer. Anyone who had received such a powerful contact with the Light, anyone so overwhelmed by its mystery and power, would at the very same moment be susceptible to the gathering of the dusk, to the emergence of the dark forces inside his or her own psyche. I eventually realized that these dark forces inevitably would be mobilized by the mere fact that one had contacted the Light. Increasingly I began to reflect upon the axiom that describes this exchange: "The brighter the sun, the darker the shadow."

At some point I began to visualize a model that would integrate this axiom with my own experience of lucid dreaming. The model contains a four-part cycle that corresponds to the four points of the compass. The four parts are: (1) dawn, (2) midday, (3) dusk, and (4) midnight. (See the diagram below.)

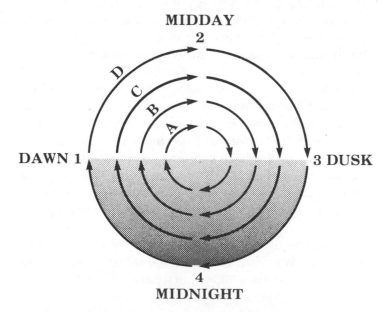

Each concentric circle within the diagram (A, B, C, D, etc.) is an orbit which represents a level of human consciousness. According to this model, each person tends to start off in life revolving in his own first orbit of consciousness, orbit A, experiencing the range of emotional intensity and contrast that is common to him in that orbit. As that orbit becomes familiar, he eventually comes to regard it as normal. Then, after some major breakthrough in consciousness occurs, a person's overall world vision (consciousness) is "bumped," so to speak, from orbit A to orbit B, from his original orbit out to the next level. He now continues to cycle around his new orbit but the size of the orbit has grown larger and the level of intensity becomes dramatically increased at both extremes of the orbit. He now experiences more light at the top of the orbit and more darkness at the bottom. As this person's joys now tend to become more intense, so also are his sorrows felt more keenly.

Any major life event or experience can jolt our human consciousness and push it outward to the next orbit. The shock, for example, could occur from a traumatic experience such as the death of a loved one. Or it could result from an intense positive experience, such as the birth of one's first child, a major recovery of one's health, the occurrence of a mystical experience or an extraordinary lucid dream. The number of "orbits of consciousness" is measureless, capable of expanding outwardly indefinitely to levels E, F, G, etc., and beyond. At this point in our evolution, we are not able to see to the far extremity of this range of consciousness because it appears to be infinite, as the universe itself appears. Each of us is like an astronomer, studying the cosmos with his own telescope and able to see outward only from that center which is his own observation point.

Every person's consciousness is constantly circling around his own orbit, touching upon the various points of his own psychic compass. The shifting is fluid and dynamic. As we approach higher levels of light, brightness, and lucidity, we also need to prepare ourselves *ipso facto* to dip into deeper and darker levels as we circle around to the bottom point of the cycle. These shifts and changes of intensity can be noticed by a careful observation of one's own dreamlife and conscious fantasy life.

In my own case, I began to see that "The Gift of the Magi" brought a substantial "energy jolt" to my psyche and pushed me into a wider orbit within my own system. With this model I began to understand how the midnight side of my cycle would become darker than ever and how the universe was making a greater demand on me than ever before to confront this darkness.

Eventually, I learned how to trust this dark side of my psyche, though I must admit that my encounters with it were frightening at times. I also learned more about "riding through" the dark phases of my newly expanded orbit and "riding through" the depressions that came and went. In a strange way, I can even say now that I feel blessed with new, firsthand knowledge of certain aspects of human experience that I had never known before except from books or hearsay. I believe now that I fully understand how one human being could murder another, if he were totally swept away in an inner torrent of wrath and helpless rage. I believe now that I understand and see more clearly, more vividly than ever before my old tendency to devalue the feminine parts of myself. I understand how I inherited this dark legacy from my father and how much he suffered from not resolving it in his own life. At one point in my reflections I remembered scenes from my childhood in which he was verbally abusing my mother and her side of the family, calling her degrading names to her face in front of all the children, or even in front of dinner guests. I felt a lot of pain then, as a child, as it happened over and over, and as my mother went passive in the face of that abuse and never defended herself. Many years later, I saw residues of these dark traits looming up into my own consciousness, more intensely than ever in the midst of my lucid dream experiment, whenever I ignore my own feelings or those of my wife and child. I saw that there would be no escape from my pains of the past. There would only be continued imprisonment or hard-fought liberation. I saw that certain old forms of victimhood remained stubbornly rooted in my psyche, and they would remain there until my conscious mind discovered them and uprooted them one by one. As a child, I was a victim as I helplessly watched my father heap intimidation and verbal abuse on everyone around him. Now, in the midst of this experiment, I began to feel the sharpness of that emotional pain, both old and new, more keenly than ever each time that I passed through the dark side of my orbit. This sharpness and increased intensity began to tell me that I could not continue forever in my old mode. In order to survive and emotionally thrive in my new orbit, I would have to become more sensitive to feelings than ever before. As I continued to cycle around and around in my newly expanded orbit, I eventually made an extensive commitment to face these old unresolved dark aspects of my inner life. This work became an integral part of my whole experiment. This work was the transformation of the shadow.

My dream "Lucid and Loose" made an important balancing contribution toward my ownership of the power of the lucid state. In essence, it taught me to be lucid *with* relaxation and *with* humor, to balance out the seriousness and emotional intensity of the overall project. The uproarious laughter and the "loose conversation" in the dream provided this counter-balance in a way that was delightful.

The next lucid dream that occurred in the series was explicitly religious in its symbols. Arriving approximately two weeks after the previous dream, it left me with an overriding feeling of strength and joy.

JOHN CHRYSOSTOM: THE GOLDEN MOUTH
March 6, 1981

I hear a powerful male voice chanting in a most vigorous and rhythmic manner. I peer into the darkness and eventually I see a priest coming into focus. He is standing at an altar, facing his congregation and celebrating the Mass. His voice is steady, deep and powerfully magnetic as he chants in a language I do not recognize. I sense somehow that it is ancient Greek, but I am not quite sure. Suddenly I realize I am dreaming, and I mentally call upon my hands to appear as my confirmation. My hands do not appear, but the familiar feeling of extraordinary clarity and mental balance appear. I *know* I am dreaming. The priest who appears is Father Gene Lucas, though I feel a bit unsure about his identity because his voice is so incredibly powerful and resonant, more resonant than any human voice that I have ever heard. I watch him very intently as I kneel in the sanctuary close by, not far from the side of the altar. I can see only Father Lucas although I know his congregation is present. Now he slowly begins to fade from sight and I telepathically call for him to return. As he fades out of sight completely I realize I do not have control over this dream.

Moments later I hear another male voice, also chanting vigorously. Again I peer steadily into the darkness and eventually a picture of another priest comes into focus. He is also standing at an altar before his congregation. The picture I see is like a beautiful black-and-white photo, very delicate and sensitive. The chanting and the power of this priest's voice are also extremely magnetic and in the same foreign language that I heard before. Suddenly I know intuitively that this priest is St. John Chrysostom and I feel delighted. I deeply appreciate the power, eloquence and magnetism that flow from his voice and presence. As I listen, I see a dim shadow of my hand gliding across my field of vision. I feel even more assured that I am lucid as I realize that my hand has now appeared in my dream. I see several women, elegant in brightly colored dresses, standing in the front row of the congregation, their faces extremely bright and radiant with energy. I realize they are alive with admiration for John, whose voice and presence are a living grace to them all, so direct and real. Eventually, the chanting priest slowly fades from view and I watch him disappear.

This dream reaffirmed for me the spiritual dimension of the lucid dream. The first priest, Father Gene Lucas, was my hero when I was a teenager. He was the assistant pastor in my parish church when I first entered the seminary at age fourteen and throughout all of my seminary years he remained a source of inspiration and support. I still carry very good feelings toward him to this day though I now see him only occasionally. The second priest, St. John Chrysostom (345-407 A.D.), was one of the founding fathers of the early Christian church. He was noted for his extremely powerful eloquence, so much so that the people of his day gave him the honorary name of Chrysostom.* This dream also emphasized the communitarian aspect of the lucid dream, implying that in certain cases altered states can be shared with people in some special context, such as public worship, for example. In both parts of the dream, the vigorous chanting was the predominant aspect of the experience, and that is what I remember most to this day. The power and rhythm of the chanting flowed from the two priests like a river of energy and passed directly into the people standing nearby, who soaked it up most eagerly.

In later reflection I saw the connection between John the Golden Mouth and the gift of the pure gold that I presented to the Christ child in "The Gift of the Magi." The beauty and value of gold are universally recognized and need little comment. For me there is an important spiritual connection between having a heart of gold and mouth of gold, for whatever is in a person's heart is that which will eventually be expressed. As a man is in his innermost being, so will he become known to one and all, eventually. Ultimately, there are no secrets. The

---

* *Chrysos* (gold) and *stoma* (mouth) are from the Koiné Greek spoken in the early Christian era. The name Chrysostom meant "golden mouth."

sounds of the chanting that came from the two priests in this lucid dream, like so much of what happens in that state, were truly indescribable. I remember the incredibly deep and resonating pulsation of those words, lilting, empowering and projecting. Each syllable was alive with energy. Each word, it seemed in the dream, was a wave-unit that flowed from the deepest recesses of the cosmos, through the two priests as human channels, to be completely absorbed, sponge-like, by their eager audiences, fully attuned and fully receptive. Indeed, the people were "en-chanted" by these vigorous chant-pulsations, which were in truth pulsations of the Spirit, and in the dream, I too was totally "en-chanted" by the beauty of God's music coming through two of His selected instruments. This was real liturgy! This was public worship as I had never experienced it anywhere in the waking state. John the Golden Mouth and Father Gene had each brought forth his respective manifestation of the divine gift. The saint was a channel through which the divine energy could flow, unimpeded—after the blocks of ego had been removed. The modern, contemporary priest was perfectly attuned to the essential pattern of his spiritual ancestor. I cannot imagine a more down-to-earth definition of holiness, wholeness or living grace.

In this dream I was able to see only a portion of John Chrysostom's congregation, those who were standing closest to the altar, erect, alert, bright-eyed and very attuned to his chanting. Neither the people nor I myself understood the meaning of the words or the intellectual content of the chant, and yet this was completely acceptable to everyone in the dream. The chant was as it was. Its *energy* was its essence. Its *vibration* was its special healing power. In the dream, I felt a deep appreciation for the vitality of the ancient language and for the vibrations coming through the voices of both priests, one ancient and one modern.

In conclusion, I have taken this dream as an invitation to develop that fullness of power and energy within myself in order to speak "my truth" with the full eloquence and conviction of "the golden mouth." I have enjoyed rereading this dream numerous times because it has such a strong sense of mystery about it. I still believe that I have not fully grasped its meaning and import, and that too is acceptable. Perhaps this dream will always have more to say to me the older I become. I am willing to wait for its fullness to be unfolded.

CHAPTER FIVE

Blocks and Barriers

"There is always light, shining in the darkness, for those who dare open their eyes at night."
—Richard Bach

The next portion of my experiment focused on understanding my resistance to lucid dreaming. Those who are familiar with the psychological growth process know that most people will somehow resist a change in life, if they are not fully prepared to change. At this stage in my experiment, about five months after its inception, I began to search more deeply within myself to understand my own readiness or lack of readiness for change. A chance reading of a book by Peter Drucker, the well-known management and organization consultant, shed some valuable light on this subject for me. In essence, Drucker says there are four conditions for a person's *psychological readiness* for change: (1) The change must appear rational; people always present to themselves as rational even their most irrational and most erratic changes. (2) The change must appear as an improvement over one's old situation. (3) The change must be comfortably paced. It must not be so rapid and so great as to obliterate the familiar psychological landmarks which make a person feel at home. (4) The change must clearly and visibly strengthen the person's sense of psychological security.* As I reflected on these four conditions, I began to see that the fourth

---

* Peter Drucker, *The Practice of Management*, p. 269.

item on Drucker's list was the one that concerned me most. I began to wonder if the intensity of my lucid dreams had begun to upset my old mental balance and somehow threaten my basic security.

It is one of the paradoxes of the psyche that we can want and not want (resist) something at the same time. Frequently, the more strongly we desire something, the more intensely will doubts, fears and resistances come into our minds as we approach or achieve our desire. This fear is actually a blessing in disguise, because it confirms for us that we place a high value on the object of our desire. The higher the value, the more intense will be our fear and anxiety as we are about to receive what we desire. For example, the typical bride and groom are usually very nervous on their wedding day and often for many days and weeks preceding the big event. They both know that the wedding is a major commitment and their high degree of fear and anxiety reflects the high degree of importance they place upon it.

After about five months of continuous, regular lucid dreaming, I entered what proved to be my first major dry period, a time when my lucid dreams vanished. I was concerned and yet knew that certain barriers, conscious and unconscious, were soon to be explored. These barriers would have to be identified and worked out of my system if I were to allow myself to enter the light on a regular basis and maintain my sense of balance in the process. At this point, I began to have a series of normal dreams that addressed my resistances and emotional blocks to the lucid dream state. The first of these dreams was as follows:

LACERATIONS ON MY HANDS
April 20, 1981

I am sitting at a table in the dining room of St. Joseph's College in Mountain View. The room is filled with seminarians and faculty who are all sitting in their places as usual. The meal is almost finished. I look under the front edge of my table and I see some clumps of stringy, thread-like, gray material clinging to the table. Vigorously, I grab it and pull it off with my right hand. There is some slight resistance and then the stuff peels off. I notice now that the fingertips and thumb of my right hand have received many fine, delicate cuts from pulling off the stringy material. (Now I feel myself about to wake up, and I give myself the suggestion that I will see my hands in my dream and become lucid. I fall back into the dream state and the dream continues.) Now I see that my hand is bleeding profusely from the lacerations. I try to hide the blood from my fellow seminarians who are now leaving the dining room because the meal is over. I wipe off some blood with a paper napkin and I plan to go to the infirmary at once and have my hand bandaged. I wake up with a strange feeling.

This dream was fairly easy for me to interpret. My hands, the prime symbol in the dream, had been the official cue that I had used from the very beginning to evoke lucidity. Isn't it strange, I thought, how my hands keep reappearing in all these dreams in so many different ways. So now I asked myself, "How am I lacerating myself in my lucid dream experiment?" The answer came in reflecting on the stringy, clumpy material in the dream. It reminded me of rolls of fine grade steel wool that I had sometimes used in my old janitorial business. Several years earlier I had owned and operated a part-time janitorial business, primarily for the sake of survival, for the steady income it provided. Sometimes I did actually incur small cuts on my fingertips in using rolls of steel wool to clean difficult spots on floors or cramped areas. The clumpy, stringy material in the dream reminded me of those earlier financial, survival struggles. Accordingly, this dream told me that I had been putting too much attention and energy into my financial concerns during the past few weeks. Specifically, since it was the month of April, I had been struggling over my income taxes and putting a lot of energy into figuring out ways to reduce my taxes. I had also been looking for ways to create a tax shelter for the coming year. This dream told me that these current survival concerns had been lacerating me, injuring me by draining my energy excessively and thereby lowering my availability for lucidity.

This dream and my interpretation of it confirmed the findings of both Scott Sparrow and Patricia Garfield, that regular lucid dreaming requires the maintenance of a high level of energy. If the dreamer is going through a period of stress or fatigue, or is exceptionally busy with activities in the external world, then the quality and quantity of his lucid dreaming are likely to diminish. I have generally found this to be true as I look back over the whole scope of my experiment.

Two days later I had another dream also portraying human hands. This one pointed out the existence and nature of my resistance even more acutely.

AMPUTATION
April 22, 1981

I am in a large prison yard that feels like a heavy-duty prison, perhaps San Quentin. I see the thick, high walls all around me, with armed guards and observation towers strategically located here and there. I am a prisoner, and I am walking in front of a cell block with a guard and another male prisoner. The cell block is like a row of small cages that have iron bars facing out onto a courtyard. Several men are placed in each cell and I am painfully aware of their cramped, inhumane conditions.

As we pass one particular cell, one of the inmates calls out to the prisoner walking beside me. The inmate is a very rough-looking Latino, with crude tattoos and self-inflicted lacerations on his huge arms. He is a tough, hardened criminal. He says to the prisoner beside me, "I see you're a married man," and points to the wedding ring on his left hand. Then he says, "Give me your ring finger." Now the prisoner beside me passively complies and sticks his left hand through the bars and into the cell. The tough Latino inmate reaches into his pocket and pulls out a small pocket knife. He calmly and deliberately opens the blade, grips the man's ring finger with his free hand, and slowly, methodically amputates the ring finger at the knuckle. The victim watches silently, passively and attentively as his finger is cut off. I am shocked at the cold, deliberate cruelty of the Latino inmate.

Now the amputation is completed. The victim withdraws his finger from the bars and suddenly begins to weep and wail profusely. I wake up feeling depressed by the whole scene.

This dream came as a shock to me. In this scenario I am completely enclosed in a maximum security prison. The dream told me that my survival consciousness or security consciousness was far greater than I had imagined, and it implied that I would have to resolve this issue if I intended to go forward with lucid dreaming. One of my resistances to the experiment was my current, excessive focusing on security and my use of money as the major security symbol in my life. This, I realized, was a major negative belief that I had held for a long time.

The dream reminded me that everyone has a major personal security symbol of some kind. Did this dream imply that each potential lucid dreamer might be asked to face and identify his or her own security symbols, whatever they may be, and work toward transcending them in the process of cultivating lucidity? These symbols inevitably vary from person to person. Some people marry for security; others cling to an organized religion or an intellectual ideology. Some seek a security symbol in prestige, fame, a successful career, close-knit family ties, a big house, a big car or any and all of these things. At this point, I received a message from these two dreams that my own preoccupation with money was a major block to my lucid dream experiment and to my total growth as a person. At some point I would have to give it up if I chose to surrender to the Light completely. The thought of surrendering this part of me seemed strange, absurd, stupid, and above all frightening. The thought of not being concerned about money seemed totally foreign to my way of being. I had always been a "worrier" about money, an old habit that I absorbed from my parents many years ago as a child, and which I had re-enforced within my own mind as an adult countless times. I easily remembered many awkward and stressful experiences of growing up in a large, working-class family, where there was never enough money and where most decisions, large and small, were made by purchasing the least expensive product or taking the least expensive alternative. These were the old values and memories imbedded in my psyche's past, and now I saw that this old layer of my mind would have to be cleared out if my lucid dream experiment was going to progress.

The tough Latino in this dream was a shadow component of myself, called "survival." He had no feelings, no connection to his feminine side at all, and was openly hostile toward the prisoner who had a connection with the feminine, symbolized by the wedding ring. My recent commitment to lucid dreams and to the intuitive awareness they foster offered me the possibility of a stronger connection to my "inner female." At the time, this inner connection felt more solid within me than it had ever been. But it was still in danger of being "amputated," cruelly cut off by ineffectual worrying about security, survival and money concerns.

The prisoner who was the victim and who lost a part of his wedding-ring finger was another aspect of myself. He told me that I was too passive and that I was being victimized by my survivor consciousness. This implied that I needed to mobilize more of my aggressive male side at the time when my income was rising. As I increased my commitment to my inner female (lucidity and intuition), I also needed to increase proportionately the strength of my inner male. He would have to react more quickly and move more forcefully to protect the total me, instead of being a passive accomplice to the "amputation" and then wailing in grief after the damage had been done. Insofar as my income tax situation gave me one specific area in which to focus these issues, from these dreams I saw what I needed to do. On one level, the level of behavior and action, I needed to seek professional tax consultation so that my inner female would feel protected, cared for and more relaxed. I saw that receiving this support from someone outside of myself would help foster my return to the creative development and cultivation of my lucid dreaming. Shortly thereafter, I consulted with a couple of tax-shelter experts who gave me a good deal of helpful and valuable information. On still other levels, this dream provided additional fuel for my ongoing meditations.

In the many years that I have worked with dreams, I have often been amazed at the creative shock value that can come from dreams that are as grotesque, painful or embarrassing as "Amputation." In the process of bringing all of this material, positive and negative, sun and shadow, into more conscious awareness, I saw that I was following the steady commitment to my own wholeness that I had originally intended. With deeper reflection I also saw that eventually one learns to have a deep faith in one's own darkness, not because it is preferable or pleasurable, but only because it is real, ever present and true. Faith is based on seeing the cosmos not as one prefers it but as God has created it, and seeing the human psyche as it too has evolved out of that cosmos. In these moments of "deep seeing" one can obtain a glimpse of the cosmic plan, so vast and mysterious that no human intellect could ever have set it in motion. The darkness exists in order that the light may shine. If there were no darkness the light itself would be imperceptible. With this dream I made still another choice to face my inner darkness, the cruelty, the insensitivity and even the savagery that it expressed. A pressing realization came to me about the sun and the shadow. We become whole when we are no longer afraid to plumb the depths of our own savagery, and no longer afraid to ascend to the heights of our own blinding beauty. As we travel in either direction, whether ascending or descending, our principal adversary is fear.

Somehow I already knew, or at least sensed, that another issue behind the dreams of "Lacerations on My Hands" and "Amputation" was *fear*. At this point in my experiment I had become so afraid of the sheer beauty and dazzling grace of my lucid dreams that my conscious mind began to scramble frantically to run away from it all. What more convenient place to run to than the old neurotic patterns and futile mental exercises of my past which I had not yet completely transformed inside of myself. During the previous three months when I suddenly became so intensely preoccupied with the trivial details of my finances, I kept sensing another faint little voice whispering inside me. It was a quiet voice, quiet but persistent, like a small child buried under the rubble of a major earthquake, still alive, still capable of being heard in its plaintive cries, still seeking to be extricated and brought up into the light of day. This quiet, subtle voice kept saying, "You *are* running. You are running away and you *know* it. What are you running from?"

As this first major dry period dragged on for another three months, I specifically decided one night to incubate a dream that would give me some insight into any additional blocks I still might have. So on the night of July 21, 1981, before falling asleep, I repeatedly asked myself the question, "How am I blocking my lucid dreams?" The next morning I woke up with three ordinary dreams, each offering some valuable insight into my question.

A CHAPEL IN THE CENTER
July 22, 1981

I am walking around exploring the interior of a large, home-like building which I know to be "our home." I am going through various closets, extra rooms and hallways just to see what is there. I open a window and am surprised to see how large the building really is. Its overall shape is that of a large quadrangle with an open space in the middle that is surrounded by the four wings. I am reminded of the basic floorplan of the old St. Pius X Seminary. I am also surprised to see that a chapel has been built to occupy the central space in the middle of the quadrangle and that there is only a small space, perhaps twelve to fifteen inches, between the chapel walls and the walls of the main building. I notice a beautiful stained-glass window. I want to explore the area between the chapel and the main building and I know it will be a tight squeeze. I fall back asleep.

This dream suggested to me that I needed to rediscover the chapel in the center, i.e., the *central* spiritual motivation for cultivating lucid dreaming. I remembered Sparrow's thesis, based on the Edgar Cayce readings, that "perhaps the most important exercise one can perform in order to insure a consistent and creative response in the lucid dream is to decide initially upon a spiritual ideal."* If a lucid dreamer forgets this spiritual ideal, according to Cayce, he will tend to lose the lucidity through losing the purity of his or her motives. I had accepted this idea and had come to believe that purity of intention was of great importance in the ongoing cultivation of the lucid state, and that the lucid dreamer would have to pay attention consistently to his motives in order to maintain their ongoing purity.

In the dream I was exploring the area between the chapel and the main part of my "home." This implied that I needed to relate this spiritual advancement somehow to the everyday parts of my world, and that this work would definitely require some effort symbolized by the "tight squeeze." In essence, this dream seemed to say: In developing lucid dreaming, keep the spiritual focus as your central concern, and explore and work through your tightness and anxiety**

---

* Sparrow, *op. cit.*, p. 54.
**An interesting etymological footnote: The word *anxiety* comes from the Latin *angustia*, which literally means "narrowness" or "tightness."

over any other aspects of the journey.

The second dream in response to my question "How am I blocking my lucid dreams?" went as follows:

BILL DASHES AHEAD
July 22, 1981

I am sitting in a pizza parlor with my younger brother Bill. It is the pizza parlor near the freeway entrance in the town of Corte Madera. Suddenly we both remember we have to be back home in Fairfax in a very short time. We quickly dash out of the pizza parlor and, realizing we have no car, we head for the nearby freeway to find a place to hitchhike. Racing down the street, Bill runs ahead as fast as he can while I run at a slower pace. I feel annoyed with him because I think he has run past a good hitchhiking spot without even stopping to consider it. I realize he can run faster than I and I can't stop him. I know he plans to run across the overpass and then position himself next to the freeway entrance. His destination is a good choice for sure, but I feel annoyed anyway because I see that he is passing up other good opportunities. Running to catch up, I intend to join him as soon as I can. I feel exasperated.

The message that I received from this dream was that my impulsive, younger, male side, symbolized by my younger brother, was rushing my pace of growth. It was moving too fast and missing the present moment with its present opportunities. Certainly, that part of me was very excited and eager about my experiment, but it was also out of control. I began to realize here that I needed to slow down so that I could pace myself properly and integrate all that I was learning about lucid dreaming. This dream was also suggesting that I didn't have the proper vehicle for the journey at this moment, indicated by the fact that we were hitchhiking, without a car of our own. The proper vehicle would probably include the fuller purification of my motives and a much deeper understanding of the inner processes and dynamics of lucid dreaming.

There was a third dream that spoke to me that night about the blocks to my experiment.

JOHN TAKES THE LEAD
July 22, 1981

I am inside the Dillon Beach house with Charlene and Erik looking out over the ocean. We are expecting a visit from some friends, John and Julia, and we are all excited. Now I see John and Julia pulling into the driveway and Erik and I dash outside to greet them. I am pleased to see John driving a beautiful, fully restored, antique car, which is in excellent condition. Its body visibly shines and glistens as sunshine gleams from the beautiful pale-green hues of the vehicle. The car looks like a late 1920s or early 1930s model.

John and Julia both get out and, as I approach them, John comes forward very fast from the far side of the driveway. I hug him warmly and he begins to talk very rapidly and very excitedly. I want to hug Julia too, but John is engaging me completely because he is expressing so much excitement. His face is very animated and he is dressed in an outfit that reminds me of a railroad engineer. He is wearing a pair of full-length bib overalls with gray and white stripes and a matching striped cap which looks like a typical engineer's cap. The cap is folded in half and perched comically on the front part of his head. In spite of the great liveliness and excitement that John expresses as he speaks, and in spite of the constant, animated movements of his head, his cap always remains in its same position, perfectly balanced and poised.

Now Julia gives up waiting for my greeting and walks back to the car to bring out a young girl from the back seat. I know intuitively that she is Julia's niece and I think, "Oh, well, I'll hug Julia later." I feel very happy to see them and can sense that Erik, who is standing beside me the whole time, is also very happy.

The internal dynamics of this third dream forced me to focus on John, almost to the exclusion of his wife, Julia. John was so forward and so animated in the dream that I had to give him *all* of my attention. My unconscious wanted me to view him as if he were a railroad engineer, with his engineer's cap folded in half and perched on the front of his head. What were all these images saying? With reflection I began to put some pieces together. The railroad engineer is an important man because he is in charge of a huge, powerful train. He keeps the train on the track! The forces within my lucid dreams, I realized, could eventually build and gather all the momentum of a roaring express train, and I would need, eventually, to become comfortable with all that power and momentum in order to keep it channeled and pointed in the right direction. In effect, I would need to keep myself on the right track if I wished to be creative with all the energy of the lucid dream state. John, in this dream, was a symbol for discipline and focused energy. In waking life John works as a professional writer, and he and I have often talked about his work and my own growing aspirations to write about my work with dreams. I have always admired his discipline and have looked forward to the day when I might bring forth enough of that discipline to write my own book. At the time I had this dream, I knew that I had the energy and the enthusiasm to write, but I frequently wondered if I really had the discipline. I now began to realize that if I could believe enough in my own capacity for discipline I could move through still another barrier to lucidity.

What about the comical and bizarre aspect of this dream? What did I make of the engineer's cap, folded in half, and delicately poised and balanced on the front of John's head? In my years of experience with dreams, I have learned to pay extra attention to the especially bizarre or incongruent symbols in a dream. The bizarreness of a dream symbol is often the clever way in which the unconscious entices or forces us to pay attention to that particular symbol. After turning the "half-a-cap" symbol over and over in my mind many times, its meaning finally became clear. I had at this point in my experiment already half lost my head, so to speak. My head (and my ego) had become inflated with the incredible potential of certain lucid dreams, and I had already concocted many grandiose fantasies and daydreams about where lucid dreaming could lead.

Julia, just prior to the time of this dream, had been a student in my lucid dream classes and in many ways had been my most enthusiastic supporter for doing this work. I often felt very moved by her enthusiasm, which added a great deal of fuel to my own hopes and aspirations for the whole endeavor. For many months before this dream arrived I had been feeling very grateful for that support and enthusiasm. Now, with the assistance of this dream, I began to see that while it was essential for me to receive such enthusiasm from someone, it was also essential for me to remain balanced about it and not let it "go to my head."

This dream outlined some kind of corrective measure for me to take in order to regain my emotional balance at this point in my journey. In effect, the dream told me to bring John into the foreground and let Julia now go into the background. It told me to bring more "John energy" (discipline) into my life and let the "Julia energy" (enthusiasm) recede a bit. The dream implied that I already had the necessary enthusiasm for my experiment and now I needed to "engineer it," to keep it on the right track, and develop my writing discipline to bring it to full fruition. I felt very good as I completed my understanding of this dream and received the clarity and power of its message.

This dream also contained a few other priceless subtleties that added their own special flavor to this "feast of images." One often receives a special reward in understanding one's own dreams over the passage of time, as the dreamer becomes further initiated into the private history and symbolic language of his own unconscious. No one else could possibly appreciate all the overtones and elements of such a dream as much as the dreamer himself, because the perfection of certain pivotal dream symbols is often so deeply personal. It is like viewing all the photographs in one's family album and allowing the flood of memories and feelings to pour forth.

I felt delighted that this dream scene took place at the Dillon Beach house, a special place for me where I often go to write in solitude. This house belongs to a friend of mine, who frequently allows me to use it as a haven for creativity and reflection. She, too, often inquires, "How are you coming along on your book?" and she urges me to persevere on it. Her voice is another voice for discipline, support and creativity in my life. I enjoyed the fact that this dream took place in this particular setting.

The beautiful antique car, in mint condition, which John drove in the dream also had a special meaning to me. When Julia first attended one of my dream classes at the local community college, the first dream that she shared centered around a beautiful, restored antique car. She entitled this dream "My 1927 Classic" because 1927 was the year of her birth. In that particular class, which I remember very clearly, she electrified everyone with the beauty and power of that dream, which eloquently portrayed so many aspects of her life. Since that day, she and I had often referred to her "1927 Classic" as a symbol for her energy and enthusiasm and for her own dreams which have been vivid and exciting to her all her life. In time, references to Julia's "1927 Classic" became a private joke between us which we both appreciated and to which we often alluded. Now her 1927 classic appeared in my dream, and John was driving it! Dream energy is contagious. The images from one person's dream are sometimes picked up and reproduced or reworked in another person's dream for special purposes. This seems to be especially true for people who actively share dreams with each other. I have seen this phenomenon many times in my ongoing dream groups where the members have developed very close ties. This dream helped me to appreciate Julia for her contributions to my work and to appreciate John as an individual as well. The dream occurred at the time I was just beginning to know them as a couple and as friends.

My son Erik was beside me throughout this dream. I saw him as the symbol for my inner child, the source of my creative self, the playful, guileless self, free of ego concerns. His joyful presence became a happy portent of my work (and play) with lucid dreaming. I took it to mean that as I dissolve my blocks to lucid dreaming, the creative aspect of my own life will emerge more fully. I could not help but remember here the saying of Jesus: "Unless you turn and become like little children, you will never enter the kingdom of heaven."*

Surprisingly enough, or perhaps not so suprisingly, my lucid dreams returned one week after I received these three dreams. At this juncture, once again I had three lucid dreams in one night and I felt my original excitement renewed. The inner spark had come to consciousness once more. Of these three lucid dreams, the second felt the most important to me, and I have often reflected on its messages.

CLOSER TO HOME
July 29, 1981

I am sitting at a picnic table with about eight other people, watching a major league baseball game. We are only about fifteen to twenty feet from home plate, sitting in the playing area near the backstop. I see Father Daniel Carroll on the other side of the batter, standing very close to him, in fact, as he watches the game. Suddenly I become aware that I am dreaming and I feel a gentle tingling sensation in my forehead. I feel very amused that Father Daniel has somehow obtained such a close perspective on the game for himself. He walks over to the table where we are sitting and I extend my hand to him as I stand up and say, "Hello, Father Daniel! Remember me? I'm Ken Kelzer, with a beard." He recognizes me and is happy to see me. We shake hands. I quip in a warm manner, "You must still have good connections with Vince Lombardi!" We both laugh

---

* Matthew 18:3.

101

and enjoy the joke.

Now I see a number of priests from seminary days. They are all dressed in their clerics as they walk up and stand around the picnic table. I greet Jim Kidder warmly and talk with him a few minutes. I am still lucid throughout the dream and I enjoy the feeling. I see Jim Pulskamp and we sit down at the table and immediately have a heart-to-heart communication. I feel wonderful to feel so close to him so quickly. I ask, "Are you still at Hanna Center?" He answers with great sincerity, "Yes, and I just love working there." I say, "How long have you been there now?" He says, "Eighteen years." I react, "Great! Maybe you'll be there another eighteen years!" He laughs and says, "No, I hope for a change someday, although I am really happy there now." I feel pleased about his commitment to change as a matter of general principle. Now the dream fades out slowly and gradually.

I found a number of valuable messages in this lucid dream. The context of the major league baseball game was a positive one for me, in that a major leaguer is someone who is playing on the highest level of achievement. Although the major leaguer is a professional and is serious about his work, his work is ultimately *play*. He is called a "player," not a "worker." His work and play are somehow *one*, so that his inner child is still very much alive and conscious as he pursues his career. I saw this message of the dream as reminding me to keep this playful, childlike tenor alive in myself as I followed the path of the lucid dream or any other path. In this context, a couplet attributed to Winston Churchill came to my mind:

> *"Those whose work and pleasure are one,*
> *Are Fortune's favored childer-run."*

I was intrigued with the image of Father Daniel Carroll in this dream. "Father Daniel," as we used to call him, was the rector of the high school seminary where I had spent four years of my life. I had last seen him about eight years prior to this dream at a special dinner banquet in Sacramento. On this occasion, I was impressed with the fact that he had recently returned from doing missionary work in rural Mexico, traveling as an itinerant priest from village to village, often riding alone by burro through roadless, uninhabited wilderness areas to reach the people he served. I sensed an unusual and very peaceful calmness about Father Daniel that night at the banquet. He carried a deep inner peace that came more from his being than from his words or from the brief stories he told. He felt very different to me, different from the way I knew him when he was the president of a seminary faculty and a rapidly expanding student body. I wondered about his career transition from a seminary rector in California to a solitary missionary, living and working with the poorest of the poor in northern Mexico. His "promotion" reminded me of the "surrender of the ego." As I drove home from the banquet that night, this impression was already forging a new symbol in my mind: Father Daniel was becoming a symbol for this surrender and its lifestyle of simplicity. His position in my lucid dream carried the connotation that he had somehow obtained "such a close perspective on the game"—that is, the game of life. In the game of life, the biggest league of all, humility and surrender were the qualities that I needed to remember once again at this juncture in my lucid dream experiment.

This dream also had an element of humor in it. The reference to Vince Lombardi goes back to my seminary days, to my sophomore or junior year in high school. In those days, Father Daniel was the athletic director and coach for the seminary sports programs. On the playing fields we often challenged him quite vociferously when he acted as referee for our games, and we often teased him about his own athletic expertise and ability. Most of us thought he was more talk than action when it came to sports. One day, in the middle of the football season, we were stunned by a large photo in the latest issue of *Sports Illustrated*. The photo showed a close-up of Paul Hornung, star running back for the Green Bay Packers, sitting on the bench next to his teammates. He had a heavy full-length cloak over him, with steam coming from his mouth as it met the cold winter air. He was huffing and puffing because he had just scored a winning touchdown on a dramatic run for the Packers. And there, standing directly behind the Packers' bench, as big as life, totally unmistakable, was Father Daniel. He wore a big smile on his face as he glanced with admiration at Paul Hornung. The seminarians were stunned with disbelief and amazement when we saw that photo. Peals of incredulous laughter rang out through the student lounge as we passed the magazine around with comments such as: "Hey, look at this!" and "I can't believe it!" The sports enthusiasts among us were especially confounded because what we saw of our coach, boldly presented in a national magazine, did not fit the image of the Father Daniel that we all had in our minds. The photo revealed a side to Father Daniel that we had never seen before or even suspected.

The students were so amazed by the photo that we went to Father Daniel "demanding" an explanation. With a lot of joking and teasing, we questioned him very persistently, because he really did not want to tell us very much. Finally, after a lot of cajoling, a story emerged which convinced us that we had indeed underestimated our "coach." It turned out that Father Daniel was a close personal friend of Vince Lombardi, the head coach of the Green Bay Packers. Lombardi had invited him to attend that particular game and had made special arrangements for him to sit down on the sidelines with the players and the coaching staff. He had just happened to be standing right behind Paul Hornung when the photo for *Sports Illustrated* was snapped. The whole incident was a good lesson for me; I learned something there about maintaining a certain respect for another person whose life I could know only partially, at best. I learned not to be too sure of myself in thinking that I had someone else "pegged" or "figured out." As far as my perception of Father Daniel was concerned, there was more to the man than met the eye. Now all of these issues and themes had come back to me in this lucid dream "Closer to Home."

This dream contained another pearl of wisdom for me in the dialogue between myself and Jim Pulskamp toward the end of the dream. Jim was a classmate of mine from seminary days, who was ordained a priest and served for many years as director of Hanna Boys Center in Sonoma, a residential treatment center for emotionally troubled boys. He had a great sense of humor, was very affable and outgoing in his temperament and was generally well liked by everyone. I had maintained occasional contact with him through the years and, as far as I knew, he had been happy in his directorship role at Hanna Center. The symbol of Jim in the dream told me, quite emphatically, that openness to change was an important mental commitment for me to maintain. As I examined myself on this score, I saw that although I attempt to remain open to change in principle, I often resist it in actual practice.

At the time that I had this dream, I was in the midst of making many big changes for myself and my family. Opening myself up to lucid dreaming was the most obvious internal change that I had already begun. This had already presented me with numerous, unexpected inner resistances. On another level, more concrete and tangible, Charlene and I were preparing to put our home up for sale at this time and had already begun to look for a new home. I was actually dreading the process of househunting, which we were planning to intensify in another month or so.

Meanwhile, the continued stereophonic assault from the teenager next door was pushing at us to make the move more quickly and we were under more pressure than I would have liked. Even when my conditions were terrible, I felt a lot of resistance toward this particular change. Perhaps, I should say, precisely *because* conditions were so terrible I felt a lot of resistance to the change. Basically, I wanted to move when *I* was ready, when conditions were favorable for *me* and when the timing suited *me*. The symbol of Jim in the dream provided a counterbalance and antidote to my dilemma. In the dream he said, "I hope for a change some day, although I am really happy there now." He opted for a principle, the principle of commitment to change even when one's present conditions are happy!

In the three months that followed this dream (August, September and October 1981), I went through another series of ups and downs with lucid dreaming. It was another relatively dry period for me. I had two lucid dreams during that time while recall of my ordinary dreams was at its usual frequency of remembering one or more dreams every morning. As I reflected upon this pattern of ups and downs, feast and famine, I formulated a metaphor depicting the current status of my experiment. I saw myself climbing through the snow-capped Himalayas and, after a long climb, I saw myself arrive at the top of a very high peak. I stood on top of this peak for a long time, enraptured with the vast vistas, the breathtaking views, and the splendid beauty of the pure white snow, the deep blue skies and the graceful, floating clouds. I gazed in wonder and awe at the other distant peaks that seemed to be just as glorious as the one I was standing on at the moment. I felt a strong desire to travel to every one of them for the sheer delight of doing so. I resolved, then and there, to make the journey to each of those mountaintops through the months and years that lay ahead. After savoring these beautiful heights for a long time and renewing my commitment, I reluctantly made my descent from my present peak into the valley below. What a contrast between the peaks and the valleys! Yet, each played an important part in the building of my awareness.

My metaphor continued. I saw myself descending now into trackless valleys and working my way around numerous obstacles, great and small, dense brush, rocks and rivers. I felt lost at times. Yet, with perseverance, I eventually reached the bottom, where the base of my former peak touched the base of the next great peak, and deliberately I began my ascent again. "Why was it such a laborious task?" I asked myself. "Why couldn't I just fly from peak to peak like an eagle, once I had reached the first summit?" Perhaps one of my blocks was the *belief* that life is a struggle, so that even now I am still "struggling" with lucid dreaming. Maybe my whole experiment would proceed much more easily if I simply allowed everything to happen and took all of the effort and expectations out of it. I did not really know the answer but I knew this question was relevant, certainly relevant for me, though perhaps not equally so for every traveler. Each would-be lucid dreamer, I thought, will have his or her own particular questions to identify and particular inner barriers to dissolve as he or she approaches the light. These were the contemplations and reflections that accompanied me as I began to climb toward the top of the next peak.

The metaphor of the peaks and the valleys has returned to me frequently as I have wondered about the overall process of becoming lucid on a regular basis. One important development was the eventual acceptance of my dry periods with more equanimity and calmness. I believe now that these periods are necessary for reflection and mental consolidation. They are also necessary for rest and emotional recuperation. I saw at some point that the entire journey is not just one of exaltation and exhilaration.

At this time in my experiment I also began to expand my earlier understanding of the need for spiritual purgation. Purgation implies a commitment to clean and purify the mind so that one can operate out of motives that are of the utmost integrity. One need not be pure in heart to begin this journey, or who would begin it? One, of necessity, becomes purer in heart as one continues the journey, or who could endure it? The fire of cleansing exacts its own price. I also saw that if I continued with the whole experiment and was not dissuaded from it during a dry period, that eventually my lucid dreams would return. So far, they always have, sometimes singly and sometimes in clusters. On one occasion I received six lucid dreams in a single night.*

As my experiment progressed, I received a number of dreams of inner cleansing. One of these was particularly unnerving and memorable.

THE HUMANOID FOX
September 11, 1981

I am walking with Yogananda** along a dirt road in the open countryside of modern India. We pass many fields of green crops and leafy vegetables, all neatly planted in rows. Yogananda has been urging me to come to India to live and work, and I feel some attraction to the idea mostly because it comes from him. We meet a workman, an American, who is installing some kind of tall, wooden pole in the ground. He appears to be a very shy man and somewhat emotionally insecure as we chat with him. Now Yogananda excuses himself for a moment and walks away as if he has some important matter to attend to. The workman straightens up his body, and suddenly appears much more self-confident as he tells me how much Yogananda has done for his life. He says that he feels totally accepted by and loved by the guru, and that Yogananda loves everybody exactly for who he is. I feel very impressed with the workman's sincerity.

Now I look out across the large field of crops nearby and I see a fox stalking some smaller animal. The fox has humanlike features, as if he were drawn by a cartoonist or were appearing in an animated movie. Just as the fox is about to pounce on his prey, he lets out a sharp, piercing screech, supposedly to terrorize and paralyze his victim. He pounces, but the smaller animal

---

* See "The Majestic Mountain," a lucid dream account in chapter eight.

** Paramahansa Yogananda (1893-1952), a Hindu master of yoga and meditation who taught in America from 1920-1952. His spiritual classic *The Autobiography of a Yogi* has had a powerful influence on my life.

escapes. Now the fox chases his intended victim madly through the field of leafy, green vegetables. For several minutes I watch this drama and can see only the flurry and flutter of the bushes and plants. For some time the fox vigorously pursues the small animal all around the field, as they both race about through the dense, green foliage. After a long and frenzied chase, the fox finally gives up his pursuit and walks over to me. He places his paws, shaped like small human hands, on my arm and in a seductive, crafty tone of voice asks me if I would be his ally in catching the weaker creatures of the world. Immediately, I grab the fox's paw with my right hand and swing his whole body with full force, round and round in the air. Quickly building up a great deal of centrifugal force, I now fling the fox away and throw him high into the air with all my might. His body at once becomes birdlike and he glides through the air for a short time, finally landing on a distant telephone wire. He perches there, precariously, with ruffled fur and feathers.

Now, Yogananda rejoins the workman and me and I feel the sharp contast between Yogananda and the fox. The silent look on the workman's face tells me what a deep trust and respect he has for Yogananda. I wake up feeling very energized.

During the week prior to this dream, I had been rereading Yogananda's *Autobiography of a Yogi* for the third time. Since I began this reading, the book had appeared in my dreams twice, and now Yogananda himself appeared. To me he symbolized the guru, the higher self, the fullest ethical commitment that a human being can make; namely, that he uses his superior power and knowledge to teach and elevate others rather than to subjugate or exploit them. He symbolized the highest potential inside myself, the full commitment to serve people with the purest of motives and out of genuine concern for their welfare.

On the other hand, the humanoid fox symbolized the direct opposite of the guru. He was the adversary to the guru and to higher consciousness. He symbolized that part of me that could exploit others less knowledgeable than myself and that might attempt to prey upon them in some way for my own personal gains. The sly fox, crafty and seductive in the dream, was a strange mixture of human and animal form, a blend of "higher" and "lower" consciousness.

I felt a lot of emotion with this particular dream because many of its symbols were highly personal. Yogananda was *my* guru—in print, at least. Through his writings, he was as close as I had ever come to finding a guru. The fields and the neat rows of vegetation in the dream reminded me of the row crops in the large fields of the Sacramento Valley where I lived as a child. The simple workman with his obvious shyness and emotional insecurities reminded me of the "common man," who in many ways is not so easily fooled after all. His simplicity was his strength. His lack of sophistication allowed him to see with his heart and to recognize and be moved by a spiritual master who was sincere. The workman symbolized a down-to-earthedness that has always been a strong part of me, something in myself that I have always appreciated. Correspondingly, growing up as I did in a small country town, I have always had a strong preference for simplicity over sophistication, especially when it comes to people.

One day, as I was rereading this dream about three years after it arrived, I was struck by a dimension to the humanoid fox that I had not seen before. Because I had previously shared this dream several times with professional colleagues and student groups, and had already received a great deal of feedback about it, I had laid it to rest in my mind. Now in this private re-examination of the fox, I focused on the fact that its paws appeared like small human hands when he placed them seductively upon my arm. What a strange and poignant image! The hands, my cue for becoming lucid, had appeared again in my series of dreams, and this time they were attached to the fox, to the trickster, the crafty exploiter! With this realization I developed another

110

important line of questioning: Was the fox part of me also interested in lucid dreaming? Was he also intrigued with this new power, just now emerging into my world? How would the fox part of me use lucidity? Would he use it to exploit others or manipulate them? Yes, I realized, there is no doubt that the crafty trickster part of the Self would attempt to use a new spiritual power for selfish or destructive purposes. This is always possible and it always poses an important question whenever a new form of power emerges into one's consciousness. I felt somewhat relieved to see that the dream scenario itself provided me with a most effective coping mechanism for this particular challenge: *immediacy of response.*

"The Humanoid Fox," in its dramatic point of climax, reinforced a crucial psychospiritual lesson. For me, the climax occurred in that split second between the fox's invitation and my own response. In that split second in the dream, I grabbed the fox by the arm *immediately* and, without a moment of hesitation or without a flicker of doubt in my mind, swung him around over my head and flung him far away. The immediacy of this response is where I have focused most of my attention in my latter reflections upon this dream. Immediacy is the ideal response to the crafty temptation. The longer one listens to craftiness, the more one is likely to be seduced by it. Immediacy is the choice not to spend any time or energy at all on the invitation to abuse power, but to reject it with full force instead. In the act of rejecting the fox, some transformational process occurred in the dream. The fox's body became "birdlike" and took on a loftier form. As it glided through the air for some distance and eventually landed on a telephone wire, the fox was changed as its outer coat became a mixture of "fur and feathers." The birdlike overtones coming out of the fox symbolized the potential of one's shadow side to be raised to a higher level of consciousness, after it is fully confronted and handled. Craftiness, I realized, when fully confronted within the Self, has the potential to become a type of

111

"worldly wisdom" that will rightly serve the higher self and become a true spiritual gift. This dream, too, confirmed the age-old principle that, in the confrontation of the inner adversary, psychospiritual transformation is effected. In my cultivation of the lucid dream state, I would need to be particularly immediate in responding to any temptation to abuse or exploit its power. I would need also to remember Yogananda, the guru, who symbolized my central spiritual motive for this work.

As I looked at myself in this dream, I also realized how important it is to remember that a dream scenario of this type does not necessarily present the dreamer with any guarantees. It does not guarantee that on future occasions in the waking world he will respond exactly as he had in the dream. It does not guarantee *that* the dreamer will do the right thing; it merely shows him *how* to do the right thing. It presents the dreamer with a model for the creative response and clearly points out an ideal way for someone to operate out of the highest motives.

About six weeks after "The Humanoid Fox" I received another powerful dream that was a commentary on my lucid dream experiment. This dream, entitled "Protecting My Golden Fruit," added further clarification about particular blocks and current emotional struggles that were inhibiting my development of lucidity. This dream invited me to attend to those particular blocks.

PROTECTING MY GOLDEN FRUIT
October 21, 1981

I am standing on the street about half a block west of my home in Fairfax. My brother Ray is nearby and we are watching several black men picking fruit off the trees in the neighborhood. It is harvest time and they are working very rapidly and industriously. There is a peach tree in the front corner of my yard next to the wooden fence, and it is loaded with beautiful, ripe peaches. All the peaches are perfectly uniform in size, slightly bigger than baseballs, and they all shine with an amazing array of brilliant colors, red, yellow and gold. Immediately beyond the fence, on my next-door neighbor's property, is another peach tree which is also loaded with beautiful peaches that glisten and gleam in the sunshine. Two black men are working rapidly there; they have almost stripped my neighbor's tree and are about to begin working on mine. I hear the workers calling back and forth, talking rapidly to another black man across the street who is standing high up on a ladder picking olives. They tease and joke about throwing fruit at each other, and I remember that my friends and I used to do the same thing when we were teenagers, harvesting peaches and pears in the summers in the Sacramento Valley.

Now I notice that one black man has completely stripped three-fourths of the fruit off my tree. I feel very alarmed and I say to my brother Ray very angrily, "Who gave them permission to pick the fruit?" Ray says that he did and I become outraged. I slap him across the face and he begins to cry. I challenge Ray to step out into the middle of the street so I can punch him out. He refuses to fight and starts to slink away. I feel surprised that he offers no resistance, and I realize he is frightened by my anger which is now very strong.

I race over to my peach tree and I command the black man to come down out of the tree immediately, which he does. I tell him I feel outraged that he has taken this fruit and that I have worked hard all year long to cultivate this tree. I tell him to pour the fruit from his bucket into a nearby box on the ground, *for me.* He obeys. Speaking again in a commanding voice, I tell him to take his ladder and leave. He complies quietly.

Now I survey the remaining peaches on the tree and see that there is still enough for the needs of my family. Still fuming with anger, I tidy up the area under the tree, gathering up some old dried limbs and branches. I see the black men, with their children, loading boxes of freshly picked fruit into their large truck across the street. Still angry, I walk up my driveway toward the house and see that the garage door is wide open. I wonder who left it open and feel annoyed. Now I see that the inside door to my office is also left ajar, and I feel even more irritated. I walk into my office, which is almost dark, and make several loud emphatic, hissing noises like psssst! . . psssst! . . psssst . . . ! intending to chase out any of the numerous stray cats from the neighborhood that may have wandered in. I look around my office and, not seeing any cats, I feel relieved. I wake up, feeling tense and very tired.

This dream offered further information and suggestions about how my own dark side was entering into my lucid dreaming experiment. The incredibly abundant golden fruit, glistening with light and sunshine, clearly symbolized for me my lucid dreams. In this dream, the gleaming peaches were being ripped off the trees by the black men. As I have discussed earlier in chapter one of this book, black people are often a common dream symbol for the shadow, the dark side of the white man's psyche. My younger brother Ray for many years had also appeared as a shadow symbol in numerous dreams of mine and his presence here added still another note of confirmation along this line. This was a dream that portrayed my shadow side in action. My conscious ego was very angry with this shadow component, as is shown by slapping my brother across the face and challenging him to an all-out fist fight in the dream. I found it fascinating that my dream ego (myself in the dream) was able to intervene in time to prevent my tree from being totally stripped, even though three-fourths of its abundant fruit had already been taken.

But what exactly was I so angry about? For one thing, I was very angry about living in that particular neighborhood, where I frequently felt "ripped off" by the primitive aggressive forces that were constantly bombarding me and my family. The constant stereophonic assault that I mentioned earlier was the prime external adversary that was draining my energy. I was angry at myself, too, for staying in that neighborhood, partly for financial reasons. I realized from this dream that my fear of financial loss and financial risk-taking had become a dark inner adversary which, by the time of this dream, had begun to drain me. My fear was "ripping me off," and, at an alarming rate. With this dream and the impact of its message, I realized more keenly that we had to move. Shortly thereafter, Charlene and I further intensified our efforts in looking for a new home.

I was also intrigued with the notion that three-fourths of my golden fruit, my lucid dreams, had been taken from me. "Was the number significant?" I asked myself. After some reflection I saw that currently I was having about one lucid dream per month. This rate was a drop from my average of four per month when I first began the experiment in October, 1980. My current rate of lucid dreaming was approximately one-fourth of what it had been at its peak. Even the math in this dream was accurate!

Although this dream delivered a powerful message about my dark side (my fear), it also conveyed a good deal of beauty as well. The images of the golden fruit were spectacular. Each inspirational peach, radiating so much light, represented a lucid dream, and the tree represented the archetype of the Self, reminiscent of the Tree of Life. The tree was absolutely loaded with this golden fruit, a symbol for the abundant potential of the lucid dream state. Regarding this particular dream, I wrote a note in my journal which read: "I must return to the cultivation of my garden, my lucid dreaming, and give less energy to money matters." This was a repetition of the same message I had received six months earlier to remember my highest priorities. This reminder was rewarded by a special lucid dream that came nine days later.

CIRCLES OF GRAPES, CIRCLES OF LIGHT
November 1, 1981

I see a large cluster of grapes in my field of vision. They look like the Thompson seedless variety, light green in color. They are all perfectly round, somewhat small, and uniform in size and shape. Suddenly, every grape on the cluster, in perfect unison and

115

synchronization, shifts its position slightly, and each grape is outlined with a brilliant ring of white light. I feel startled and wonderfully dazzled by the light, and I realize I am dreaming. The wonderful feeling of the light, tingling sensation, so familiar in lucid dreaming, returns now and travels throughout my chest, head and forehead in particular. Now, all the rings of light, perfectly circular around each grape, move again as one, in perfect unison and synchronization, as each takes on a slight hexagon shape of light which appears just inside each circumference. All these magically illumined grapes still are perfectly identical in size, shape and color. Now, as if by the twist of a brilliant giant kaleidoscope, the entire cluster spreads out and expands with a brilliant white flash, creating thousands of identically illuminated grapes that spread gloriously to the left and right as far as I can see across my entire field of vision. The impact is absolutely dazzling. I remember my friend Julia's dream in which she saw hundreds of moonlit wavelets in the ocean, each one with a tiny, identical silver fish poised in its crest. I feel myself irresistibly drawn into this myriad, crystalline structure, as I continue to enjoy its beauty immensely. I think to myself, "Relax... relax... focus... focus..." as I seek to fuse myself fully with these images and enter more deeply into the light. I feel myself starting to awaken, and I continue to focus on the beautiful, clearly etched, crystalline circles. Slowly, I feel them slip away as I gradually awaken, feeling delighted.

Upon awakening, it was obvious to me that this lucid dream was a companionate dream to "Protecting My Golden Fruit." The perfectly circular shape of each grape reminded me of the perfectly uniform size and shape of the peaches in the earlier dream. There was a clear cut similarity between the peaches and the grapes, as if to suggest that all the fruits of the lucid state are somehow related to each other. The circles of light around each grape, so dazzling in their own way, reminded me of the dazzling colors of the golden peaches and their perfect circularity. It was an immense pleasure to see the light in this dream and to contemplate merging myself with the brilliant crystalline structure, containing thousands upon thousands of circles, all interconnected and interwoven into that fascinating fabric of light and images. The first dream had warned me that three-fourths of my lucid dreams had been taken away, and this dream told me that lucidity can return and does return in abundance.

How little did I realize what a powerful return the Light was going to make. Five days after the arrival of this exhilarating dream, I was the recipient of another awesome, overwhelming lucid dream that carried me in a giant swoop back to the mountaintop again. On this occasion, approximately one year after I began my lucid dreaming project, I received an overpowering dream in the middle of the night that left me reeling from its emotional intensity and from the gripping power of its symbolism. This dream was another peak experience, worthy to be compared with "The Gift of the Magi." Ready or not, I was carried back to the summit once again. This lucid dream I entitled "The Arrival of the Serpent Power."

CHAPTER SIX

The Arrival of
the Serpent Power

"Be ye wise as serpents and guileless as doves."*
—Jesus of Nazareth

THE ARRIVAL OF THE SERPENT POWER
November 6, 1981

I am standing somewhere inside a small dark room and I see two square window frames in front of me. The frames are simple, open spaces in the wall, and I see a bright light streaming in from the outside. I see someone's hand coming in through one of the windows, reaching toward me as it holds out some small object of art, perhaps a jewel or a crystal. I see only his hand and wrist and the beautiful small object, as the room itself is in total darkness. Suddenly, I realize I am dreaming and I feel a powerful jolt of energy shoot through my body. I rise up off the floor and enter the light, flying head-first through one of the open window frames.

Instantly, I enter a whole new scene. Still lucid, I am now outside in a remote area in the woods, standing beside a small log cabin. A beautiful blanket of freshly fallen, white snow covers the entire scene, with many trees and a lovely valley that extends before me. I am with an unknown woman companion, and we are held captive by a small band of Indians. As I look out across the valley below me and up the crest on the opposite side, I see two strong-willed, determined cowboys, mounted on horses. Swiftly, they ride through the deep snowdrifts and in a matter of seconds they cover the distance between us and rescue us from the Indians. There is no

---

* Matthew 10:16.

shooting or violence; they simply *arrive,* emitting so much power out of their bodies that I *know* we are liberated.

The scene changes abruptly. Now I am lying face down on the ground somewhere on a patch of bare, brown earth. Still fully aware that I am dreaming, I see a huge serpent approach me from the right. Quickly, it glides over my back, then turns and passes back beneath me, silently sliding between my body and the ground. Then it rises, turns and comes up over my back again, strongly gripping me around my chest in its powerful coil. Its gray-brown body is about three to four inches thick and about thirty feet long. Its eyes are a strange yellow-green in color, and they gaze at me calmly and steadily, continuously emitting their soft, yellow-green luminescence from within. Finding its position now, the serpent pauses, its head poised in the air about three feet above me, and it watches me through its glowing eyes with a calm and amazingly neutral objectivity. Arching my neck backward and straining to lift my head, I look upward. Our eyes meet and the impact is extremely powerful—absolutely unforgettable as I gaze for a long moment into the serpent's profound yellow-green eyes, utterly perplexed and fascinated at the same time. Now I drop my head and begin to wrestle with the serpent. Trying to free myself from its grip, I discover that I am no match for its incredible strength. I feel afraid that it will crush me. I wrestle with all my might for some time until, exhausted, I decide to stop struggling. Soon I perceive that the serpent is actually very gentle, merely intent on holding me in its relentless grip. I am very surprised to feel that its body is warm blooded, not cold blooded as I would expect. Suddenly, it makes a quick, jerking movement with its coil which rotates my prone body onto its side. After a few moments it quickly jerks me back again to a face-down position. The serpent seems to be playing with me in some strange, uncanny fashion, rotating me back and forth in its gradual, deliberate manner. Several times it rotates me from my face-down position up onto one side, then back again to face down and then up onto my other side. I feel totally subject to its will as these movements are repeated several times, each time with a quick, powerful jerk of its massive coil.

Suddenly the whole scene vanishes. I feel many confusing, swirling energies moving through my body and I feel a lot of dizziness in my head. After a while my field of vision gradually becomes clear again, and I see myself lying on the same spot of bare, brown earth, face down with my body fully outstretched once again. I am still lucid, fully aware that I am dreaming. Now another large, gray-brown serpent approaches me from my right in the exact same manner as the first. This serpent is fully identical to the first in every detail of its appearance, except it is slightly smaller in size and length. Quickly and smoothly it glides over my body and passes beneath me, going between my body and the ground and coming up over the top again, making one full coil around me exactly as its predecessor had done. Though it is slightly smaller in size I can feel that this serpent too is extremely powerful. It also positions its head about three feet above me and gazes down upon me with full steadiness and inner calm and with the same abundance of amazingly neutral, universal objectivity. Again I stare upwards for a time into the amazing powerful eyes of the serpent, trying to fathom its intent. I am entranced with the soft, yellow-green luminescence that steadily flows from somewhere deep, deep within the serpent's eyes and even from beyond its eyes, as if from the untold reaches of another world. I feel totally in awe as I absorb the air of mystery that emanates from the serpent continuously. I return its steady gaze for a while and then I drop my head as I begin to wrestle with it, struggling with all my might to free myself from its powerful grip. I thrash and thrash about, struggling in every way that I can while the serpent remains virtually motionless, calmly gazing at me from above. Effortlessly it holds me in its single coil, exactly as the first serpent had done, until at last I finally surrender, knowing that I am no match for its incredible strength either. As I lie there quietly for several long moments, I realize that like its predecessor, this serpent, too, is quite gentle toward me, in the same, strange, neutral way. I am surprised to feel that it, too, is a warm-blooded creature.

Suddenly I awaken, and I feel very dizzy and confused by multiple, swirling energies surging throughout my body, flowing directly from the dream. I feel overwhelmed by the sheer power of the dream and very excited by it as well.

The imagery of the two serpents in this dream is so

powerfully impressed on my memory that I know I will remember them for the rest of my life. This dream was definitely another peak experience in my experiment with lucid dreaming. The power contained within the dream was rather frightening this time, because I felt so dizzy after I awakened. Only with difficulty was I able to get out of bed, stand up, and stay on my feet as I walked to the bathroom to urinate. My head felt like a giant whirlpool, with strong, multiple, swirling sensations going through it, round and round, over and over. The swirling and surging of energies was coming up my spine, up through the base of my neck and into my head.

As I tried to stabilize myself a couple of questions entered my mind: "Am I going crazy?" "Am I, at the moment, overwhelmed with some sort of powerful, psychic energy released by this lucid dream?" I decided, rather quickly, that I could not possibly deal with these questions at that moment. I also decided that I did not even dare to write down the dream right away because its energies were so overpowering. It was about three o'clock in the morning, and I knew I had best return to the mental safety of slumber as quickly as possible. I carefully walked back to the bedroom, bracing myself with my hands against the walls and furniture in order to retain my balance. I slowly and carefully crawled into bed and was immensely relieved to fall asleep quickly. Under these conditions, the unconsciousness of sleep was a welcome return, a haven from the turbulent swirling that I felt throughout my whole being, body and mind. When I awoke in the morning, I entered the dream in my journal, as its power and haunting imagery came flooding back into my mind again with indescribable vividness.

For several days after this dream the images of the serpents returned to haunt me. At the time of this writing, three-and-a-half years after the dream, I can still see, above all, that strange, eerie, yellow-green luminescence emanating from those deep, bottomless eyes with such a calm, impartial, other-worldly glow. In my memory the consciousness within these two serpents still seems totally objective, totally neutral, and absolutely detached from this world. They have no great mission to accomplish or task to perform; they just ARE. Those eyes simply BE. They radiate the THUS-NESS OF EVERYTHING THAT IS, a perfect manifesto of the way it all IS. Their way of BEING is almost indescribable in any language or medium. If I were a painter, I would regard it as the consummate artistic challenge to convey those beautiful glowing eyes from the depths of my memory onto a piece of canvas.

After several days of reflecting on the powers and qualities of the serpents, I began to wonder if they symbolized the awakening of the kundalini energy into my conscious mind. I also began to wonder if they not only symbolized the awakening, but somehow conveyed the awakening as well. These questions have concerned me ever since, and I do not have a fully satisfying answer to this day. My growing opinion is that the answer to both questions is "yes." After a few months of reflection, I began to consider still another question: How do I take care of myself if I have inadvertently tapped into the kundalini energy and awakened it through my experimentation with lucid dreaming?

My own understanding of kundalini energy is that it is a form of psychic power that lies hidden at the base of the human spine. The Hindu yogis and sages, both ancient and modern, have likened it to a coiled serpent, which is capable of uncoiling at some point in a person's evolution and capable of rising up the spine through the various centers of consciousness. These centers of consciousness they called chakras, meaning circles or wheels. At some point in the evolution of the various teachings and esoteric writings on this subject, the uncoiling of the serpent became a symbol for the rising of this psychic energy.* Accordingly, the appearance of

* See Gopi Krishna's book, *Kundalini: The Evolutionary Energy in Man*, *passim*.

the serpent in someone's dream, vision, or deep meditative trance was often seen as a portent that the kundalini energy was indeed rising in that particular person's consciousness. As this energy began to move up the spine, the recipient would, supposedly, experience more and more shifts in his thinking and ways of seeing the world. Among the benefits received would be an increase in his psychic powers of perception and in his intuitive abilities. In everyday life this often fostered an increased ability to see clearly through the maze and complexity of the world, and to discern the truly essential issues and concerns of any given situation.

At first, the biggest single change that I noticed in myself around the time of this dream was an increased sensitivity to my own feelings (on all levels) and an increased difficulty in being in prolonged contact with negative feelings and negative energies from other people. I seemed to be exercising less tolerance than ever for the average foibles of everyday life. More and more I wanted to "get away from it all" and rechoose my personal contacts very carefully. Increasingly I felt a strong desire only to be around those people whose energy lifted me up or, at least, did not pull me down.

Secondly, I began to develop an "energy awareness" in which I saw the entire physical world as a huge mass and sea of energies, all vibrating at different frequencies and moving in different directions. I began to see in a very real way that everything is alive, and there really is no such thing as an "inanimate object." The old distinction between animate creatures and inanimate objects no longer held much meaning for me as a frame of reference. Above all, I became very aware, perhaps even hypersensitive by some standards, to all the emotional shifts and mood swings in the people around me, both with my clients and students in professional work and with complete strangers in public places such as street corners, supermarkets and restaurants. Gradually, I ceased to perceive people according to my old sense of them. Each person I now met became more like a living, glowing, dynamic ecosystem, whose thoughts, emotions, words, tone of voice, breathing and body movements became more and more vividly impressed upon my mind than ever before. At times I felt mentally flooded with all these impressions and had to learn a new set of skills in relating to others and responding to them. I had to work more quickly and actively to sort through all these impressions and choose more consciously what I wished to respond to in the people around me.

While these changes brought a good deal of excitement and inner freedom, they also brought me some concern about becoming an "elitist" or socially isolated. I wrestled with this particular issue within myself for over a year after this dream arrived before I managed to create a new and comfortable inner balance for myself. With this new balance, I eventually began to feel comfortable again in the presence of negative vibrations from other people. I somehow learned how to retain my newly acquired sensitivity and not be drained by the dark energies or negative thoughts of others. I felt as if I were learning how to be "mentally tough," in a way that I had never been conscious of before. My new strength was all internal, like an invisible blanket, an energy field that I could call up out of myself in an instant and throw on top of some obnoxious situation, covering up its negative vibrations and thereby protecting my heightened sensitivities. This mental blanket of toughness often proved to be invaluable in certain social situations and, above all, in certain psychotherapy situations where clients were working to release their own pain, anger or depression. Somewhere during this time, I learned to encourage their full release while protecting myself at the same time, on a deeper level than I had ever done before.

At this point in my experiment I began to see how the cultivation of lucid dreaming aided the cultivation of intuition as well. The more intuitive one becomes, the more one focuses on becoming a "seer" as distinct from becoming a "thinker" in the world.* Increased clarity of perception is tantamount to increased lucidity. To be lucid means to be clear, full of light or enlightened. As I reflected on these plays of words and their related similar meanings, I could see how they all seemed to be leading to the same end. The cultivation of lucidity in the dream state promoted lucidity in the waking state and perhaps the arousal of kundalini energy for some individuals and probably an opportunity for advancement along the spiritual path and progress toward personal enlightenment for most people.

One must remember, here, that I am addressing these issues in a framework of evolution and not in a framework of finality. The cultivating of lucid dreams does not mean that one *is* enlightened; it possibly means that the dreamer *is becoming* more enlightened. One must remember also that the points of comparison are completely internal. The lucid dreamer is becoming more enlightened than his former self, not necessarily more enlightened than anyone else. This "becoming" is a miracle in its own right, as has been so aptly expressed in this quotation from Willa Cather: "Where there is great love, there are always miracles. Miracles rest not so much upon faces or voices or healing power coming to us from afar off, but *on our perceptions being made finer,* so that for a moment our eyes can see and our ears can hear what is there about us always."** [Emphasis added.]

To me, this has become one of the greatest miracles of my experiment with lucid dreaming in that I have been able to see, through my own experience, how my own human perceptions were made finer as I advanced into

---

* The Latin derivation of the word intuition is interesting: "in" (into) + "tuere" (to see). "To see into" implies that to intuit is to see into the insides of a person, problem or situation, to see beyond the level of external appearances or symptoms. To intuit is to see the essence of someone or something and to distinguish clearly between what is essential and what is nonessential.

** Willa Cather, *Death Comes for the Archbishop,* p. 50.

this frontier of consciousness. With the experience of lucidity, it became easier for me to understand how the whole truth is always fully present, directly in front of us at any moment, simply waiting to be seen. Only the cloudedness of our ordinary perceptions prevents us from seeing the truth all at once in a single, unified flash. Our human challenge is to remove the cloudedness that customarily covers our own eyes, so that our perceptions *can* be made finer, our eyes *can* be opened and we can see as if for the first time.

The ancient Greeks apparently knew about this mystery of the cleansing of human perceptions. In their language, the word for truth was *aletheia*. Aletheia was actually a compound word: "a" (non) and "letheia" (hiddenness). In their minds, to discover the truth about something meant to see its non-hiddenness, to see through the illusion of appearances. This way of thinking implies that they knew that much of reality is hidden from our awareness, and that to mature as a human person is to refine and cleanse our perceptions and to bring the truth out of hiding into the light of consciousness.

One of the more intriguing aspects of my experiment with lucid dreaming is the sudden "jolt" of energy that often shoots through my dream body immediately upon becoming lucid. This jolt occurred with the onset of lucidity in "The Arrival of the Serpent Power" and has occurred in one form or another in many of my other lucid dreams. Sometimes I feel this energy rising up my spine; sometimes I feel it coursing through my chest, arms and legs; and very often I feel it moving through my face and settling solidly at the point between the eyebrows.* These energies usually feel delightful and

---

* This point between the eyebrows is commonly referred to as "the third eye" in the esoteric writings of Hinduism and Buddhism. According to these teachings, the third eye is located in the sixth chakra, the "ajna" chakra. The opening of the third eye creates another channel of conscious perception for the seer and supposedly is another valued and demarcated step that occurs at some point in one's spiritual evolution.

uplifting. This, however, was the second lucid dream where I felt overwhelmed by the energy to the point of feeling dizzy and confused when I awakened.

The symbols in this dream were filled with multiple meanings for me and I doubt that I could ever write a complete account of them. The dream was archetypal in that it presented the universal theme of passage from captivity to freedom by flying out of the dark room and entering the light. The new world which I entered in the dream, enlightened as it was by the beautiful blanket of white snow, was still, however, one that contained polarities and struggles, as along with my "unknown female companion" I was held captive by Indians, symbolizing some primitive forces within myself. The dream then suggested that release from those primitive forces could be accomplished in an instant, and without violence, through the mobilization of my male power, symbolized by the cowboys with the uninhibited and forceful way in which they arrived on the scene. I have come to think of their forcefulness as a type of "creative aggression," a virtue that, unfortunately, is hardly ever discussed at length in a spiritual context. These themes and images have helped me to pinpoint those moments and situations in the waking state when I need to give myself a push in order to grow. Patience and tolerant waiting are not always appropriate to every dilemma that life presents. Sometimes taking powerful, aggressive action is exactly what I need in order to liberate myself from the destructive powers that are holding me prisoner. The cowboys in the dream were a symbol of silent, indisputable strength, a strength that simply liberates through the mere force of its presence and through its *way of being.*

I appreciated the fact that this dream appeared in two distinct parts and I saw a clear relationship between the parts. The first reminded me of a major theme that appeared in "The Gift of the Magi," that lucid dreaming is a liberation from darkness and captivity, and that even when liberation is achieved on one level the dreamer will be called to continue to advance and achieve it on subsequent levels as well.

The second part of the dream showed me wrestling with the two serpents. I interpreted this to mean that I would be in a position to wrestle and grapple continuously within myself toward the cultivation of higher states of consciousness (for example, kundalini) *after* I had mobilized a lot more healthy aggression (male energy) into my life. With reflection on these themes, I realized more and more how much I needed this to protect my sensitive inner life, an inner life that had become much more sensitized than ever since I began the development of lucid dreaming.

"The Arrival of the Serpent Power" and the life context out of which it came has often led me to reflect upon one of Carl Jung's statements: "I would much rather be a whole person than a good person." His message was a criticism of the commonly misunderstood and truncated version of moral goodness that is so often held up for emulation in civilized society. Goodness has often been equated with qualities such as niceness, patience, kindness and tolerance, with the expectation that these qualities should be displayed at all times and in all circumstances. Such "goodness" unfortunately often makes people into victims because it may unconsciously invite more aggressive individuals to abuse, attack or exploit. In this setting, I was relearning once again that a whole person is someone who feels his own anger and aggression on those appropriate occasions when someone else is exploiting him and can speak out or take effective action to prevent the attack from proceeding any further. In essence, it is not always appropriate nor spiritual to turn the other cheek. For me, Jung's basic idea is so vital because it implies that there is a dark side to love which actually turns out to be a positive human force in the long run. It throws out absolute behavioral guidelines for people to follow and encourages us to commit to the wholeness of the psyche as our overall

128

guiding principle. This means responding appropriately to each situation that one is in at the time that one is in it. I saw once again that "love" might make some strange and stressful demands upon those who follow its path. It might require of us that we tell someone else how angry we are with him. Or a true act of love might mean taking someone to court, ending an abusive relationship or sending a hardened criminal to prison.

Let me now return to the dream. The act of wrestling with the powerful serpents was its highlight. This wrestling suggested to me many possibilities, including that I had now become "gripped" or seized by the path of lucid dreaming as I was seized by the serpents. At first I fought against the seizure in the dream, only to discover that true safety and peace come with "surrender." Surrender of my own will has never been particularly easy for me, and now the dream was suggesting something that felt strange and new to me, that I stop struggling in order to discover. It also suggested that I will face this challenge repeatedly in life, over and over, until my surrender is complete and final. Learning through repeated surrenderings was beautifully portrayed in the dream by the advent of the second serpent. The second serpent was identical to the first in every respect, except it was slightly smaller in size and length. The actions that it performed, and which we performed together, were exactly the same in every minute detail as those that occurred with the first serpent. With both serpents it seemed as if we were performing some strange kind of ritual together, and the repetition of this identical ritual with the smaller serpent suggested that if I persevered along this particular path, I would eventually be able to handle the powerful energies that are symbolized and conveyed by the serpents. Each successive serpent, perhaps, would become somewhat smaller, closer to my own size, as I wrestled with them through time. No one knows how long this might take and that concern is essentially irrelevant. The numerous times in which the first serpent rotated my prone body in its massive coil seem to have some significance to me also. These serpents were almost playing with me; they, not I, were completely in charge, moving my body according to their rhythms and timing. In that portion of the dream, after giving up all my resistances and my needs to struggle, I finally fully surrendered to them in the end.

The light coming from within the eyes of the serpents was one of the most engaging images I have ever seen in any lucid dream or anywhere. That soft, yellow-green bottomless luminescence was totally unique in my experience and I know of nothing in my life upon which I could base any comparison. The light was completely "other" in its quality, and words like eerie, fathomless or cosmic scarcely begin to convey the all-pervading sense of mystery emanating from those eyes that seemed like glimmering windows to the universe. As I reflect on those images now, I find a deep feeling of peace and tranquility coming over me. The serpents ultimately were my friends, I realized, and their inner messages and gifts were very soothing and comforting in their own incomparable way. Ultimately, their path is one of comfort and the deepest consolation. The path of the lucid dream must, of necessity, have its own contemplative rewards along the way. These deepest consolations are the unexpected gifts that await the traveler, much like a moment of reverie when one contemplates a single blade of grass, holding a single drop of dew glistening on a shaft of sunlight, and suddenly one feels like a child all over again, reborn in a moment. Such intensity and deep, quiet consolation are the elements of which the lucid dream is frequently made.

About three weeks after "The Arrival of the Serpent Power" I had another unusually powerful dream. This one gave vent to another strong force in my psyche that was operating at the time of my lucid dream experiment. The force was rage—blind rage, and it opened another dimension to the unraveling of my story and the exploration of my own inner labyrinth.

CONFRONTING THE POLAR BEAR
November 26, 1981

I am somewhere in the wilderness of Alaska standing beside an outdoor campsite. I am speaking with a man who looks about thirty-five to forty years old. He appears to be the rugged, sturdy, outdoorsman type, with a mustache, blue jeans, boots and a flannel shirt with long sleeves rolled up to his elbows. I think of him as a lumberjack. He starts to tell me a story about an encounter he once had with a blind polar bear. Suddenly, the scenario of my dreamscape changes and I now see the man's story portrayed before me, like a cinema flashback, as he continues to tell his tale.

I see the lumberjack standing alone in the wilderness on the bank of a wild, tumbling river. He is fishing. I see a polar bear come out of the forest on the opposite side of the river. It enters the surging waters and heads directly for the fisherman. I know intuitively that this polar bear is about one year old and that it is totally blind. In spite of its blindness, however, it heads for the man with an amazing, unerring accuracy. I am not sure whether the bear is friendly or hostile, though I am very aware of its power and directness.

Now the lumberjack starts to leave the riverbank, somewhat hurriedly and frightened, as the polar bear has successfully completed the crossing and is emerging from the water. The shaggy white giant quickly pursues the fleeing man and easily overtakes him. In desperation the man turns and pulls a pistol from his coat pocket. For a long moment he points the pistol directly at the polar bear which suddenly stops its pursuit, and rising upright on its hind legs, stands motionless, as if frozen, and glares intently at the frightened man. Then almost at point blank range, the lumberjack shoots the polar bear in the head. Immediately, I see two huge, white scales fall from the eyes of the polar bear. Now for the first time in its life the bear can see. It repeatedly blinks its eyes and gazes blankly off into space, becoming accustomed to the light as man and beast stand there facing each other with a prolonged, intense feeling of uncertainty in the air. I wake up feeling a lot of energy and power in the dream.

This graphic dream was yet another that captured my full attention as I awoke. I began to put some pieces together quickly, even as I lay in bed. The polar bear connoted a "polarity" within myself, some two-sided inner struggle. I recognized the thirty-five to forty-year-old outdoorsman lumberjack as an old part of me, another symbol for the survivalist aspect of my ego, equivalent to the tough Latino inmate in my "Amputation" dream. With amusement I reflected upon the fact that I was forty years old at the time I had this dream. This lumberjack part of me has always believed that I have to struggle for my survival. His prime concern in life *is* survival. He is tough and sturdy and believes in rugged individualism as the key to survival and success. His long-sleeved, flannel shirt reminded me of the four or five similiar style shirts that I have in my own closet and which I enjoy wearing, especially in the wintertime.

The polar bear, on the other hand, represented a relatively new, yet very powerful, instinctual force in my life. I could not figure him out at first, but with the help of two professional colleagues with whom I frequently discuss dreams, I discovered that it symbolized the powerful rage that had been building up inside of me for the past year. This rage was to a large extent "blind" or unconscious. My conscious mind simply did not want to feel how fully outraged I really was over the constant bedlam from my neighbors next door and how enraged I was at the survivalist ego part of myself for the way in which it responded to that ongoing stress. As I began to decipher this dream, I saw another example of how a dream's mathematics could be important, since the ages of the two dream protagonists, the survivalist ego and the blind rage, corresponded quite accurately to the actual ages of these two parts of myself in waking life.

132

By the time that "Confronting the Polar Bear" appeared, my conflict situation with my teenage adversary had become even more aggravated. A number of new hellish developments had taken place just prior to the arrival of this dream. A tough-looking bunch of young males had recently begun to use the house next door as their hang-out. They would gather at all hours of the day or night, often appearing to be drunk or on drugs, interacting with a lot of loud yelling and cursing, frequently punctuated with the sounds of breaking glass. I never knew whether the crunching or shattering glass was just another beer bottle dropped onto the concrete or perhaps another windowpane knocked out of their own back door. After a few months of guessing, I got to the point where I couldn't care less. Still, the rising bedlam was particularly unnerving as I could see it steadily escalating. Eventually, we began to suspect that heavy drug traffic was taking place on the premises, judging from the general chaos, mysterious arrivals and departures at 2:00 and 3:00 a.m., and the steady flow of tough-looking, "spaced-out" strangers coming in and out the back door at all hours. On several occasions the police arrived in the middle of the night and made arrests, dragging one or more of these toughs into a police car amidst volleys of more loud cursing, screaming and yelling. I was appalled, shocked and saddened at how the family next door had fallen apart in the few years that we had known them. In short, the neighborhood had become a nightmare.

In the face of all this, my feelings of helpless frustration, anger and rage returned with a vengeance. My violent fantasies also returned as I thought about picking up my baseball bat, going next door myself, and smashing everything and everybody in sight. I had never felt anything like this before and I knew that something had to change.

From an internal point of view, too many of my own shadow components (aggression, hostility, insensitivity, etc.) were still projected onto that teenager and had remained projected onto him for too long a time. In this case, as the projector, I now easily became extremely irritated and agitated toward him and his friends, so much so that every disturbance that they created became intolerable to me. I was now "overreacting" to all their bedlam and adding my own internal bedlam to the situation. My lucid dream breakthrough had intensified these unresolved inner tensions and was heating me up internally to the point where I desperately needed to change by reclaiming those projections. Unfortunately, in the heat of the conflict, I did not see this part of my dilemma at the time. Several years after we moved away from the neighborhood, this dimension of the conflict became perfectly clear to me; the "young hoodlum" too was a part of my inner makeup. I remember the day I fully reclaimed that projection, as I sat in a deep meditation with a special group of people and chose to bridge the gap between myself and my teenage adversary by visualizing his image in my mind very clearly and saying to myself: "You, too, are a part of me."

As we groped toward a solution to this conflict on its external dimension, Charlene felt this rage building up inside of me, and she strongly urged that we sell the house and move. After a number of stormy arguments and painful discussions, I agreed, having made my decision under extreme duress. Although I felt terrible about our arguments, I knew on some deeper level that Charlene was right. It was time to move on, whether I was ready or not. Very soon thereafter, we found a new house, decided to buy it, and moved in mid-March, 1982.

As I reflected further on "Confronting the Polar Bear," I saw that although the bear was totally blind in the dream, it was able to attack the lumberjack with pinpoint accuracy, swimming across that wild, tumbling river. In this same fashion, my rage was pushing against that rugged, individualist ego part of me and pursuing it to some accurate, inescapable point of confrontation. The confrontation meant that I would eventually have to admit how strong the rage really was and that it could have destroyed me if I had not moved out of that neighborhood. In the dream, the lumberjack at first panicked and fled rather than face the powerful bear. This flight was a clear portrayal of all the overwhelming feelings that my conscious mind experienced when that murderous rage was tumbling around inside of me at that time in my life. Finally, when the pursuing bear caught up with the lumberjack in the dream and only when he could flee no longer, the lumberjack turned and shot the bear in the head with a pistol. How typical, I realized, that often the ego confronts its buried rage only when it is at the absolute end of its normal avoidance patterns and can flee no longer. When psychological escape and flight are no longer possible, then comes the moment of full confrontation! Though the lumberjack's method of defense appeared feeble and futile to me in the dream, when I reflected upon the dream after I awoke, I realized that it did nevertheless have a significant impact on the bear. When the ego will give its all to confront the unconscious, then something will change!

The ending of this dream is a classic in its ambivalence, air of suspense and simple beauty. The moment of impact, when the lumberjack shot the bear, symbolized the moment when my common sense and survival urge pushed back on my rage in the waking state, in an effort to halt its destructive charge. The two large white scales that fell from the bear's eyes indicated that the blindness had been removed and that this unconscious part of me was going to "see the light" in some new way. As I examined these protagonists, man and beast, facing each other at the end of my dream, I imaged two questions emerging from their mouths: "Where do we go from here?" "How do we create a new inner balance of power that will serve the totality of this dreamer?" The dream ended with an air of wondering and incompletion. The all-important questions of the hour had not yet been answered, but they certainly had been posed. I felt a certain amount of relief in simply knowing that the right questions had been raised, and that some day I would have all the clarity I would need on this issue and this turbulent period of my life.

I have often wondered how this strong undercurrent of rage affected the quality of my whole experiment with lucid dreaming. The purist in me wishes that the rage had not been a part of the larger picture. The purist wishes that I had never felt murderous rage toward anyone. The purist in me wishes that I did not have to confront the problems of bedlam and chaos, inner and outer, at that particular time in my life. But I have often reminded myself that this experiment was conducted in the laboratory of real life, with real feelings, real events and real people, not in some ivory tower laboratory under artificial and sterile conditions. The experiment was conducted with my reality, inner and outer, my environment, beliefs, values and personal history, such as they actually were at the time.

Obviously, it could not have been any other way. I have also often reminded myself how deeply vulnerable I became from the mere process of opening to the lucid state and from the pouring of so much extraordinary dream energy into my conscious mind. Knowing what I know now, I would have taken more precautions to protect that vulnerable part of myself, perhaps in postponing the experiment until after I had moved out of my old neighborhood. I believe now that anyone attempting to explore lucid dreaming in depth would be wise to establish as a prerequisite a living environment that feels completely safe, comfortable and secure, fully conducive to such sensitive, inner work. I would also choose to work under the close tutelage of an experienced guide, a spiritually oriented psychotherapist perhaps or someone who has a thorough firsthand knowledge of both psychological and psychic processes of development. In retrospect now, five years after beginning the experiment, I can delineate more clearly the ideal conditions under which I would have preferred to conduct my investigations.

One of the most valuable keys for unlocking dreams is to examine the context in which the dream scenario takes place. I have learned from my professional work to place a special emphasis on this aspect of the dream's message. "Confronting the Polar Bear" took place "somewhere in the wilderness of Alaska," a milieu that aptly symbolizes my experiment with lucid dreaming. For me, the wilderness is the frontier, a term that I have used often in referring to the lucid state. Moreover, the phrase "the land of the midnight sun" came into my mind early in my experiment and has returned to me numerous times as another apt metaphor for the lucid dream state. In the lucid dream the light comes to the dreamer in the midst of our time of darkness, during sleep, the nocturnal phase of our daily cycle. As my experiment progressed and as I reflected extensively on this simple fact, I began to develop a deeper respect for darkness and a deeper appreciation for its untold, fertile potential. The further I go with my experiment, the more I feel the special value of darkness in all its forms: the vast limitless void of outer space that beckons the astronomer and astronaut, the internal psychological darkness of the shadow within each person, the darkness of the winter months that calls for quietude and slowing down the pace of life, the darkness of the ocean floor that is another gateway to a world unknown, and the impending darkness of evening that signals the end of each day. In all its forms darkness can deeply nourish the human spirit, if we allow it to do so. So often I now look forward to the night and to my time of sleep, perhaps to dream lucidly, perhaps to receive another special gift from the realms of inner darkness. The unconscious mind is our mother in countless ways. Out of its inner darkness, the light is born.

I still often think about the wilderness of Alaska as a special environmental stage, a theater where the interplay between light and darkness is re-enacted dramaticaly and vividly. Some day I hope to travel there in person. In the meantime, in more ways than one, my dreams have already introduced me to the "land of the midnight sun."

With the passage of time and the passage of my fears, and with the full recognition of my rage, I have created a synthesis in my understanding of these two dreams. "The Arrival of the Serpent Power" and "Confronting the Polar Bear" have now become co-messengers in my dream journal and my dream journey. The serpent power aspect of my lucid dreamwork was certainly overwhelming and yet deeply sensitive at the same time. I have a much more healthy respect for that power now and a realization that its sensitivity must be protected adequately if it is to flourish. One of the mental exercises that I consciously practice now is to mobilize the male side of my psyche even more quickly when my female side (my sensitivities) feels trapped or assaulted. In silent inner practice, I choose to keep demonstrating to myself that my "cowboys" are capable of arriving instantly into the moment to liberate my "unknown female companion" when necessary, in both the waking state and in the dream state. The cowboys are essential companions to the serpents because of the feeling of basic inner safety which they provide. When this stronger level of male energy has become readily available to me in an instant's notice and when I have developed the easy habit of calling it up within myself in an instant, then I will eventually pave the way for my entrance into ever deeper levels of the mysterious serpent power. Through ongoing meditation on these themes and images, I have created a new affirmation for myself: "Be ye wise as serpents ... guileless as doves ... and tough as silent cowboys."

CHAPTER SEVEN

The Second Return

"You must give birth to your images. They are the future waiting to be born. Fear not the strangeness you feel. The future must enter into you long before it happens . . . Just wait for the birth . . . for the hour of new clarity."

—Rainer Maria Rilke
Letters to a Young Poet
Letter #3

I worked my way down from the mountaintop again. This time I bore in my memory the vivid impression of the giant serpents, with the mysterious, yellow-green luminescence emanating from their eyes, an image unforgettable to the end of my days. I also carried some sadness and disillusionment this time, since I was now so much more cognizant of my limitations, oversights and vulnerabilities. I was limited in how much intensity I could bear from my lucid dreams. Yet I was so entranced and intrigued with my inner explorations that I knew I would not stop. I determined to find a way to work within my limits and protect my sensitivities.

I continued to have lucid dreams on a fairly regular basis ever since "The Arrival of the Serpent Power." In the months and years that have passed I occasionally would have another dry period, usually of three or four months' duration. After going through several such periods, I finally reached a point of feeling no anxiety or concern about them. I began to compare them to the fallow field which the wise farmer allows to remain "unproductive" for a deliberate purpose, to restore the soil, give it rest and allow time for regeneration from within. I began to see that I actually needed these fallow periods and I increasingly accepted them when they emerged, growing to understand and appreciate these deeper rhythms and learning that fallow time was time well spent.

As the months went by, I continued to receive a steady flow of inspiring lucid dreams, as well as maintain good recall of my ordinary dreams. Because I cannot recount them all here, I am making a special selection of those that were the most important and nourishing to me. The writing of this account is, by its very nature, limited in space and time. This text can describe my experiment only up to a certain point and then must, of necessity, have an arbitrary ending. My lucid dream experiment itself, however, is presently ongoing. It may never have an ending point and may well continue for many years, perhaps to the end of my life.

One of the more inspiring and memorable of these dreams occurred several months after Charlene, Erik and I were settled in our new home.

BEAUTIFUL DREAMER: WAKE UNTO ME
June 2, 1982

... I have been dreaming for a long time, and now I see myself lying on a brass bed in what looks like an old hotel room. The decor of the room looks like the 1920s era. I hear a man's voice, loud and clear, coming from an adjacent room. He is talking to someone about maintaining the stylish plumbing fixtures on the sinks and bathtubs of this quaint, old building. Now I remember an earlier part of the dream, in which I had vomited out a long, steady stream of chalky, white fluid into the sink in this very room. I shiver convulsively, and I feel very relieved that I got all that poison out of my system.

Now I stretch out my body full length and begin to fly. My feet stick out through the bars at the foot of the brass bed, and without any effort or intention on my part, I lift the bed up off the floor. Soon the bed and I are flying together around the room as I seek a way to explore all the rooms in this huge hotel. Suddenly, I realize I am dreaming, and I feel exhilarated as the familiar, light-headed tingling sensations begin. I decide to look for my friend Julia as I fly around and around in the room but I do not find her. I hold her image in my mind as I search everywhere. Still I do not see her. I begin to sing, "Beautiful dreamer, wake unto me, Starlight and dewdrops are waiting for thee." I deeply enjoy this song, and I sing it with my heart wide open. As I sing, I hear the gentle tinkling of a music box. The music box plays "Beautiful Dreamer" in perfect accompaniment to my voice, its modulations, its pacing and its rhythms, as I sing the words over and over. I feel how wonderful it is to be lucid again, and I realize that "Beautiful Dreamer" is the perfect theme song for me. I remember the little brown music box that Julia had given me for my fortieth birthday, and I appreciate its perfection all over again.

Now I see many beautiful colors and lights flashing about me. I see hundreds of rainbow droplets, tiny little spectrums, floating and spiraling circles of white light, and many small, shiny objects of art swirling everywhere. I feel very uplifted as I enjoy this dazzling display of music, light and color. It is a fantastic feast for the senses, a miniature psychedelic light show, though much more delicate, sensuous and uplifting than any that I have ever seen. Unfortunately, I now feel myself losing my balance as I start to fall from the lucid state. I attempt to stay lucid by focusing on one of the small illuminated objects in the dreamscape, but slowly I slip away from it, and soon I wake up.

For several minutes I lie quietly in bed feeling my physical body and deliberately keeping my eyes closed. I can still see many of the beautiful colored rainbows and images from the dream gently swirling by, and I focus steadily on one ray of light in an attempt to re-enter the lucid state as Eleanor, one of my students, frequently does with her images. I feel I am very close to success but somehow I don't quite manage it. After several attempts I let go and drift back to a normal sleep.

The positive qualities of this dream have remained with me for a long time. At the point where I became lucid, I began searching for my friend Julia.* In my mind she had become a prominent symbol for my lucid dream experiment, because she had been one of my most ardent students and had had numerous, splendid lucid dreams herself. In the dream I did not find her, but I felt her presence in a powerful way. The tinkling of the music box in the dream, so delicate and so sensitive, was a beautiful re-creation of her spirit. These gentle and steadfast tones tinkled in a perfect accompaniment to the words, tempo, phrasing and other subtle variations of my voice as I sang the words to "Beautiful Dreamer." It is impossible to describe in words the subtle blendings, the soft touch and the exquisite precisions of these two sources of music. My heartfelt singing and the delicate tinkling from the music box were two sets of vibrations that somehow became one in the dream. All the modulations, variations and nuances of expression had magically united in a blending that transported me. One source of the music, my voice, came from inside me. The other source, the tinkling music box, came from outside, from some undetermined place in the hotel room.

In waking life, Julia had, on my fortieth birthday, presented me with a small music box that played the theme "Beautiful Dreamer." I enjoyed this gift immensely; it was perfect in every way. Now after hearing its simple melody, so clearly imprinted on my mind because of my heightened receptivity within this lucid dream, I have appreciated her gift more than ever. And, of course, Stephen Collins Foster's classic song "Beautiful Dreamer" has a deeper meaning for me now than ever before.

The countless hundreds of brilliant rainbow colors and flashing beautiful lights in this dream grew to bear a special heartfelt significance for me, one that grew steadily with the passage of time. The more I reflected upon them the more I grew to appreciate the image of the "rainbow droplets" in particular. Shaped exactly

* Julia is also mentioned in chapters five and twelve of this book.

like tiny tear drops, each droplet was perfectly identical to all the others in size and shape. As they swirled about the room by the hundreds, dancing through the air and gliding along the walls, each one contained within itself all the colors of the rainbow. Each droplet contained and portrayed a tiny, potent spectrum that shone brightly from within as they swirled and sparkled everywhere. These brilliant, tiny spectrums were the most outstanding images in my vision, as I also saw many other bright, small objects of art, jewels, diamonds and shining beads, dancing and whirling about in an array of lightbeams and brilliant colors. This splendor created a clear example of how a delight to the senses can also be a delight to the soul. I experienced there, in those lucid moments, a full blending of sensuality and spirituality. No wonder that I wanted to return to that lucid level of vision immediately, as soon as I felt myself losing it. Yet, try as I did to remain lucid, the lucidity and all the beauty of the vision nevertheless slowly slipped away this time in a feeling of "falling from lucidity," which by now had also become a familiar experience, one that I quickly recognized in the dream.

As I fell from lucidity I did not know exactly where I would land. By now my previous experiences with lucid dreams had taught me that, as I begin to drift or fall out of lucidity, there are generally three possibilities as to where my consciousness would go. I would either return to a normal dream, or fall asleep and go totally unconscious, or I would awaken. In this instance, I returned to the waking state.

As I lay in my bed in the aftermath of this lucid dream, I deliberately chose to remain immobile and kept my eyes closed for a long time. Many of the beautiful colored rainbows and brilliant images continued to flash by in my mind. They were almost like a river of bubbles, as they flowed steadily past my field of vision. I still savored their luminous beauty, absorbing and soaking up every detail in my memory and imagination to the best of my ability.

Awake in my bed with my eyes still closed, I attempted an experiment using a method that one of my students, a woman named Eleanor, has used quite successfully to induce lucid dreaming. Over the past few years Eleanor has become a prolific lucid dreamer. One of her most effective techniques for entering the lucid state is to focus on some specific image, any image which may come to her, as she lingers in the hypnagogic state* just before falling asleep. As soon as the image comes to her, she concentrates all of her attention upon it and maintains the concentration for a few minutes, while remaining deeply relaxed all the while. Then she "merges" with the image as she imagines herself becoming one with it, and eventually allows all of her consciousness to "enter" the image. As she enters the image, she usually feels a building sense of momentum, an energy that soon pulls her completely into the image through the image and bursting out on the other side. At this point she usually finds herself in a "whole new world," that is, a whole new dreamscape, which invariably for her is a lucid dream. Often she then begins to fly, thereby launching herself fully into the lucid state. As she repeatedly reported these experiences in one of my dream groups, I began to picture them as similar to the well-known "breakthrough" exercise of the circus lion, in which the lion jumps through the large paper hoop and bursts out on the other side.

In attempting to use Eleanor's method on this occasion, I focused all of my attention on one ray of light that lingered in my memory from the dreamscape. I focused and concentrated on it for several minutes to

---

* The hypnagogic state is referred to by psychologists and sleep researchers as the zone between consciousness and the unconsciousness of sleep. It is easily and commonly experienced by most people as an "in-between" state, a twilight zone between wakefulness and sleeping. I describe some of its characteristics at length in chapter ten and point out how the hypnagogic state, while essentially distinct from the lucid dream state, can be used as a vehicle for entering the lucid dream state.

see if I could merge with it and possibly re-enter this alluring lucid dream. Though I did not succeed on this occasion, I nevertheless acquired a better feeling for this particular technique and decided that I would attempt it again at some future point in my experiment when the opportunity presented itself.

This lucid dream was so uplifting for me that it inspired a series of meditations. The flashing lights and the swirling rainbow droplets remained in my mind for a long time. In one meditation I received the insight that the words to "Beautiful Dreamer" could be interpreted as words spoken by God to each human being. In calling out to humanity, God is telling each person that he or she is already a beautiful dreamer, and that we are all invited to awaken unto Him. This is an archetypal theme, I soon realized, as it appears explicitly in the Christian tradition* as well as in most of the major religious traditions of the world. The lucid dream is a perfect metaphor for the awakening of the human soul into a higher state of consciousness. In addition to being *a perfect metaphor for the awakening, it is sometimes a concrete experience of the awakening as well. In lucid dreaming we awaken IN the dream; in ordinary dreaming we awaken FROM the dream.* These were the primary reflections that came to me, leading me to deepen my own understanding of Stephen Foster's original lyrics. To anyone who accepts God's invitation to awaken in the dream, He has promised numerous rewards: "Starlight and dewdrops are waiting for thee." This poetic promise refers to the cleansing of our perceptions and the refining of our consciousness that often accompanies a direct experience of the Light. Out of these rewards the dreamer is able to see the exquisite beauty of creation on a level that was heretofore unimaginable, and on a much finer and much more subtle level of perception than was previously possible. I am convinced that these

---

* "Awake, O sleeper, and arise from the dead, and Christ shall give thee light." (Ephesians 5:14)

rewards exist on all levels of our being. They bring delight to the physical senses, sensitivity for the emotions, clarity for the intellect and conscious realizations on how to bring the lucid awareness into ordinary living as much as possible. Since the arrival of this dream I have often wondered if its beautiful flashing lights and rainbow droplets were my personal equivalent of "starlight and dewdrops." They were every bit as delicate.

Approximately two months after the arrival of "Beautiful Dreamer: Wake unto Me" I had a rewarding and successful hypnagogic experience followed by a lucid dream. I was lying in my bed one night in the hypnagogic state, half-awake and half-asleep. An image came to me in which I saw myself standing before an old concrete wall about ten feet high. The wall surrounded me on three sides—front, left, and right. In the vision, I levitated my body straight up into the air and at the top of the wall I saw the opening of a cave or tunnel. The opening was square and I flew directly into it head first. I began flying faster and faster, speeding through this long, dark, square tunnel, until I saw a tiny speck of light at the far end of it. I thought to myself that I could be approaching a lucid dream by staying focused on the image of the light at the end of the tunnel. Though I could still feel my physical body lying in bed, I deliberately chose to remain focused on the light as I continued to fly toward it and continued to gather speed. I thought, "So, this is how Eleanor does it!" An instant later I burst out of the tunnel into the following lucid dream:

THE SUTTER BUTTES: A NEW PERSPECTIVE
August 2, 1982

I am flying gloriously over a beautiful, mountainous countryside. I see gorgeous rock formations, trees and peaceful, green valleys. Everywhere I look the beauty of nature is breathtaking. I am fully aware that I am dreaming and I thoroughly enjoy flying about, taking great pleasure in the clear, blue sky and the white, fluffy cloud formations. I am still aware of my physical body, however, as it lies in my bed, and yet I am able to stay lucid and enjoy the gorgeous scenery that lies everywhere below me.

As I fly I look closely at a mountain range in the distance and I recognize it as the Sutter Buttes where I often hiked and explored in my youth. However, since I am now approaching the buttes from the west, their profile on the horizon is exactly the opposite of the eastern profile that was so familiar to me in times past. I continue to fly past them and I enjoy looking at them from this new perspective. As I leave the buttes behind, I fly past many other scenic, beautiful mountains and valleys. Finally I awaken, feeling good about the lucid dream.

This episode provided me with my first success in entering the lucid dream through merging with an image from the hypnagogic state. I was pleased to have obtained positive results this time with this particular technique, which I think would be an effective one for many people to use.

This dream had another interesting feature in that I was again conscious on three levels simultaneously, as had first occurred for me in "The Gift of the Magi." This simultaneous, trilevel awareness did not seem so amazing or important to me this time. I took this as a good sign, a sign that I was starting to become more accustomed to and familiar with this particular phenomenon of the lucid state. What had originally struck me as a "miracle" in "The Gift of the Magi" was now starting to feel more ordinary or, at least, not quite so extraordinary. I began to realize here how this was all part of my growth process. I fondly remembered the words of Baba Ram Dass from one of his workshops many years ago. He said: "The word 'miracle' is merely a cover for our own ignorance." By this he meant that whenever we encounter something new and mysterious in the world, something impressive which we do not understand, we are likely to label that event as a "miracle." However, once we begin to understand the event, we become less likely to consider it a miracle and more likely to view it as ordinary. Even if we never come to understand the "miraculous" event with our rational mind but come to lessen our excitement about it simply by the frequency or repetition of its occurrence, then once again we begin to view the event as ordinary. The ordinary is that with which we are familiar. Once "miracles" become familiar to us, we usually cease to regard them as miracles and begin to view them as normal occurrences.

I do not mean to imply that familiarity *necessarily* makes dull or ordinary those parts of a lucid dream experience that are repetitive. Based on my own experiment with lucidity, I do not believe that it has to be that way at all. There is another human possibility that often becomes real in the lucid state, namely, that many lucid dream experiences maintain an almost miraculous quality of freshness and aliveness in each occurrence. The Zen Master Shunryu Suzuki spoke of this quality of perpetual freshness of mind in his book that has now become a spiritual classic, *Zen Mind, Beginner's Mind*. According to Suzuki, the beginner's mind is that extraordinary ability to see the world afresh in each passing moment, no matter how many times we have seen it before. Whatever the particular person, place or thing we are seeing in the moment, the mind has the capacity to see it afresh and never grow tired of it. This was his understanding of grace: to see everything with the mind of the beginner. "In the beginner's mind there are many possibilities; in the expert's mind there are few."*

The lucid state can truly be spoken of as a state of mental and emotional grace. I believe it can teach many of us what it actually feels like to experience the state of "beginner's mind" to which Suzuki refers. In the lucid state I have often experienced this freshness, original vitality and marvelous beauty in the images, sounds,

* Shunryu Suzuki, *Zen Mind, Beginner's Mind*, p. 17.

sensations and energy currents of the dream. Lucidity offers us the opportunity to enjoy the miracles that will constantly surround the lucid dreamer, the miracles of the extraordinary and the miracles of the ordinary as well. Lucidity provides a path for the visionary reunification of the extraordinary and the ordinary.

One week after "The Sutter Buttes: A New Perspective" I had another strange and mysterious lucid dream.

APPROACHING THE PRESENCE OF GOD
August 9, 1982

I have been dreaming for some time, and suddenly I become aware that I am dreaming. I see a huge, all-pervasive flash of light that illumines my entire field of vision with the power of a bolt of lightning against a dark night sky. I feel my whole consciousness elevated rapidly to that familiar feeling of the lucid dream. My mind suddenly feels extremely clear as I find myself standing in a room in a modern, tract-style home. The room is totally empty, and the bare walls are painted a uniform white all around. I particularly notice the ceiling which is covered with the typical acoustical ceiling spray, the white "cottage cheese" lumpy material commonly used in contemporary homes.

Now a strange, eerie feeling comes over me as I realize that I am in this room to look at God, face to face. I feel the powerful presence of God somewhere on the left side of the room beyond my present field of vision. Slowly I begin to turn my head to the left to take in the unseen portion of the room. As I turn, I feel a tremendous fear building up inside me, and I remember someone once told me that God had warned Moses not to look directly into His face, because any man who looked directly into the face of God would surely die. With continued effort I slowly turn my head toward the left, moving it in very small increments, because the fear and inner resistance have now become very strong. Finally, out of the leftmost corner of my left eye I see a large, dark, shadowy silhouette. It has the shape of a very large man, dressed in a long, black robe with a large hood covering his head and face and with a black cape draped over his huge, extremely broad shoulders. I can see only his silhouette, portraying the upper half of his body and only the left side of his body, head, shoulders and torso, since the huge, dark image is facing me. The figure is shrouded in darkness and I cannot discern anything distinguishable about him. Nevertheless, I feel a tremendous and overwhelming power emanating from him, and I wonder how much longer I can bear to look.

For a moment I turn my head away, giving myself a short mental rest, and then I slowly turn it back toward the left again. I feel my inner fear and resistance building once more as I slowly, gradually turn my head. Again I see the same dark, shadowy, male figure as before, motionless and faceless, still emanating his tremendous power. I turn my head away again and now the dream slowly fades out.

I found this dream to be stunning in its straightforwardness. After it ended, I fell back into a normal sleep and awoke later in the middle of the night with clear recall and feeling very uplifted. Even before I began my experiment, based upon my reading of Patricia Garfield and Scott Sparrow, I had come to believe that the primary purpose of cultivating the lucid dream was union with the Light or union with God. I had come to hold this personal belief quite strongly. The literalness and simplicity of this dream reflected the accumulated power of this newly acquired belief. The huge, all-pervasive flash of light that began with the onset of lucidity was a marvelous and powerful sight. Once again in this dream I saw the Light! The Light, in and of itself, was instantly elevative and transformative.

With this dream one of the chronic, nagging questions emerging from my experiment now became clearly formulated in my mind: "Wasn't this dream a clear-cut example of inflation of the ego?"* I wrestled with this question for a long time. Finally, I answered: "I do not know." Still later, I began to realize this was a question that a person cannot answer for himself. The

---

* In my own terms I would define inflation of the ego as the state of feeling puffed up with one's own sense of self-importance and harboring illusions of grandeur that feel excessive or offensive to others.

conscious ego cannot really serve as its own policeman. To ask the ego if the ego has become inflated is to invite the answer "no." Any inflated ego would, of course, tend to deny that it had become inflated. Though I could not possibly answer this question for myself, nevertheless, it was my responsibility to ask it. Perhaps, I eventually thought, the course of responsibility on this matter is to ask the question continuously at regular intervals, knowing that the universe will answer it for me. If I were willing to "live this question," then reliable feedback would come, primarily from sources outside myself. After I began looking for it in the proper places, this particular item of feedback did come, from colleagues and friends, from my own therapist, from the subtle hints and remarks of clients, students and casual acquaintances. I began to discover that at times I was suffering from ego inflation.

Working through my initial judgmentalism about it, I eventually began to see that inflation of the ego really wasn't such a "bad" thing itself after all. Rather, at some point I realized that it is a common and normal response for someone who has had some new and marvelous event added to his life. How often, for example, have we observed proud parents, practically bursting their buttons, as they strut about displaying their newborn child to friends and family. This is especially true for their firstborn. The exultant papa and mama are naturally swollen with pride and many other emotions, as they mentally adjust to the new arrival and attempt to imagine all the impact the child will have on their lives. At some point I began to speculate that there must be some wisdom and purpose in this type of emotional reaction, because it seems to be universal. I began to see that the inflation of the ego is the first stage of a very rapid expansion of consciousness that comes to assist a person who has just experienced a major change or advancement in his or her life.

This first stage of reaction, the inflation, can be

compared to the rapid construction of the exterior shell of a high-rise skyscraper. The construction is, at first, only the empty, external shell of the edifice. Though crude, incomplete and unpolished, it clearly foreshadows its potential. Some day this exterior shell could be brought to completion and serve many useful purposes. Just as the empty shell of the skyscraper cries out for completion, so too must the initial inflation of the ego be brought through all of its growth stages in order to result eventually in a positive outcome for the individual. Reflecting upon my lucid dream experiment as my prime working material, I gradually was able to distinguish a working model that outlined four distinct stages for the transformation of ego inflation. They emerged in my mind as (1) internal solidification, (2) internal and external beautification, (3) accustomization, and (4) social communication. With a successful passage through these four stages, giving each its own due time, it appeared to me that ego inflation could possibly become a positive and creative force in human endeavors. Without the successful passage, however, the very same inflation would remain as a negative force, untransformed, unrecognized and unconscious, and thereby potentially destructive to the spiritual and psychological growth of the individual.

The first stage of growth, according to this model, is the internal solidification of the ego inflation. Here the recipient of grace seeks to stay balanced while acknowledging those times when he may fail completely at this and become swept away with his own excitement. He also recognizes that he only barely understands what has recently happened in his life and he seeks, above all, a fuller understanding of the initial experience. He needs to understand that the initial, rapid inflation could be the beginning of a much larger growth experience if he makes room for this possibility inside himself. Therefore, he will need to "allow" for the inflation to occur, not attempting to stop it or stifle it, and above all not criticizing himself for it. Instead, he aims at merely observing it with as much self-objectivity and detachment as possible, while obtaining feedback about it from those who are closest to him. At this stage, the person needs to intend to stand firm against his or her own inner sweep of euphoria, excessive pride of self-aggrandizement coming with the initial burst of excitement.

One practical tool to promote this solid stance is the willingness to communicate to some trusted person any grandiose feelings and fantasies that may have arisen. Thus, the person aims at not becoming intoxicated by inflation on the one hand or excessively fearful of it on the other. Eventually, in this fashion, a person can internalize the new spurt of growth, feel solid around it, and expand his own awareness so that he eventually comes to the next stage of his growth where he reacts differently to the "great event" in his life. Using the metaphor of the skyscraper, this first stage would correspond to the proper installation of the heating, electrical and plumbing systems of the building, making the structure functional and operable and moving it closer to serving people in some practical way.

Stage two in this growth process would be internal and external beautification. The person undergoing genuine transformation at some point will begin to feel more ennobled by the initial experience that set off the inflation. I have come to believe that this inner beautification is a universal and fundamental human need, and that everyone needs to feel uplifted and transformed by the major events of his own lifetime in order to continue his life journey with energy and enthusiasm. A life crisis that remains untransformed lives on in the psyche as a strong negative force, a deep regret, a cause for depression that often becomes stronger, not weaker, with the passage of time. Using the skyscraper metaphor, the process of beautification is analogous to painting the building, landscaping the grounds and furnishing the interior in an uplifting way.

Stage three in this growth process of the ego I have chosen to call accustomization. Through repeated reflections, meditations and communication about the experience with close friends, confidants and colleagues, the person eventually becomes accustomed to the new major event in his life. As he grows he no longer feels the overpowering urge to "tell the world" about his experience though he may calmly and forthrightly talk about it when the time and circumstances are right. The crusader urge, often felt initially, now begins to fade, and the person in transition is much more relaxed about his experience. With the skyscraper, accustomization is the stage in which people have seen the building often enough to become accustomed to its appearance on the skyline of the city, and they now realize the contribution the building will make to society.

Finally, stage four in this process of transformation appears to involve social communication. The person may feel some desire and some need to share the extraordinary experience with society at large, with a larger group of people beyond his own immediate circle. This need to communicate, however, feels quite distinct from the earlier urge to "tell the whole world," often marked by feverish excitement and the crusader spirit. At stage four, the desire to communicate is much more peaceful, free of ego attachment, free of anxiety about results and free of concerns about how others will respond. The sharing may also be actively supported by friends and colleagues who have given feedback that they see some social value in this broader outreach. Not every miracle-event, I believe, needs to reach this fourth stage of resolution through wider communication. The decision can only be made by the individual himself weighing the specific factors involved. At stage four, the skyscraper becomes a more widely accepted landmark, recognized beyond the scope of its own city, a source of civic or national pride, or perhaps a symbol that conveys some special meaning to the culture as a whole.

As I reflected at length upon ego inflation and its potential for either good or evil, these four stages gradually appeared to be the internal stepping-stones that I could identify within myself as I worked actively toward my own inner transformation. Ego inflation was the major two-edged sword that came out of my experiment with lucid dreaming. It was capable of cutting both ways: positively or negatively, creatively or destructively. I see this inflation now more as if it were a branch growing from the trunk of a tree. Somewhere in my experiment I made the choice to face, accept and understand that branch as one more particular spurt of growth, an offshoot of mental and psychic energy. Somewhere along the way, I came to see that "that, too" could bear fruit in the end. One of my biggest challenges here was to move away from my initial judgmental attitude and simply allow the whole drama to unfold, in a burst of watching, waiting and trusting. Now I have come to see that all my feelings, thoughts and emotions, all those bursts of energy within myself were working toward some contribution to the life of the Self that was much larger than I could ever have imagined from the beginning of my experiment.

To inflate or not to inflate, that is *not* the question. How to respond to one's inflation, if it occurs, *is* the question. For as Rilke wrote to the young poet, we must give birth to our images, and we must give birth no matter what happens as a byproduct in our psychological development. To be human is to love, create and give birth in the real world and to wrestle courageously, if need be, with any negative byproducts that may emerge from one's choice to be fully alive.

A person's own beliefs have a great deal of creative power as to what he or she will eventually experience in a dream, or in life itself, for that matter. My singlemost positive belief about lucid dreaming from the very beginning of my experiment was that it is a pathway to the Light. One of my oldest negative beliefs about God, apparently, was that if anyone looked directly into the face of God he would surely die. This lucid dream, "Approaching the Presence of God," was somehow reminding me of that old belief and testing its validity at the same time. This belief, I later remembered, had originated from an animated remark made in a religion class by one of my high school seminary teachers many years ago. I still remember how alarmed I felt at the impressionable age of fifteen when I heard this priest's strong comment about a certain passage in the Old Testament where God issued a dire warning to Moses.* Accordingly, it became part of my lucid dream experiment, then, to exhume and re-examine this old belief at this time. I now began to speculate that to come face to face with God may somehow be related to coming face to face with the Light in the lucid dream state. To see the Light in its overwhelming power was as close to seeing God as anything I had ever experienced. With this dream I also remembered another of the classic teachings of the New Testament: "God is Light."**

Of all the concepts and images of God that have been handed down through the centuries, the image of the "Light" or the "White Light" is one of the most commonly found and deeply ingrained in the psyche of Western civilization. This light is often referred to as "dazzling," "blinding" and "overwhelming" by those who claim to have seen it. The list of superlatives is seemingly endless.

At some point, I began to realize that the belief that a person will die if he or she looks directly at the face of God refers to a psychological rather than a physical death. This "death" and the rebirth that implicitly follows are metaphors for the transformation of consciousness that occurs as the result of a powerful inner experience. Here another nagging question arose for me: could this death also be manifested on the physical

* "You cannot see my face; for man shall not see me and live." (Exodus 33:20)
** I John 1:5.

level as well? Would my body die if my old consciousness died? Since the time when my experiment reached its peak, I had at different times feared that I was going to die. Usually this fear was vague and general, a persistent, indecipherable, steady gnawing at my insides. Sometimes I would have a specific fantasy of dying in a plane crash or auto accident. Sometimes I would wonder if I had gone too far and was somehow going to be punished for stealing the sacred fire. All of these thoughts and concerns were present and, as I can see now, were being melted down inside me, as if my psyche had become a giant crucible with a raging fire beneath it. This intensity was particularly true in the first two years of my experiment. The intense internal heat seemed to be melting down a lot of my old beliefs, fears and concepts that I had acquired in my first forty years of living. This melting down, I see now, was the essence of the death alluded to in "Approaching the Presence of God." An internal "dying" was, in truth, actually taking place, and it was preparing me all along for a new consciousness, a new way of being in the world. At the time, I knew all of this in principle and in theory from the extensive reading that I had done on the subject of personal transformation. But even so, at times my fear, confusion and internal panic were great. I still found myself, at times, clinging to whatever blind faith I could muster, to keep going forward with the experiment, and to trust somehow in the principle of the death-resurrection cycle. Somewhere ahead of me I believed that an experience of rebirth was awaiting. I was already something like a prisoner, enthralled in a swinging cycle of doubt and conviction, vision and lack of vision, alternating back and forth. At certain times I found myself deeply longing for the stillness of inner peace. At other times I knew that I had already found it or, rather, that it had found me.

So in place of my old belief a new belief would eventually arise, that if one must "surely die" then one must also "surely live again," and this time on a higher plane of consciousness. The image of this higher plane came to me in my dream of "Confronting the Wildebeest" (June 8, 1983), which I have related and discussed in chapter one. In that dream, I climbed up the steep rocks until I reached the higher plane, or plateau, where the main action occurred. There I met new dangers and challenges face to face and also found within myself the lucidity to transform them.

This dream, "Approaching the Presence of God," left me with a very clear awareness about "increments," a series of graduated steps for the overcoming of fear. When I remember this dream, I clearly recall the process of turning my head very slowly to the left, carefully and deliberately looking out of the leftmost corner of each eye. Bit by bit, inch by inch in the dream, I eased my field of vision toward the God image. This process reminded me of some of the basic Gestalt awareness exercises that I frequently use in group therapy in which a person will be encouraged to feel every part of his or her scenario very deliberately. In this type of exercise the person who is working on himself is guided to feel the fear, feel the resistance, and feel each gradual step of the way toward transformation. Every step of the journey is important and valuable. Even turning my head away, which occurred twice in the dream, did not necessarily indicate a defeat or a failure. This too was part of the incremental process which can be used in any situation calling for confrontation. After this dream, I felt more respect for the "little steps" that we can take each day toward our goals and aspirations. When taken with full consciousness, every little step somehow becomes a giant step. It is the conscious quality of our steps and not their size that determines their true stature. Transformation comes from the quality of a human thought that is lived with full awareness. Expansion and joy are the children of the incremental vision.

Within the context of this dream, it seemed fitting for me to ask the basic question: "Who is God?" or "What is

God?" The image of a large, dark, man-shaped, shadowy silhouette, dressed in a dark robe with a long, black cape draped over his shoulders, was the image that appeared in my lucid dream. I never saw the entire figure, only about one-fourth of it, the upper left side of its body. Could it be, I wondered, that God too has a dark side? In the dream, the blinding flash of light appeared first, followed by this mysterious and somewhat foreboding figure. In my own personal growth, I have become quite comfortable with the idea that God is All, a mixture of light *and* darkness. I believe, too, that God has a dark side, a chthonic spirit as many Jungian writers are saying today. However, the more I look at this dream, the more I end up feeling speechless about the image. I am beginning to think that the best I can do is describe the image to others, remember it myself, and keep it relatively free from analysis.

Most serious seekers, I believe, need a healthy antidote to the countless volumes of rational theology that have been written about God. One of my favorite heroes in this respect is Thomas Aquinas (1225?-1274), considered by many to be the greatest thinker that the Catholic Church ever produced. The voluminous writings of this medieval scholar are viewed as the high-water mark of philosophy and rational theology reached during the Middle Ages. There is an intriguing story told about Thomas, who, even while he was still living, was regarded as a mystic by some of his contemporaries. One day, according to this story, about three months before he died, Thomas was overcome by a powerful experience. According to the account of one eyewitness, a fellow monk named Dominic of Caserta, Thomas was observed to be in a state of ecstasy as he was praying alone in a small monastery chapel. Dominic claimed that he saw Thomas' entranced body raised in the air and that he heard a voice coming from the image of the crucified Christ on the cross above the altar. The voice said, "Bene scripsisti de me, Thoma. Quam ergo mercedem accipies?" To which the entranced Thomas responded aloud, "Nil, nisi te, Domine."*

Such stories usually raise a great deal of doubt and skepticism in the minds of modern people, as well they should. Tales about miracles and mystic events should not, I believe, be taken lightly but are best greeted with an initial dose of healthy skepticism. However, for the sake of this discussion and to deepen our understanding of the relationship between rational knowledge and mystical knowledge, I would like to assume here that the eyewitness account of this event was accurate and factual and that it was accurately recorded by Thomas' biographers. What then? What could we make of such data if the data were accurate?

Thomas' story continues. Immediately after this event, this experience of grace if you will, Thomas seemed to be a different person according to the first-hand reports of several people who knew him. Thomas now seemed to be living in another world, going in and out of trance states frequently, totally absorbed in his inner contemplations. But the most dramatic change of all was his refusal to proceed any further with his theoretical writing despite strong protestations from his colleagues. According to his biographers, after this alleged mystical experience, Thomas did not write another single word in the theological treatise on which he was working at that time. To his closest confidant and companion, Reginald of Piperno, he said, "Reginald, my son, I adjure you by the omnipotent and living God, by the vows of your order and your affection for me, not to reveal during my lifetime what I am about to say. The end of my labors has come. All that I have written appears to me as so much straw after the things that I have witnessed and that have been revealed to me. For the rest I hope in the mercy of God that the end of my life may soon follow the end of my labors."**
Approximately three months later, Thomas died at the

* "You have written well of me, Thomas. What will you accept as a reward?" "Nothing, except yourself, Lord." Reginald Coffey, O.P., *The Man from Rocca Sicca*, p. 123.

** *Ibid.*, p. 126.

age of forty-nine while traveling to Lyons to attend the ecumenical council that had been convened in that city.

While such an intense reaction to mystical experiences does not occur in every case or probably even in the majority of cases, it is important, I believe, to speculate about the particulars of Thomas' story. Whatever the content and emotional impact of Thomas' experience, it was enough to plunge his brilliant mind into a "psychological death" and stop the flow of his prolific pen in mid-sentence. By his own statement, it appears that his actual physical death was in some way hastened by the power and suddenness of that "inner death" or transition. Whatever halted his life's work must have been the beginning or perhaps the acceleration of a significant psychic change, one that prepared him and perhaps even invited him to leave this world.

What, I wonder, was Thomas' problem? What must have been the intensity of his personal dilemma when, after the impact of his revelatory experience, he immediately cut off his brilliant career as a writer and systematic theorist? At the time of this inner event, he had been writing and teaching continuously for almost thirty years. His fame, acclaim and notoriety had spread through much of Europe, through many of the major universities that were flourishing at that time. He had also been the subject of heated controversy and had been suspected of heresy by the witch hunters of his day, no small matter in that society, insofar as heretics were sometimes burned at the stake for their views. By reintroducing Aristotle's philosophy of natural science to the West and creating his own synthesis between Aristotle's thinking and the Christian tradition, Thomas was in the midst of performing a monumental intellectual task conceived on a grander scale than any scholar before him had ever attempted.

So what then was Thomas' inner understanding of his mysterious experience? Did he himself regard it as a problem? Or is it only a problem for us when the most acclaimed intellectual leader of an era suddenly declares his voluminous life's work to be "as straw" and ceases to produce a single additional word?

Looking at Thomas' story through the lens of my experiences with lucid dreaming, perhaps we could safely speculate that, in part at least, his problem was that most of his revelation remained *uncommunicated.* We do not know if he shared it in full even with his closest colleague, Reginald. Was Thomas personally struggling inside, unable to integrate within himself the contrast between intellectual, rational knowledge and direct, suprarational, mystical knowledge? Was he perhaps at a total loss for words, as I myself have often felt after certain of my lucid dreams? I find it beneficial to pose these questions even though we cannot answer them in Thomas' case. Above all, it appears that Thomas lived in a society, the direct antecedent to our own rationalistic culture, where there was very little support for the integration of rational knowledge with suprarational knowledge—two very distinct ways of knowing. Today, over seven hundred years after his death, it is safe to say that our own society has not yet evolved very far in the healing of this particular psychological split. From this aspect, I have come to view my experiment with lucid dreaming as necessarily having a social and cultural dimension. As a society and as a culture we still need to legitimize the human potential for mystical experiences. We still need to acknowledge further, much further than we have done so far to date, that ordinary people do have these kinds of experiences, that they can sometimes be earthshaking to the psyche when they occur, and that, above all, we need persons, places and resources to integrate these experiences fully into our lives when they occur. Above all, I believe, the recipients of grace need to communicate about their experiences. Although such experiences themselves in their essence can never be *communicated,* they, nevertheless, can be *communicated about.*

Let us return now to my lucid dream "Approaching the Presence of God" and ask the basic question again,

"What is God?" The most compact statement that Thomas Aquinas ever wrote about God was: "Quid Deus sit, nescimus." The sentence translates: "What God *may be,* we do not know." I have always appreciated the subtle humility in this sentence, because Thomas did not write, "What God *is,* we do not know," but rather, "What God *may be,* we do not know." This *may be,* the subjunctive mood in both Latin and English, implies a sense of uncertainty, indefiniteness and openness. The very question itself, implied Thomas, is shrouded in uncertainty. This openness, this sense of mystery, this sense of potential discovery amid perpetual searching, is the spirit that I felt surrounding the dark, vague, shadowy silhouette in my lucid dream. The course of my experiment with lucid dreaming perhaps inevitably led me to approach the Presence, only to find in the dark image a poignant reminder of Thomas' concept which I had first heard many years before and which had always remained as one of my most cherished beliefs. Even now as I write, the thought occurs to me that if I would be fully honest, then I must also remain open to any new event that might radically challenge this cherished belief tomorrow. Where the exploration of consciousness may ultimately lead us, we know not. What potential may lie within the lucid dream state, we know not. As I proceed with my experiment, I have only one viable choice: to remain open and waiting, wondering and wandering through the dream world to discover its further dimensions, whenever and however they may be revealed.

As the poet Rilke wrote, we must continue to give birth to our images. They are the substance of our dreams. They are the material of life and death. In essence they enable us to speak to one another about things that carry us far beyond any words, things that carry us beyond all rational understandings that are presently possible. In essence, we are able, through our images, to speak about those things that seem to matter most.

CHAPTER EIGHT

The Majestic Mountain

"The color of mountains is Buddha's pure body,
The sound of running water is his great speech."
—Dogen Zenji
13th Century Zen Master

I have always had a special love for mountains. All of my life, beginning with childhood, I have preferred to recreate, play, and explore in the hills and valleys that were accessible to me. Especially during the summers of my early teenage years, I often climbed and hiked with my companions in the Sutter Buttes, a small, indigenous mountain range rising up from the floor of the Sacramento Valley. We found excitement and adventure in those buttes, wildlife that we might chance to see such as deer, huge turkey vultures, red-tailed hawks, skunk, opossum, fox, coyote, raccoon and jackrabbits in abundance. We found danger there too. Rattlesnakes were not uncommon in those hills, especially in the hot, dry summer months. And there was always the chance that some angry rancher or sheepherder might discover us trespassing on his land and try to run us off, giving us the exciting chase that we always seemed to be looking for.

As wholehearted young adventurers we used to add more zest to our expeditions into the buttes by firing up each other's imaginations with daring "what if" questions: "What would you do if you saw a live rattlesnake coiled right next to your foot on this narrow, stony ledge?" "What would you do right now if someone drove up in his pick-up truck and yelled at you to get off this land?" "What would you do if a farmer took his rifle and fired a shot, and you heard the whine of a real bullet sailing over your head?" We enjoyed tossing these quick challenges at each other. We didn't think about it at the time, but such "manly" dialogue served the purposes of fueling our imaginations and strengthening us against our fears as well. These mental and verbal exercises were typical preparations for growing up and entering the adult world. For me, much of it took place in the mountains.

Today, as an adult, I still feel a very strong affinity for the mountains. One of my greatest satisfactions in living in Marin County, California, is the delight in looking at Mount Tamalpais from as many different angles and viewpoints as I can as I go about my regular tasks. Climbing on the mountain itself, exploring its many trails and vistas is one of my favorite recreations. Any tall mountain, and especially Mount Tam, does something spiritual for me. It grabs my attention and raises it skyward, inspiring me by its mere presence to look upward. I have not been at all surprised, then, through the years to see so many mountains and peaks, hills and valleys, appear in my dream world as well.

One particularly memorable mountain image came to me in a lucid dream on July 1, 1983. On this particular night, I had a series of six lucid dreams in a row, all in rapid succession. As I progressed through this series of dreams, at the end of each dream I fell back into a normal sleep for what seemed like a short time before the next dream began. I remained asleep throughout this whole series of lucid dreams with a brief "intermission" of non-dream time occurring between each dream.

However, in this series of lucid dreams, something new happened in my experiment for the first time. Upon becoming lucid in the second dream, I immediately remembered with full, clear recall all the details of the first lucid dream and watched that dream replayed in its entirety in my lucid memory, exactly as it had just appeared only a short time before. I felt astonished and pleased to be aware of both lucid dreams simultaneously, each presented fully and in an intelligible sequence of imagery. In this experience I felt as if I were watching two distinct movies on two separate screens at the same time, fully realizing that I had just seen the first movie only few moments before. I enjoyed this simultaneous "double feature" very much, especially since the remembering of the first lucid dream did not interfere with the sequence of symbols and the spontaneity of images in the second lucid dream in any way. Because I was lucid to a rather high degree throughout this process, the remembering of the first dream and the simultaneous playing out of the second dream were completely distinct in my mind, two completely distinct tracks of consciousness. I felt amazed as the second dream ended and as the replay of the first dream also ended with it at the same time.

Then, after another "brief intermission," the third lucid dream began. Immediately upon becoming lucid in the third dream I remembered in full detail and full exactitude both the first dream and the second dream of the series. These also were now fully replayed in my "lucid memory," as I watched and enjoyed the third lucid dream from beginning to end. I felt more amazed than ever, because now I felt as if I were watching three movies all at once, enjoying them all, keeping each one fully distinct in my lucid mind and fully aware that two of these lucid dreams were now recurrent, since they had both originally appeared only a short time earlier in the night.

In similar fashion, this entire process continued to escalate and compound itself all through the entire series of six lucid dreams. As each successive dream began, I immediately became lucid and, upon becoming lucid, I remembered without any effort or intention all of the previous dreams of the series in full detail. By the time the sixth lucid dream was in progress, I was

166

dreaming it and simultaneously remembering all five of the previous lucid dreams, replaying them all in my lucid memory. At this point the experience was like watching six movies on six different screens at the same time and keeping them all distinct in my mind! This experience of cumulative lucid consciousness and cumulative lucid remembrance was totally new and unique for me, one that I had never known before on such a broad scale. It expanded my horizons once again, illustrating what the human mind is capable of. In the lucid state apparently, the psyche is capable of holding a vast amount of material in consciousness at the same time and capable of playing many distinct "tracks of consciousness" simultaneously.

In reflecting upon this series of dreams, I remembered a story that I had heard ten or twelve years earlier from Baba Ram Dass recounting a legend from the life of the Buddha. According to the legend, after he became enlightened, the Buddha on one occasion remembered 10,000 of his previous incarnations. He also remembered every single detail of each of those distinct lifetimes, understood the exact meaning and purpose of each event in each lifetime, and fully understood how all these lifetimes interconnected and influenced each other in his own particular vast, karmic pattern. For years I had never particularly believed this story or even known how to approach it. Now, after this experience in this series of lucid dreams, I remembered the story and began to wonder. Perhaps through the lucid state I had obtained another glimmer of human possibilities and potentialities. Perhaps, I began to wonder, there is some truth to this legend about the Buddha. What once appeared to me as impossible now merely appeared as overwhelming. Once again, I began to watch a few more of my old opinions about human consciousness shake and crumble.

After I awakened from this lucid series I wrote down only the first dream, because I felt completely overwhelmed with this new phenomenon of the lucid state and with the vast amount of material that all six of these dreams had presented. I entitled this dream "The Majestic Mountain." Its theme and images seem to blend harmoniously with the metaphor of the peaks and valleys that I have often used to describe my experiment.

THE MAJESTIC MOUNTAIN
July 1, 1983

I am walking alone down a country road. The road is well paved and a bit narrow. It curves gracefully through many hills and valleys that are covered with lush, green grass and many beautiful trees. Suddenly, I realize I am dreaming and I decide to fly. Feeling the exhilaration of the lucid energy arising within me, I spring off the pavement with a light bounce of my toes and begin to fly, following the contour of the road. I see a young girl, about ten or eleven years old, flying toward me from the opposite direction. She is wearing a bright red knit blouse and blue jeans. Just as we pass each other in mid-air, I quickly stick out my arm and catch her around the waist. I pull her over in front of me and playfully wrestle with her and tease her. I realize at once that she does not enjoy the game at all, and so I let her go. She flies away, looking nonchalant and unexpressive, as if nothing had happened.

Now I see a beautiful, tall snow-capped mountain far ahead in the distance and I fly directly toward it. The peak is a highly visible landmark, perhaps an extinct volcano, and it rises majestically far above all the other mountains around it. I focus on it intently as I fly. Suddenly it disappears from view and I feel completely disoriented. I veer to the left and see a sky full of grayish dark clouds. Their hue is strangely beautiful and a bit ominous at the same time. I see a solitary black bird, like a crow, flying with the dark, gray clouds in the background. Now I focus my full attention on the bird and fly toward it. The bird becomes larger as I approach it and I know it is too large to be a crow. I wonder what kind of bird it is, when suddenly it disappears. Again, I feel a swirling, confusing sensation all over and slowly I begin to descend to the ground. My lucidity slowly fades out, and gradually I lose sight of the dreamscape as well. I fall back asleep.

The majestic mountain symbolized for me my long-range goal of cultivating lucidity and the dream reminded me that distractions and digressions are easy and numerous. At the time that I had this dream I had interrupted my regular writing schedule for this book, mostly because of numerous household projects that I thought required my time and energy. I felt a lot of conflict and inner restlessness about these interruptions. "Who was the young girl in the dream?" I began to ask. "What did she symbolize?" I decided to use the Gestalt therapy dialogue method here, an active and conscious fantasy process in which the dreamer carries out an imaginary dialogue with each of the major symbols in the dream. I asked the young girl who she was and she answered that she was only another frivolous distraction. She was headed in the opposite direction of my path and she really did not want me to grab hold of her and play. She just wanted me to ignore her, let her fly on past, keep to my own course and follow the road that the dream had created for me. She was expressionless in the dream, an empty distraction that held no real excitement. Just as I let go of her in the dream, I needed to let go of certain people, places and situations that were not fun or playful for me, not investing them with any of my energy and not allowing them to pull me off course.

What were those ominous, dark clouds in the dream? Upon reflecting, I began to see that they represented a number of worries and depressing situations that had already taken up too much of my attention and were distracting me from my prime goal, the majestic mountain, the inspiration of lucid dreaming.

The largest of these "stormy" situations had been brewing for some time. About a year-and-a-half earlier, Charlene and I had been named, along with six or seven other parties, as defendants in a personal injury lawsuit by one of my female clients. This woman, whom I felt very concerned about at the time, had fallen into a tragic predicament. She had been seriously injured, almost killed, in an auto accident that occurred on the street near my office. Unfortunately, she had no medical insurance at the time to cover the overwhelming costs of numerous surgeries and very technical medical procedures that followed her accident. Because the driver of the car that hit her also had no insurance, my client and her husband soon became financially desperate. Though Charlene and I were convinced that we were totally blameless for the accident, we were named in the suit by her attorneys anyway and had to spend a great deal of time and energy to defend ourselves. The lengthy and tedious process of answering interrogatories, talking with attorneys and giving depositions, which dragged on for almost two years, was now depleting a great deal of my creative energy. It also left me feeling enraged and helpless before the onslaught of our present legal system which allows an attorney who is representing someone in a personal injury suit to name numerous defendants in this kind of legal action, even if there is no just cause for naming them. In popular terms, this legal procedure has become known as "searching for a deep pocket," and in our particular case one of the "deep pockets" happened to be our auto insurance company.

My emotional responses to this whole tedious process were intense: dismay, pain, betrayal, disbelief, outrage, helplessness and depression. At the time that the lawsuit struck, I was already feeling exhausted from the flood of overwhelming pressures, inner and outer, that I have recounted earlier in this story. This lawsuit now became one more stressor from the world that seemed to be carrying Charlene and me further into a state of exhaustion, confusion and disorientation. I also knew that I really wasn't coping with it all as well as I would like. Looking at it later, in hindsight and restrospect, I saw that this "legal assault" was one more dramatic example of the universe's basic demand upon me at that time in my life: *"Ken, stand up and fight!* Stand up and mobilize all the aggressive energy you can muster to protect your insides from assault wherever you find it and in whatever form it comes!"

One of the more intriguing symbols in "The Majestic Mountain" was the large black bird that eventually became larger than a crow. As I examined it reflectively, it began to symbolize my need to focus more on worldly power, and in particular it became another symbol for creative aggression used in self-defense. My situation with my desperate client had now created another opportunity for me to mobilize this all-important, particular type of power. Involvement in the lawsuit, I realized, was turning into a swirling, confusing battle for me, one that I had to go through because there was no other alternative. My easy-going, gentle exterior had inclined me initially to be far too patient and "understanding" when the summons first landed on my doorstep. I had been feeling a lot of sadness and a great deal of empathy for this particular client at the time that she was first injured. Eight months later, when the summons arrived and *we* were named among the numerous defendants, I was totally stunned and thrown off balance by this unexpected turn of events. I suddenly found myself to be in a very difficult position. Someone whom I had supported, first in her therapy work and then throughout the aftermath of her accident, had now suddenly turned against me and I did not know what to do in my relationship with her. This was the hour in which I definitely needed to wield my "worldly power" in ways that I had never done before.

I struggled inwardly with this problem for some time, consulting with my attorney and talking it over extensively with Charlene. Eventually, I realized that I had been, in an unconscious way, betrayed by my client and her husband, and that the pain and stress of that was more than I could bear. Even though my intellect knew that they and their attorneys were not after our personal assets but were only seeking reimbursement from our auto insurance company, I felt deeply betrayed anyway. That explained why, in spite of a great deal of dialogue and explanation between us, I was never able to reach a state of inner peace about it. Finally, with a lot of pain and sadness, I asked her to leave my practice. I realized I had to sever my relationship with her completely because of her choice, active and passive, to put me in the position I was in. I also realized that it was in the original moment of betrayal, when the legal documents first landed in my hands, that I needed to demand that she drop me from the suit or leave my practice at once. Such a timely and immediate wielding of worldly power would indeed have been the most wise, loving and ethical act for all concerned. Unfortunately, at the crucial hour of decision, I was paralyzed by my own shock and excessive compassion for her suffering.

Of course, it was easier for me to see all this in hindsight and difficult for me to act with fullness of power and clarity at the time of betrayal. My major lesson in all this was basically the same once again: I needed to be as tough with my client as I needed to be with the out-of-control adolescent next door. God must be a very patient teacher, I thought, as I finally put these pieces together. The Cosmic Teacher was giving me the same lesson, but in a different form. He was asking me to dance the same dance again, but this time with a different partner.

As I went through this conflict, symbolized by the dark, threatening storm clouds and the large, black bird flying against those clouds, I remembered that my unconscious had already given me some precious assistance in the form of two unforgettable dreams. The first was a dream fragment, short but potent.

THE KITTEN THAT CLAWS
May 21, 1982

I am standing somewhere with a group of people and I see that my entire midsection has been cut open as if with a sword. My stomach and my intestines are hanging out, dangling loose from my abdominal wall. Suddenly a small gray and black kitten jumps onto my insides and hangs onto them tenaciously with its claws.

The weight of the clinging kitten starts to pull my intestines out even further as I watch it hanging on with its claws. I feel passive and immobile in the situation.

Given the context that I have described, this dream was so self-evident that it needed no commentary on the day it arrived. I knew that the clawing kitten was my litigious client, who in desperation was hanging onto me, and I in my passivity was allowing it to happen. This dream was exactly what I needed at the time. It was shockingly grotesque and revolting because my conscious mind needed to be jolted and pushed in the direction of my own salvation. With the shock of this dream I began to resolve my inner paralysis.

The second of these two dreams offered me further internal resolution. I found its beauty exceptional and comparable to the raw material and rich imagery out of which some of the classic fables and folk tales are made.

HOW THE CROW FOUND ITS TONGUE AND ITS NAME
October 19, 1982

I am standing alone on a high mountain looking over a large, beautiful, green valley that extends for a great distance below me as far as the eye can see. The panoramic view is inspirational and I see a long river that winds gracefully through the valley. I hear a male voice calling aloud and directing my attention to a whale swimming upstream in the river. I see the whale in the distance and at once I lift off the mountain and fly toward it. For a moment I think I might become lucid, but I do not. Soon I am flying directly above the whale following it as it swims upstream. After a short time I fly on, leaving the whale behind. I am astounded to see thousands of large fish, uniform in size and shape, swimming in a huge school in the wide river. They all move in complete unison, speedily darting about in the deep, clear water. I continue to fly upstream and at every major bend in the river I see another similar, giant school with thousands of large fish moving in complete unison beneath the water. I enjoy watching them very much as I fly. Slowly this scene fades out . . .

173

The scene changes. Now I am watching a strange, gray prehistoric bird. I sense it is a crow even though it does not look like a crow. It has a very long bill and a long shaft of brightly colored feathers coming out from the back of its head. The bird impresses me as very powerful though a bit sluggish and passive in its movements. It is standing on a flat sawed-off tree stump. Now I see a black and gray cat stalking the bird, approaching it very cautiously and stealthily. Soon the cat has positioned itself quite close to the bird and is gathering its legs up under its body, preparing to pounce. Then the cat pounces, gripping the bird tightly in its claws and carrying it to the ground. For a few moments the ancient crow is completely immobile as the cat clutches it tightly in its claws and teeth. Suddenly the bird jerks powerfully and easily frees itself from the cat's grip. Immediately it flies back to the tree stump and perches there again, its body stiff, erect and proud.

Now a second cat, gray in color, begins to creep slowly and stealthily up toward the bird. In due time, it attains a favorable position, crouches, waits and then pounces, pinning the bird to the ground, gripping it tightly in its claws. This time the bird waits only a few seconds and then very forcefully jerks itself free from the cat's claws. Quickly, the ancient crow flips itself around and suddenly it is standing on the cat's back, gripping the cat fiercely with its claws and pinning it to the ground. With its sharp beak it strikes a clean blow to the back of the cat's neck and blood begins to flow from a round, red hole. As the bird is about to strike again, fiercely intent on killing the cat, a tall man approaches dressed in a brown khaki safari outfit. In a loud voice he commands the bird to stop. The ancient gray crow obeys. Now the man grabs the bird firmly with one hand and with the other he breaks off a large portion of its long beak. Then he opens the bird's beak and begins to pick at its tongue forcefully with his fingers. As I watch, I think that he is trying to teach the ancient bird to speak by splitting its tongue. The man finally tears off a portion of the tongue and immediately the bird becomes a modern crow with shiny, black-purplish feathers that glisten in the bright sunlight. He releases the crow and it takes to the air at once, flying around and around in a large circle directly above him. Now, in a loud voice, the man commands it to speak. I wait for the sound of the familiar "caw, caw, caw" and am quite surprised to hear the bird call out instead, with great exuberance: "Crow! Crow! Crow!" I watch, amused, as it continues to circle around us calling again and again with high enthusiasm and power in its voice: "Crow! Crow! Crow!" I wake up feeling very good.

This dream strongly impressed me with is primitive beauty, its creative imagery, and the depth and range of its symbolism. The gray and black cat that first attacked the large, prehistoric bird was the exact same color as the gray and black clawing kitten of the previous dream. When I saw this recurrent symbol, I knew that the unconscious was now delivering the next installment of my intricate, inner lesson plan. The gray, prehistoric bird (the predecessor of the modern crow) was the symbol of my worldly power moving passively and sluggishly in regard to the lawsuit. This passive and sluggish quality in the dream was "prehistoric," suggesting that it might date from a very early stage of my own development, perhaps from the pre-verbal stage of infancy, further back than I can now remember. It was portrayed as ancient, very much in need of being modernized and brought up to date. This old archetype, my old mental and behavioral pattern, was desperately in need of being changed in my life and under the onslaught of numerous pressures its basic survival was at stake as the dream itself suggested. This old part of myself, symbolized by the mute, prehistoric crow, needed to be transformed into a form that would be truly powerful, assertive, and properly vocal.

The principal themes of this dream were struggle and survival, victory and transformation. With an interesting twist to the dream story, one of the victimizers, the second cat, almost became a victim itself as the ancient bird turned the tables on it. As the bird freed itself, it clearly felt the urge for revenge and was about to act on it. That was an accurate reflection of the extent to which my own anger and pain had led me, in that I had felt a desire for revenge against my former client and her husband for what they were putting us through. But a powerful inner voice, the modern, civilized man in

175

the brown khaki outfit, forcefully transformed those destructive urges in the dream as he began to work on the beak of the primitive crow. This man was the dream archetype for the higher self, willing to reshape and reform the beak and tongue of the ancient bird, to bring out its voice and thereby its noble potential. In real life-and-death conflict situations, the higher self always commands us to change ourselves rather than to try to change others; it always commands us to change our old ways of being rather than succumb to primitive urges such as revenge or vindictiveness. The higher self always commands us to use our present miseries and sufferings to expand our consciousness and to go higher, like the flying modern crow at the end of the dream.

From this dream scenario I learned a great deal about my ancient difficulty in being fully assertive. One problem has been that I often feel the urge to be vindictive or cruel when I have to defend myself from someone else's aggression. I learned this old behavior pattern, I realized, from my father, who often mixed his assertions toward me as a child with a good deal of verbal cruelty and punitiveness. He was commonly quite aggressive and dominating in his ways toward all the members of our household and apparently unconscious of his cruelty. Somewhere I realized in working with this dream that a long time ago I began to hold back my power in this world for fear of provoking my father's cruelty. Later in my adult years I continued to hold back my power when under attack for fear of releasing my own cruelty, for my father's cruelty had now become my own. No matter how much I hated and feared this quality in him when I was a child and no matter how much I had consciously vowed to be "different," that cruelty had, nevertheless, seeped into my own psychic reservoir.

This realization reminded me of an old saying: "The sins of the fathers are visited upon their children." In either case, both as a child and as an adult, the end result in conflict situations would be the same for me: I would hold back. This dream was calling for the full transformation of my ancient, prehistoric pattern. This dream invited me to give up my old ways of feeling, thinking, and acting and to believe that transformation was possible. My lucid dream experiment, combined with my life journey, would facilitate my willingness and indeed my need to advance into a stronger assertion framework. These dark sides of myself were already being worked out as a part of the journey. I resolved that in the future I would react more on a gut level and risk more. I would risk the possibility of being cruel to someone rather than hold back my reactions. For me, it would be better to react and risk in the moment, than not to react at all.

As I awakened from this dream, I felt exuberant and fully identified with the flying modern crow, circling overhead in the final scene of the dream. His call of "Crow! Crow! Crow!" has been an important affirmation for me ever since. To this day I frequently look to the shining black crow as a symbol for the validity of raw personal power. As a meaningful coincidence, soon after I moved to a new home and new office, I began to "see" and "hear" the numerous crows that frequently fly and "crow" around me in my new community. I often pause and pay them special attention, feeling pleased with this example of what Carl Jung called "synchronicity."* Often now in a silent, inner way, I stop for a moment when I hear these dark, black birds

---

* Jung coined the term "synchronicity" to refer to the special phenomenon of a *meaningful* coincidence, in the coming together of two or more events in a person's life. These events are usually a combination of inner and outer experiences, such as the appearance of the crow in my dream, followed by its frequent appearance in my physical environment. Jung spoke of synchronicity as an "a-causal connecting principle," meaning that the two events are not caused one by the other. They are instead *associated* to one another, linked somehow by other kinds of mysterious forces which we still do not understand in a rational and scientific way. However, we are capable of training ourselves to become more conscious of these coincidences (comings together) and, as we become more aware of their existence, we can notice how frequently and commonly they actually occur, and we can learn how to use them for the cultivation of intuition and for "individuation," Jung's term for the process of becoming a conscious, self-realized being.

and draw some of their raucous, beautiful power into myself. For me, they have become a living totem.

In the end, the lawsuit was settled in a way that is typical of such things. After almost two years, we were dropped from the case when our auto insurance company agreed to pay a substantial settlement to the injured woman out of court. I felt a lot of relief when we were eventually dropped from the case. The dark clouds had blown over in due time. However, numerous scars upon my psyche and several broken relationships were the damages that remained, along with a lot of mixed emotions about how the legal "system" works. In human terms, the emotional wreckage it left behind was substantial.

My lucid dream of "The Majestic Mountain" took on a deep significance for me as I contemplated its dynamics and its symbols over and over. Because it was placed in first position during this unique display of "multi-screened, inner cinema," I actually viewed this dream a total of six times on the night that it occurred. There must have been a reason why I was supposed to watch it six times and with full lucidity each time. The messages of the dark clouds and the solitary large, black bird are clear to me now. Unfinished business from my ancient past and from my immediate past had coalesced, had come together within my psyche, and had become strong enough to deviate me from the mountain. In the midst of my lucid dream experiment I was sent on a "detour," and this detour became the perfect point of departure for learning other specific and mandatory lessons that were most valuable in their own way. These lessons were both multiplex and complex. My stance toward my injured client had become too "lofty." This dream brought me back down to earth and clarified what my genuine limitations were.

About a year and a half after the lawsuit was settled, I meditated one day in a deep way on this whole unfortunate experience with my former client. I focused on the theme of "the victim" and took this symbol to the level of full conscious ownership. In meditation, I said to myself: "Let's pretend that this whole tragedy is a dream or, more accurately, a nightmare. In that case, every character in the story is also, somehow, a part of *me*. If she is a part of me, exactly how is this true? How am *I* the victim? How have I been a victim in this world?" It was not very difficult for me to think of numerous examples from throughout my life in which I felt, looked and acted like a victim. The tally began to mount up as I went fully into this conscious exercise of internal ownership of the victim symbol. I remembered my first day of school in the first grade, when a big fourth grader threatened to grab my lunch bucket and take it away. I remembered how hard it was to stifle my panic and try to act tough, and how relieved I felt when a friend came to my rescue. I remembered another scenario in which I felt intimidated by a sadistic college professor who during his first lecture proudly boasted to the whole class that one-third of us would fail the first quarter exam in his course, because his material was just too difficult. I remembered clenching my teeth as I sat in the lecture chair resolving that *I* would not be among those who failed. I succeeded. I passed the first quarter exam and did not become one of his overt victims, but ended up carrying covert resentment toward him for years. Thus, in another way, I did become his victim. As dozens of related examples came to my mind in this meditation, I realized some personal value from my client's victimhood. She became a victim, and then I became her victim, the victim's victim. We were, ultimately, co-victims. The extreme value in this tragedy for me was that I had received from the universe the unforgotten reminder that I needed to become fully conscious of all the shades, degrees, variations and situations of victimhood of which I had always been capable.

Ultimately, the lucid dreamer is someone who seeks to become a lucid or conscious being in the world. He or she is someone who will, with increasing frequency, move his awareness to the level where he sees every part of the physical world around him as reflecting some part of his own psyche. In relating to an adversary, he begins to say to himself: "You too are a part of me; you too, somehow, somewhere, exist within me." Eventually, as he becomes more steeped in this concept, the lucid being learns to communicate with others *not only by reaching out, but also by reaching in,* into the deepest recesses of himself. By reaching deep within, he seeks to find that part within his psyche that corresponds to the person or problem he is currently facing in his environment.

My dream of "The Majestic Mountain" and the life context from which it emerged reminded me of something important about the stages of spiritual growth: The higher stages could only be built upon a foundation that was purged of my primitive emotions and yet operating with full respect for them at the same time. In a path of full spirituality there can be no such thing as "trying to be above it all," that is, denying or minimizing one's true feelings about anything. The higher self must always exist in harmony with the lower self if true inner peace is to be attained. Just as the higher parts of a building (the walls, rafters and roof) must ultimately rest on a solid foundation, so too, self-love and love for the other in a conflict situation can only be built upon a full acceptance of one's own basic (or base) emotions. When one's anger, whether justifiable or unjustifiable, is fully discharged and one's personal injuries are adequately and truly compensated for, then, and only then, will true inner peace be reached in a relationship. One's higher self in its truest integrity always rests upon a full honoring of one's lower or primitive emotions. Eventually, I realized, I would approach and dwell upon the majestic mountain after I completed the crucial lessons presented in the "detour" of this pivotal dream.

At the time of this dream, when I was grappling with so many seemingly trite and banal problems all at once,

I often felt disgusted with myself. "How can you be so petty?" a voice within me nagged. "Why don't you just 'let go' and forget the whole thing? Why don't you get on with your higher pursuits? Why don't you get on with your creative pursuits, such as writing your book?" All these nagging questions and self-accusations were coming from my inner critic. The "shoulds" and "ought to's" were part of my old judgmental framework, and I began to sense more clearly than ever before that as long as I operated out of that framework I would never reach genuine spiritual purgation. Full inner cleansing, I realized, would mean that I would eventually honor and trust every single feeling that I have, large or small, trite or magnificent. It meant that I would follow through on becoming conscious of each nagging or persistent feeling, tracing it to its roots, past or present, in my psyche, in order to understand and appreciate its contribution to my overall growth as a person. The intensity of my anger and my feelings of betrayal were not evil or wrong. Even if I were "overreacting," the overreaction, I realized, was also a gift offering me a pathway to fuller understanding. The overreaction told me that I was indeed particularly sensitive to being manipulated and betrayed precisely *because* this type of thing had happened to me before, somewhere and somehow in my past, even perhaps my ancient past.

Sometimes my lucid dreams have returned in a burst of splendor. At different points in my experiment I have received other outstanding lucid dreams with their wonderful qualities and enriching symbols. Such dreams suggest that I may be standing on still another mountaintop as I continue this inner journey. Of course, I can never predict exactly when one of these special dreams will emerge, though sometimes I can "feel a lucid dream coming on" as I crawl into bed at night. Interspersed between the highest peaks are many less elevated peaks, "ordinary lucid dreams," as I now call them, which are also valuable in their own way. As I explore all of this terrain, I see more and more that it is all perfect just the way it is. The high peaks, the middle ranges, the low valleys, the winding pathways and the obstacles in between are all a part of the journey. More and more I realize too that, at the present time, I could not dwell permanently on the mountaintop anyway. I would probably "fry my psyche to a crisp" if I were to feel every day or every night the full intensity of the lucid dream state. At present, I feel content simply to aim at building an increasing inner tolerance for ecstasy as my journey progresses.

I know now, too, that it is important to be aware of the danger of "dream burn-out," and especially "lucid dream burn-out." What I am referring to here is a mental state of exhaustion that comes from overdoing a good thing, from exposing oneself to too much mental-emotional intensity for too prolonged a period of time. I know now that I need a certain amount of "down time" to balance out and countereffect the moments of "up time" that I am experiencing on this journey. Just as advanced practitioners of intense, daily meditation have discovered the possible danger of "meditation burn-out," so too I have discovered that there is a similar corresponding danger in working with dreams, and lucid dreams in particular.

Recognizing this danger makes it all the more mandatory for those who follow lucid dreaming as a spiritual path to remember the principle of *balance* in their daily lives. This principle cannot be emphasized enough. For myself, I have come to see that I need to balance out my work with lucid dreams on five distinct parameters, five distinct sets of inner scales as I proceed with these explorations. These five scales are: (1) I need to balance my inner reflection on lucid dreaming with outer conversation, that is, talking about it to other knowledgeable persons; (2) I need to balance the "peaks" with the "valleys," the highly intense lucid dreams with those of low intensity; (3) I need to balance the abundant periods of lucid dreaming with the dry periods, allowing the field of the psyche to lie fallow as needed; (4) I need to balance my attitudes of *wishing* for lucidity with *allowing* for lucidity to happen in its own right; and (5) I need a certain amount of physical exercise and physical labor in my life to give my mind regular recesses and vacations from my inner world. There may be other important inner scales to balance as well, but at present I am particularly aware of these five.

"The Majestic Mountain" has become another sustaining and guiding image for me as I follow the path of lucid dreaming. Its image often comes back to me, especially when I feel that the ordinary demands and pressures of everyday life may be consuming too large a portion of my time and energies. Though I know full well that the routine demands of life are important in their own way, my prime task now is to keep my mind and my vision focused on the mountain. The mountain reminds me now of many things. It reminds me of a verse, a part of song that I wrote when Charlene and I were first married:

> There's a mountain in me
> I know you can see
> There's one in you
> It's tall and true,
> I feel it best
> When I face to the west
> In the evening
> When the sun goes down.

It reminds me too of certain teachings from the Zen Buddhist tradition: "Nature is the true teacher of Zen, but not all who enter the mountains see them as they really are. Only a man who knows himself can see the true nature of mountains."*

And through the soul of the thirteenth century Zen Master, Dogen Zenji, come the words: "The color of mountains is Buddha's pure body, the sound of running water is his great speech."

I have always had a special love for mountains. I am beginning to understand why.

---

* Suzuki, *Zen Mind, Beginner's Mind, passim.*

CHAPTER NINE

The Warrior Hero: Back to Basics

*"Those who live by the sword shall perish by the sword."**
—Jesus of Nazareth

"Those who ignore the sword shall also perish by it. Who will teach us the path of wholeness and balance?"
—Anonymous

At various times during my experiment with lucid dreaming, I have had key, integrative dreams. These dreams have pulled together many of the pieces of my experiment that had previously felt scattered, confused or disjointed in my own mind. Such integrative dreams, when they were clearly understood, have had a strong settling effect on my mind. They were like the impact of a zestful ocean breeze or a brisk shower of rain that could wash away the accumulated mental smog of my past. Sometimes a bit startling at first, they have been so refreshing in the long run that I have learned to place a special value on them. One such dream arrived about three years after I had begun my experiment.

---

* Matthew 26:52.

THE SWEET HORN OF GENEVIEVE
December 16, 1983

I am in a huge, well-lighted social hall with a large group of attractive, energetic people. I am standing behind a long "L"-shaped table that is elegantly set for a banquet. The table is covered with a long snow-white tablecloth with beautiful china, genuine silver and sparkling, clear crystal goblets at each place setting. The table runs the entire length of the hall, then makes a 90-degree turn and runs its entire width. I stand straight and tall at my appointed place with my hands touching the back of my chair and look around at all the people who are formally and elegantly dressed in tuxedos and long-flowing evening gowns. I am wearing a crisp, black tuxedo and I feel wonderful and excited to be here.

Suddenly a large door opens in the wall on the far side of the room and four or five medium-sized black bulls come running into the open area of the banquet hall. They seem like adolescent bulls, rambunctious, clumsy and out of control. They stamp and snort and stomp their feet, bumping into each other while stumbling and staggering about, moving closer and closer to the elegant banquet table. Several male waiters, dressed in white, rush in and attempt to grab the young bulls by the horns and control them. They are all unsuccessful as the bulls easily toss them aside with quick movements of their powerful necks and bodies. Now the head waiter, a determined and bright-eyed young man also dressed in white, runs into the open center area of the hall. He is brandishing a huge axe and with two deft and powerful swings, he cuts off both horns of the bull nearest to him. His cuts are extremely accurate and clean, severing each horn perfectly at its base. As the two severed horns fall to the brightly polished floor, the dehorned young bull settles down at once and all the other bulls calm down with him in unison, as if their bodies were all one. Now the young head waiter picks up the two severed horns from the floor and places one in his lips pretending to blow on it. I feel amused as I realize that the horn of the bull is a primitive musical instrument. Now he walks directly over to me, reaches across the table and offers me one of the horns, gesturing silently, inviting me to blow on it. Feeling a bit unsure of my ability for this new task, I take the horn, place the small end into my mouth and blow. The first two notes that come out remind me of the opening two notes of

"Sweet Genevieve." They come out so clear and mellow that I feel a strong desire to continue. I play the rest of the song all the way through, deriving the greatest pleasure from the extraordinarily deep, beautiful sounds and tones of the horn. I am surprised at how effortless it really is, as I pour all of my heart and soul into the melody. In the hushed banquet hall, everyone listens with rapt attention as I both play the melody and play with the melody, improvising on it in ways that are very innovative, yet rich and moving. I feel the music come from way deep down inside me as if from the bottom of my soul. As I finish the melody, I lower the horn from my lips, feeling wonderful and uplifted. I see the head waiter standing nearby, nodding brightly and smiling a big broad smile of appreciation toward me.

Now I hand the horn to my friend Arnie Kunst, who is standing next to me on my left. He too plays his rendition of "Sweet Genevieve." It is not nearly as mellow and soul-touching as my own though I enjoy it nevertheless. As he finishes playing, I feel wonderfully content. I wake up feeling exhilarated and feel a lot of warmth and harmony in my heart and stomach area from which the music came, so freely and absolutely effortlessly.

I woke up with a wonderful glow from this dream. Though it was not a lucid dream, it contained many of the hyperconscious qualities of the lucid state. The music as I played it from the bull's horn in the dream was so rich and mellow, so deeply felt in every cell of my body that it remained with me for some time. For days after the dream, I would catch myself humming or singing the melody to "Sweet Genevieve" and pouring all my heart and soul into it, just as I had done in the dream. I thoroughly enjoyed carrying the feeling tone of this dream into my conscious, waking life.

Upon first awakening, I lay in my bed for several minutes before I arose to write down this dream. I sensed at once that it was filled with meaning. The first image that immediately caught my attention was the strange placement and design of the banquet table. It was not arranged in the center of the room, nor were its two wings shaped like a "T" as my conscious mind would expect. It was placed along the sides of two walls like an enormous

"L." I began to play with the letter "L" in my mind, asking what in my world begins with "L." I focused on the incredible elegance of the table, and for a moment I looked at the clear crystal goblets at each place setting, perfectly clear and sparkling with light. Then I saw the connection: "L" stands for lucid. The clear translucent glass and the sparkling light are the hallmark characteristics of lucid dreams, exactly the type of images that they frequently convey. "Of course!" I thought, and my heart began to beat and my mind began to race. "What is this dream saying about lucidity?" I asked myself. The exquisitely elegant banquet, I realized, was a perfect image for the world of the lucid dream, an inner realm that is full of beauty, grace, poise and delicateness. I was reminded too of one of Jesus' parables in which "the kingdom" was compared to a great banquet. "A man once gave a great banquet and invited many . . ."*

In the dream I was standing at my appointed place at the banquet table, wearing my tuxedo and feeling in harmony with all the other beautiful people at the banquet. With my hands touching the back of my chair, I was calmly waiting to be seated when suddenly the major disruption began. Who or what did the four or five rampaging, black bulls symbolize?

These disruptive and aggressive forces were totally incongruous and out of place in the dream, like the proverbial "bull in the china shop." In the months that followed, I shared this dream with many people, including several professional colleagues. I also shared it with Charlene and Erik and with students in my various dream groups and workshops. I actively sought out and took in a lot of feedback and clarification about the bulls, the obvious symbols of conflict and trouble in the dream. Finally, a comprehensive picture began to emerge. The four or five young bulls were the four or five major aggressive forces, both from the environment and from my unconscious mind, that barged in upon me,

* Luke 14:16-24.

unexpectedly and violently, both in the beginning and throughout my lucid dream experiment!

Collectively these forces constituted *overwhelm!* They had the collective power to overrun me completely and perhaps even to destroy the beauty and delicateness of my lucid dream explorations. These forces constituted a tremendous challenge and, in examining the imagery of the dream thoroughly, I began to appreciate exactly how much stress I had been through in the previous three years of my life. Finally, my integrative question emerged: "What lessons were these rampaging bulls and that amazing head waiter trying to teach me?"I soon realized that they were attempting to teach me something about efficient coping and taking good care of myself when I am in a situation of multiple stressors, feeling overloaded and overwhelmed by them. I felt excited as I discovered this basic key to the dream. "The Sweet Horn of Genevieve"* came about a year and half after my stress was at its peak, but its clarity was most welcome nevertheless.

On the morning that I received this dream, I shared it at the breakfast table with Charlene and Erik. Erik was seven years old at the time and, as usual, he enjoyed hearing the dream. We were discussing the adolescent qualities of the bulls, and we had related them to our former neighborhood and to the out-of-control teenage boy and his adolescent friends. We were laughing and joking about how they had not been intentionally cruel to us; they were simply behaving like the bulls in the dream, completely out of control, noisily stomping about, insensitive and potentially destructive. As we talked about these ideas, Erik hit the nail right on the head with a cryptic comment: "Yeah, those young bullies!" Charlene

* St. Genevieve (422-500 A.D.) is the patron saint of Paris. She is said to have predicted the invasion by the Huns. When Attila and his army were threatening the city (451 A.D.) she persuaded the inhabitants to remain on the island, encouraging them by her assurance, justified by subsequent events, that the attack would come to nothing. Attila later abandoned his seige, and Genevieve was credited with having saved the city. This historical reference has deepened my appreciation of my dream's central theme.

and I laughed, enjoying the truth-telling insight of a child's clear vision. I had, indeed, often felt bullied by those "young bullies."

Was this dream, perhaps, going to supply some missing piece to my longstanding puzzle? For over three years I had been searching in vain for an answer as to how I could have dealt with the young bullies next door. I was very impressed when I saw how the rambunctious bulls were finally stopped in my dream. As I reflected on the principal characters of this dream, I began to collect some valuable observations. The first three or four waiters, dressed all in white, who rushed in and tried to grab the bulls were easily and promptly tossed aside. These young men symbolized the "Mr. Nice Guy" part of my personality. They had good intentions (they wore white); they put out a lot of energy and gave their all, but they were totally ineffective. They were ineffective because they were *too gentle* in a potentially violent situation and did not apply the necessary force and highly focused skill that such a situation calls for. What was needed to stop the bulls in my dream (and the teenage bullies next door in my waking world) was a type of raw, personal power, freely used, highly focused, with full attention placed on the precise spot where the adversary could be hit and stopped, as if struck in his Achilles heel. I was stunned and pleased to realize the special significance of the head waiter, the man who wielded the axe! *He was the missing piece to my puzzle!* He was the symbol for raw personal power, wielded with consummate skill.

The young man who brandished the axe in my dream soon became a hero symbol for me. Like the other waiters, he too was dressed in white (motivated by good intentions). He too threw himself completely into the fray, but he stood out from all the others because he was very skillful. This man was a *warrior,* as portrayed at length by Don Juan to Carlos Castaneda.* In

---

* Carlos Castaneda, *The Teachings of Don Juan: A Yaqui Way of Knowledge, passim.*

meditating upon his behavior, as it appeared in my dream, a whole series of thoughts quickly came to me. A warrior is someone who knows and who is fully clear that there will be times in one's life when one has to take up the sword. A warrior is not afraid to swing the sword, or the axe for that matter. He is able and willing to see evil and danger exactly for what they are. He does not delude himself with excessive idealism about the world. He does not believe in the practice of "Hear no evil, see no evil, speak no evil." He is not mired down in middle-class niceties" nor is he paralyzed by popular convention. The real warrior is extremely conscious, skillful and deft in the way he swings his sword. The warrior understands the laws that govern aggressive energies. He knows the futility of meeting an aggressor with gentleness, placating or appeasement. He knows that these qualities usually invite more aggression, and intensify and prolong the impending conflict. The warrior knows how to meet oncoming aggression on its own level, while positioning himself in a place of effective leverage. The skillful warrior does not engage his adversary in a head-on collision. Such collisions are unskillful, unnecessarily brutal and exhausting to everyone involved. This type of "spiritual warrior" aims to become fully conscious of the exact, precise spot where he needs to strike his adversary, to render him harmless with the least possible damage to everyone. The true warrior is a *precision* swordsman and his blows are *merciful* and *loving* in the larger view of life. Jesus' way of responding to the Pharisees and Mahatma Gandhi's way of confronting his British adversaries provide many excellent examples of this type of "spiritual swordsmanship."

The further I explored this dream, the more it amazed me. I saw that as the head waiter swung his axe, he made two swings, and with each one made a perfectly clean cut, with balance and grace, and with a minimum expenditure of his own energy. As both horns fell to the floor, there was an immediate energy shift in the bull who lost his horns and in all the other bulls as well. In unison, as if they were one organism, they all became perfectly calm and perfectly peaceful together, through a mysterious, but shared unconscious connection. The warrior had made the perfect strike.

"The Sweet Horn of Genevieve" pointed out to me, ever so clearly, that the warrior hero had been the missing part of my personality in my attempts to cope with the overwhelming flood of events and emotions that struck me during those many months. I had been far too patient and far too tolerant. With this insight I began to meditate and reflect frequently on this warrior hero, my waiter in white, wielding his large axe. I soon thereafter began to give him much more space and conscious acceptance in my inner life and could feel myself frequently exercising more of this "creative aggression," in words and deeds, where I saw that this quality was appropriate for creating something beautiful in the world. This dream in conjunction with my experiences illustrated how conscious warriorship, when used for self-defense and at the proper moment, is indeed a virtue. It is an act of heroism.

In this dream, the warrior hero extended a most important invitation to me. After he subdued the bulls, he offered me the severed horn, the trophy of his skillful victory, and he invited me to blow on it. To accept the horn, as I did in the dream, was to accept the prospect of following his direction and incorporating him more and more into my conscious awareness and behavior in the waking state. The dream contained a valuable pun here. I was invited to "blow my own horn," another metaphor for putting out more of my own power into the world.

In many ways, the horn struck me as the most important symbol in the dream. I say this primarily because the horn was the dream's most prominent symbol of transformation. As such, it was the positive counterpart to the axe, also a symbol and instrument of transformation. The true warrior hero, one who is whole and balanced, knows how to use both instruments. Through his fully balanced participation in the dream scenario, this hero initiated with the axe and completed with the horn two distinct stages of transformation. The horn, while it remained on the head of the rampaging bull, could have been an instrument for destruction. And yet, when severed (confronted and contacted) and placed in its proper position, it became the instrument for creativity, peace and beauty. In this dream the horn became the channel for some of the most moving and deeply soulful music that I have ever heard in a dream or anywhere. The horn became the instrument through which I, the dreamer, was transformed, for as I played it in that dream moment I felt myself become a different person. The music that came from the bottom of my soul was my living proof of change, because it was so rich, so sweet, so mellow, so deep, so ultra, so beyond description. The horn and the music and the dreamer became one! Many accomplished musicians have acknowledged this type of experience, claiming that when they are performing at their very best, giving peak performances, they often feel as if their instrument is a part of their own body. They become one with their instrument and with the music that flows through it, as they feel the music arise from the deepest part of themselves, flow through the instrument and out into the world. This experience of at-one-ment with the horn and with the soulful melody of "Sweet Genevieve" led me to a deep feeling of inner harmony and beauty. The moment of tranformation can be very sweet, and in the dream I savored every single note and every single trill and vibrato that I placed upon each note as I blew. The music and sound within this dream transported me into another realm. I still find it most difficult to describe that realm in words or re-create its sound in the waking state. That dream moment meant a great deal to me then and still does now, as I completed the melody with a deep sense of fulfillment. The rapt, hushed attention of the people who listened in the dream spoke volumes to me and the broad, beaming smile of the head waiter came as no surprise. I needed his appreciation, and in this dream I opened myself to receive it abundantly.

The ending of "The Sweet Horn of Genevieve" seemed a bit anticlimactic to me. In the dream, as I handed the horn to my friend Arnie, I listened as he played his rendition of "Sweet Genevieve," which was not nearly as mellow and touching as my own. In waking life, Arnie is a very good friend of mine; I have known him for over thirty years. Musically, he is much more gifted than I and his talents are so far above my own in that area that I have never made any comparisons between us. Yet in the dream my music was much more moving and inspirational to me than his! In the dream, I noticed this turnabout with complete calmness and acceptance. There were no feelings of competition or jealousy. As I reflected further, I began to see that this anticlimax, this final punctuation mark, was somehow related to the whole experience of transformation.

I believe that the ending of this dream may have taught me something new about the nature of a genuine moment of transformation. In such genuine moments, I now believe, a person is so filled from within by the beauty of the spirit that all external considerings are hushed in the mind. In this state, the customary ego-chatter of the mind ceases. In such a moment, we do not compete with others, we do not compare ourselves to others, and we do not look outside of ourselves in any way for satisfaction or fulfillment. Nor do we seek to change anything or improve upon anything for satisfaction or fulfillment. In a transformative moment the mind is totally conscious of WHAT IS and WHAT IS NOW, and finds a fullness of joy and exquisite perfection in *this* moment, in *this* situation, in *this* time and place. In a transformation experience, the mind does not race backward or forward in time. It is totally attuned to the present and stilled by its incomparable beauty. In such a moment we are filled with awe and fully immersed in the peace of WHAT IS SO.

These were the realizations that came to me from the flood of inner sensations that I gathered at the conclusion of "The Sweet Horn of Genevieve." I felt wonderful as I awoke from this dream and as its energies began to carry over into my waking mind. I knew, at once, that the voice of the unconscious had spoken again and I opened myself widely to receive its gifts.

My experiment with lucid dreaming could continue forever. A book, however, is limited by space and time, and at some arbitrary point an author is forced to bring his account to a conclusion. I feel certain that my openness to my dream channel will remain a lifelong process for me and that my dreams will continue to serve a major role in my life, no matter what happens. My venturing into the lucid dream state has become a specific dimension and plateau in my dream explorations, which have been a major part of my life for almost twenty years. I feel quite confident now too, after five years of regular lucidity, that my lucid dreams will return and remain as my companions for the rest of my life.

I remember, too, the ups and downs, the "energy bursts" and the "energy drops," the dry periods and the abundant periods that can be clearly delineated in my experiment. I have watched these cycles come and go in myself often enough, to understand that they too are an intrinsic part of what is so. I understand their existence and I accept them now completely. I can feel a deeper inner peace about them now, a peace that was lacking when my experiment was in its earlier stages. I don't fully understand *why* these cycles are so and I don't really need to understand *why*. I only need to understand *that* they are so and live in harmony with their movements.

As a psychotherapist, I have frequently observed in

my work that if we will fully commit to living in the moment and consciously feel our feelings of the moment, that eventually all of our important *why* questions will be answered. So often, we ask *why* prematurely. So often we ask *why* in the midst of a powerful experience, a question that slows down the flood of feelings from that experience, seeking to satisfy our intellectual curiosity about it. So often we need to put the *why* questions on the inner shelf of the mind and let them rest there until the emotional work is completed first. "Eventually," I tell myself and my clients, "the intellect will catch up with the emotions." The intellect simply cannot move as fast as the emotions, especially when the emotions are at flood stage. Later, the clear and rational understanding of an experience often emerges into consciousness. Later, the important why questions will be answered and the unimportant will have fallen by the wayside. The numerous cycles of dreaming and the many levels of understanding, rational and nonrational, are all a part of my whole experience with lucid dreaming now, and I approach them with a fuller sense of detachment and surrender.

Surrender—this concept has been one of the most difficult for me to grasp and to practice in my experiment with lucid dreaming and in my whole life as well. Ever since childhood I have been a very goal-oriented individual and have built into my mind many major belief systems and minor supporting belief systems that emphasize and reward the ethic of hard work and individual effort. At this point in my experiment, the surrender of the ego and the continued practice of that surrender loom larger than ever in my view as a necessary overall state of mind for a cultivation of lucid dreaming that promotes genuine spiritual growth.

In my classes on lucid dreaming, I have often emphasized to students that the lucid dream state is readily accessible to those who both *wish* and *allow* themselves to become lucid. Wishing and allowing: these two states of mind are quite distinct. They are a pair of opposites that together comprise a whole. In traditional Jungian terms, wishing in this context would be seen as the "masculine" quality of mind, and allowing as the "feminine." When we wish for something, we mobilize our intentionality, focus on the object of our desire as a goal, and visualize it in our imagination as already having taken place. In pursuing this process we are using the masculine (or yang)* qualities of the mind. At this point, I have confirmed through my experiences that the mobilization of the yang energy is not sufficient to induce lucid dreaming. We cannot simply *make* it happen; we must also *allow* it to happen. This attitude of allowance is the feminine (or yin) state of consciousness, in which a person immerses his or her conscious attention into the qualities of acceptance, patience, vulnerability, receptivity and passivity (in a positive sense). These qualities provide a mental matrix, a fertile soil in which the desire to cultivate the lucid dream can sprout and grow. In my own particular case throughout my experiment I have had to cultivate consciously more of these feminine qualities. I have frequently needed to remind myself to "trust the process," to "allow" the lucid dreams to come, and be receptive to all the cycles and rhythms within myself as I went deeper into my unconscious mind and deeper into the lucid state.

In addition to balancing the yin and the yang, there seems to be another important quality that governs the conscious inducement of lucid dreaming. I would call it a deep sense of inner readiness. I do not know whether this internal readiness has to be felt consciously by each particular seeker. Yet I have come to believe that it is somehow crucial to the outcome of each person's experiment. In my own particular case this sense of

* According to Chinese philosophy, everything in the universe is composed of a mixture of yin and yang, the feminine principle and the masculine principle. The Chinese, however, applied these concepts not only to the psyche and to human relationships, but to every part of the physical and natural world and, by extension, to the entire cosmos as well.

readiness was quite conscious and strong. For several weeks before I actually began my experiment, I began to sense some quiet and gentle prodding within myself, like a persistent inner voice that kept saying to me: "Now! Now! Now is the time to begin." This quality of readiness also seems to be present in those students who eventually reach the lucid dream state, learn how to prolong and maintain their lucid dreams, and receive the numerous benefits and joys that they have to offer. What creates this state of internal readiness, whether conscious or unconscious, within the individual aspirant? At this point in time I do not know. At best I can only speculate that it too is some kind of free gift, given by some source that is beyond our control or rational understanding.

It may seem strange for some of my readers to hear the implications for popular mysticism that I have emphasized throughout this book. Many, perhaps, do not believe that "mystical experiences" and "peak experiences" happen to a sizeable number of ordinary people. Many times, as a teacher and seminar leader, I have taken a classroom poll of my students, asking them to raise their hands in response to such questions as: "How many of you have ever actually seen a vision?" "How many of you have had an experience of extreme bliss or cosmic ecstasy, without the assistance of mind-altering chemicals?" Usually about 60 percent of each class will raise their hands, answering "yes" to these questions. Then, after their show of hands, I usually follow with another question: "How many of you have spoken of these experiences, communicating about them to another person?" Usually, at this point, approximately 10 percent of each class or group will signify "yes" by raising their hands. Then I ask: "How many of you have *never* spoken of your experience to anyone?" Often about 40 to 50 percent of the class will answer "yes" to this question.

I have often been impressed by the natural reticence that many people seem to feel in talking about their own religious or visionary experiences. These experiences are some of the most private, sensitive and delicate areas of our lives, and in general I think we are wise to guard them carefully. However, it is also possible and even probable that when people feel sufficient support, respect and trust from others, they will become more willing to speak about these most intimate events. In surrendering this heretofore private communication, we enter into one more aspect of the surrender of the ego. Many people today, I believe, are crying out on the inside for this very kind of communication, or perhaps I should call it communion. My fondest wish in writing this book is to contribute to a growing social and spiritual context in the world today, where more and more of us are seeking and finding this kind of communion. As T.S. Eliot said so well: "Mankind will have communion, in one way or another."

I fully intend to continue my experiment with lucid dreaming. Reluctantly and because of the limitations of space and time, I must bring this part of my account to a conclusion. Even now, I am wondering what I would say if I rewrote this book ten or twenty years hence, and wondering what new discoveries I might make in that time that would warrant a sequel to the present volume.

As I examine and appreciate the many things I have learned from my experiment, my thoughts return to the very beginning of the experiment and to deeper reflection on the "basics" from which the experiment was launched. Recently I received another lucid dream that refocused this issue in my mind once again. The theme and principal images of this dream have filled me with a deep sense of tranquility every time I reflect on them.

BABY HANDS: BACK TO BASICS
April 25, 1984

I have been dreaming for some time and I see my right hand. I look at it very closely and carefully, bending down close to it. I think that if I see my hands in my dream it could become a lucid dream. Now I see both hands, and I say aloud several times: "I see my hands in my dream; I *know* I am dreaming." I feel a definite and familiar energy shift inside myself and the quality of my consciousness changes as I enter the lucid state. My head feels very light and very clear.

Now my hands gradually shrink down in size until they remind me of Erik's hands when he was about four years old. They are plump, pudgy and cute, like a baby's hands. I realize very clearly that there is something very basic and elementary about lucid dreaming that I need to relearn. I am going back to the beginning to learn it all over again. I wake up feeling a lot of mixed emotions and wondering what the basic lesson is.

As I turned these images and ideas over and over in my mind, I felt amused to realize that my son, Erik, was four years old when I first began my experiment with lucid dreaming. I began to return in my reflections to that time in my life and felt the excitement of my original expectations once again. In this dream, *my* hands became like baby hands. Now these hands were somehow guiding me back to the beginning and back to the basics. For several days after this dream arrived I asked myself repeatedly: "What is the basic lesson about lucid dreaming that this dream urged me to remember?" Eventually an answer emerged. It was time again to re-examine my original, basic motives. So I asked myself, "What was my basic motive for this project? What was it in October, 1980? What is it now? Did it change along the way? Did the basic motive become sidetracked or corrupted by ego concerns?"

I remembered reading in Scott Sparrow's work,[*] based on the Edgar Cayce readings, that the prime motivating force for pursuing lucid dreaming has to be some spiritual ideal. This spiritual ideal, according to Cayce, could best be symbolized by a single word and the word could be used as a mantra, a device for keeping our awareness centered on the ideal. The ideal that I had originally chosen was the word "love." Had my

* Sparrow, *op. cit.*, pp. 54-57.

experiment always been motivated by love? I had to conclude that my answer was "no." Then I performed an act of self-love by not expecting perfection or full consistency of myself, by forgiving myself if I had deviated from my ideal, and by choosing to purify my basic motive with a gentle hand now that I realized the need to do so.

As I reflected further on my lucid "baby hands" I realized that I am still a beginner on this path of lucid dreaming. In this realm an honest, alert seeker would always regard himself or herself as a beginner, always cultivating the attitude of the "beginner's mind" toward a dimension of life that is so mysterious and replete with endless possibilities. I also remembered that the deliberate use of the lucid dream for personal growth originated many centuries ago, in a spiritual and religious context, the Tibetan Buddhist school of meditation, where the cultivation of lucidity in dreams was known as "the yoga of the dream state."* This yoga, or pathway toward union with the divine, was but one of a whole series of pathways through which the advanced students of Tibetan Buddhist meditation passed as they continued to work on their inner life. This discipline that springs from one of the world's great religious traditions can certainly be adapted to other religious traditions and cultures as well, as my experiment and the writings of Patricia Garfield, Scott Sparrow and Stephen LaBerge have amply demonstrated. As we now begin to study and explore the lucid dream state in our own culture, it will be most important to remember its original parentage and its basic spiritual and religious nature. This basic remembrance will become increasingly important here in the West, as more and more professional pyschologists and researchers study lucid dreaming with their vast array of scientific and laboratory equipment, using the basic attitude of the scientific method.

* W.Y. Evans-Wentz, *Tibetan Yoga and Secret Doctrines*, pp. 215-222.

If the lucid dream becomes excessively secularized, its spiritual dimension could easily be overlooked. Like a beautiful flower scrutinized under the rays of a high intensity lamp, it could all too easily wither and die. In a context that is spiritually barren the lucid dream could all too easily become just another "object" of scientific inquiry, wilted by the hot desert wind of contemporary rationalism and scientism.* It is imperative now, I believe, especially for professionals exploring this newly developing field, to understand and to heed this concern. Otherwise, this field of human discovery and human inquiry could, in a very short time, become filled with credentialed "experts" who pretend to know a great deal about lucid dreaming and who in some sad and empty way know very little.

To go back to the basics for me has meant to remember those qualities of the heart that can guide one's approach to the lucid state with the purest of motives. These are the motives of surrender of the ego and love for the Self within. The baby hands in my dream clearly reminded me of this childlike state of mind and its qualities of simplicity, directness and openness that foster the life of the Spirit. "Unless you become like little children, you cannot enter the kingdom of heaven."** The lucid dream state is truly an inner kingdom. This older word "kingdom" has now been replaced by our modern word "state," as we speak of a "state" of mind and a "state" of consciousness. But the inner reality which both words convey is one and the same, and it transcends time, history and culture. Just as "the kingdom of heaven is within,"† so too the

---

* The distinction between genuine science and scientism is a vitally important one. True men of science, such as Albert Einstein, Albert Schweitzer, and Louis Pasteur, have held a deep respect for the ultimate mysteries of the universe, a reverence for life, and a personal affiliation with spirituality in some form. Above all, they were keenly aware of the limitations of the scientific method and did not pretend to explain or understand everything with the limited categories of reason, logic and science.

** Matthew 18:3.

† Luke 17:21.

kingdom-state of the lucid dream lies within each person, waiting to be awakened and brought into our conscious awareness.

In many ways, the mystical poets have said it best. Down through the centuries they have spoken of these inner realities with force and clarity. William Blake wrote: "If the doors of perception were cleansed every thing would appear to man as it is, infinite."* In the lucid dream state, we are now discovering a very concrete way to stand at the doors of perception and marvel at the clarity of which we are truly capable. Sensing the awesome beauty of this "kingdom of consciousness," this altered state, many of us may pause and reflect before we open these doors of perception and volunteer to pass through. A whole new world awaits us on the other side.

My "baby hands" are an image that brings my journey and my experiment to a full circle, to a place where an arbitrary ending to this account could perhaps be made. These "baby hands" have become a powerful, though tender, teacher reminding me of that original purity of motives with which the journey began. These tender, young hands frequently call out to me now: "Ken! Return to the source. Remember your inner child. Purify your motives once again; repurify them at regular intervals in your journey. Surrender and keep on surrendering. Your inner child shall lead you. The divine Light is the gift of the Magi; the divine child brings that Light into the world; the divine child brings the fullest joy; the divine child brings the peace that passes understanding. This child brings the love that heals all pain. Ken! Remember the child. Ken! Remember the Light!"

My full circle has led me to a special ending, to an image which has carried me back to the beginning of my experiment. I have seen that beginning anew, and have loved it once again with a renewed freshness.

* William Blake, "The Marriage of Heaven and Hell," *The Portable Blake*, p. 258.

Pausing here now, as if at an oasis, I remember the words of T.S. Eliot:

> *"We shall not cease from exploration*
> *And the end of all our exploring*
> *Will be to arrive where we started*
> *And know the place for the first time."**

---

* T.S. Eliot, *Four Quartets*, p. 59.

PART II

Understanding the Experiment:
An Evaluation

CHAPTER TEN

Toward a Descriptive Definition of the Lucid Dream State

"Any man who bows down to no one will some day be crushed by the burden of his own weight."

—Fyodor Dostoevski

The basic definition of the lucid dream, one that most contemporary psychologists and dream researchers have more or less agreed upon, is: A lucid dream is a dream in which the dreamer knows that he is dreaming while he is dreaming. This basic definition as well as the term "lucid dreaming" were created by Celia Green in her ground-breaking book, *Lucid Dreaming* (1968). Even though the definition is succinct and straightforward, some people seem to have initial difficulty in grasping the concept or in applying it consistently, perhaps because of its very simplicity. Knowing from my own teaching experience that students sometimes have a tendency to make things difficult, I have felt the need to provide here an elaborated "descriptive definition" of lucid dreaming. I will proceed in two sections: First, I will describe what the lucid dream is *not;* second, I will describe what it *is.*

207

SECTION I: What the Lucid Dream Is Not

The lucid dream is not the hypnagogic state. In lecturing to audiences on lucid dreaming, I have frequently met people who assured me that they have had lucid dreams, and who then proceeded, usually with great animation, to tell me of an experience that most psychologists would classify as the hypnagogic state of consciousness.

The hypnagogic state is that borderline state of consciousness that occurs between wakefulness and falling asleep. Most people can readily experience this state. In it a person is aware of the images that are coming from his or her unconscious mind, sometimes a single image or sometimes a series of images that form a sequence and fit together like a dream. In the hypnagogic state one is able to exercise some conscious control over these images because one is still partially awake. Furthermore, in this state a person may focus his attention on any of these images at will or choose to let one image pass in favor of selecting another on which to focus. Or, he may ignore the images altogether and allow himself to "fall asleep" and go completely unconscious. Or, with some deliberate effort, a person could pull himself up and out of the hypnagogic state and return fully to the waking state.

Although there are some similarities between the lucid dream state and the hypnagogic state of consciousness, the two states are not identical. Their prime similarity is that in both states a person knows that he could, if he chose, exercise some conscious direction over the images that are rising into consciousness. One of the major differences between the two states, as I see it, is positional. The hypnagogic state lies between wakefulness and unconsciousness, whereas the lucid dream lies completely within the normal dream. I will discuss this item in more detail later in this chapter. Thinking in spatial terms for a moment, we could say that the lucid dream state lies completely surrounded by the normal dream state, much as the city of Sacramento lies completely surrounded by the state of California.

Sometimes the hypnagogic state can be used as a vehicle for entering the lucid dream. (Please see chapter seven where examples of this technique are described.) However, even in these instances, it is clear that the two states are distinct, and the dreamer usually has a clear awareness of crossing the boundary as he or she passes from the hypnagogic state into the lucid dream. Once the dreamer has fully entered the lucid state by this means, he or she usually loses contact with or interest in the hypnagogic state, leaving it behind as the lucid dream unfolds.

The lucid dream is not the experience of waking up in the middle of the night. Some dream researchers have begun to refer to the lucid state as one in which the dreamer is "awake" in his sleep or "awake" in his dream.* The term "awake" could be misleading here if the reader interprets it literally. The term "awakening" in reference to lucid dreams is a metaphor, analogous to the concept of a spiritual awakening as propounded in many of the religious and mystical traditions of the world. The term *awakening* as used in this context is an attempt to describe the definite shift in consciousness that occurs as the dreamer moves from one level of awareness to another, as he moves from the normal dream into the lucid dream. This shift of consciousness often feels like an expansion or opening and is often quite exhilarating, so that it is easily compared to an awakening. However, this awakening to a new level of consciousness occurs *within the normal dream.* As I have elaborated at length in the text, in a normal dream we awaken *from* the dream, whereas in a lucid dream we awaken *in* the dream.

In most of the lucid dreams that I have personally experienced, I knew with certainty, after becoming lucid, that I had not awakened from my sleep. Recent laboratory dream research has demonstrated conclu-

---

* Stephen LaBerge, *Lucid Dreaming, passim.*

sively that lucid dreamers are normally still asleep as they become lucid and as they progress onward through the lucid dream.* These laboratory subjects were definitely observed by the researchers to be still asleep after they had become lucid and after they had signaled to the researchers by a prearranged means that they had entered the lucid state.

The lucid dream is not identical to the pre-lucid dream. In a pre-lucid dream the dreamer may be on the verge of or very close to becoming lucid. In these dreams the dreamer typically asks, "Am I dreaming?" or "I wonder if this is a dream." Or, he may say, "This couldn't be a dream," in a type of voluntary denial. In these types of dreams, although the crucial question of lucidity has been posed, it remains unanswered and unclear in the dreamer's mind. Pre-lucid dreams are of special value because the dreamer is at least raising the creative question about lucidity and pointing his attention in that direction. Usually these dreams are important as self-confirmatory steps along the path to lucidity, assisting and stimulating the dreamer to persevere in becoming fully lucid.

Pre-lucid dreams are also characterized by other phenomena, such as false awakenings,** flying dreams, or seeing one's cue for lucidity in the dream without subsequently becoming lucid. Since the technique of seeing one's hands in one's dream† has worked so well for me, I have recommended it generally to all my students. Many have subsequently reported dreams in which they saw their hands in their dreams, but did not become lucid. I now refer to this process as "missing one's cue" and regard it as another important and amusing aspect of the pre-lucid dream. The partial

---

* *Ibid.*
** The false awakening is a common dream phenomenon in which the dreamer *dreams* that he awakens. Usually this part of the dream is so literal and convincing that the dreamer does not realize that he is still dreaming. Upon awakening, however, he is often surprised to realize that the earlier "awakening" was actually a part of his dream.
† See my own experiments described at length in the text in chapter two.

clarity of mind that often develops with the pre-lucid state is a valuable and enjoyable harbinger of things to come. The *full clarity* of the lucid state, however, will be recognized by its intensity and impact when it eventually arrives.

The lucid dream is not identical to self-observation in the dream. A dreamer may be a completely neutral, objective and impartial observer of himself in a normal dream as well as in a lucid dream. The experience of being the observer could occur in either type of dream and is, therefore, not one of the essential characteristics of the lucid dream.

The lucid dream is not identical to being completely in charge in one's own dream. It is possible for a dreamer to exercise full power and authority in his or her dream without becoming lucid. Many professional dream therapists and dream students are by now quite aware that people can be trained to fight back successfully in a dream in which they are attacked or threatened by some dream adversary. In many cases these dreamers have learned and developed this technique by giving themselves the suggestion in the waking state that they will fight back in a conflict situation in the dream state. In effect, this is a basic form of self-hypnosis, in which people have learned that they can use the power of suggestion and intentionality to influence the outcome of future dreams. For most people the successful counterattack and the transformation of a potential nightmare into a dream with a happy ending is an exciting, or even exhilarating, experience. I have had such dream victories and dream transformations many times and I can endorse this concept and technique wholeheartedly.* However, this method, popularly known now as the Senoi method, can be used without becoming lucid in the dream.

Judging from my own dream experiences and from the dreams of students and clients, there seems to be one salient feature distinguishing the transformation of

* Cf. Patricia Garfield, *op. cit.*, chapter five.

nightmares in lucid dreams. That feature is tremendous ease. In the lucid dream, where the dreamer is fully conscious that the enemy who is attacking is a dream image, the dreamer usually responds to the attack with the greatest of ease, fullest of courage, and with extensive creativity in finding a solution. These qualities emerge from a state of mind in which fear is usually totally absent. Therefore, a lucid dreamer, for example, could easily change a ferocious charging lion into a singing canary in a split second simply by holding the thought of such a transformation in his mind. And if this particular lucid intention failed to transform the charging lion, it is quite probable that some other highly imaginative and creative solution to the conflict would appear in its stead. This element of unpredictable creativity always remains possible in lucid dream scenarios and is part of the delight of lucidity. A threatened lucid dreamer, then, can usually project any thought, conscious or unconscious, from within his own mind into his surrounding dreamscape and thereby transform his dream scenario simply by wishing for a transformation to occur.

Being completely in charge in one's own dream, then, can occur in either the normal dream or within the lucid dream. In the lucid dream, however, the dreamer often expends much less effort in such transformational work and feels a much greater sense of ease in the ownership and exercise of this creative power.

Lucidity, essentially speaking, is not a power for exercising "control" over the dream; it is rather a conscious opportunity to be "in charge" within the dream. Although some readers may deem this distinction to be inconsequential, I have come to believe that it offers a substantial contribution to our understanding of lucidity and to our use of the lucid state for expanding personal growth. This distinction is much more than a matter of semantics. It expresses a concept that I believe is vital to our precise understanding of the lucid dream state.

I think it is unfortunate that the term "dream control" has become so widely used in dream literature in recent years. I have always found this terminology to be somewhat misleading, because in an indirect way it advocates the impossible. It is impossible for the conscious mind to control the unconscious, even in a lucid dream, and in my opinion such control would be a most undesirable state of affairs anyway, even if it were possible to attain.

Based on my personal experiences and in listening to the lucid dreams of others, I have concluded that the lucid dreamer, at best, is able to *take charge of* his personal experience within the dream but is not actually able to *control* the dreamscape itself to any great extent. With lucidity, the dreamer can shift and move his own dream body about with greater freedom and dexterity so as to suffer no harm or even fear of harm in the dream. He may also, through his power of visualization, be able to control or change the dream-scape around him for a while, but usually only for a limited time. The tremendous power of the unconscious mind seems to be able to reassert itself at almost any time during a lucid dream, making any attempt at "control" on the dreamer's part tenuous or temporary at best. Witness, for example, the frequency with which a lucid dream scenario, controlled for a time, can suddenly flip about and go completely beyond the dreamer's control once again. Or witness how a so-called controlled lucid dream can abruptly end, vanishing completely from the dreamer's field of vision. Or witness how a controlled lucid dream could abruptly change and, in a flash, present the still lucid dreamer with a whole new dreamscape. All of these possibilities, well known to experienced lucid dreamers, will force us to redefine the term "dream control." To summarize this point, a lucid dreamer could remain completely in charge of his own experience throughout any of the above variations, and retain his poise, balance and fearlessness in the face of them all. But to be fully in charge of self during a lucid dream is a concept quite distinct from controlling the dream scenario or the dream environment.

What, then, is the essential difference between exercising control over the dream and being in charge of oneself within the dream? To exercise control is to regulate, dominate, and manipulate the elements of the dreamscape, that is, to focus one's attention primarily on the world *outside* of oneself. By contrast, to be in charge within the dream is to be empowered internally, that is, to focus one's attention primarily on the world that exists *inside* of oneself. Perhaps the best way to make this distinction clear is to use an analogy. In the lucid dream, the dreamer is like the skillful, conscious sailor who is in charge of his sailboat as it moves about in a powerful and highly unpredictable environment. In a sailboat, the sailor is surrounded by powerful forces of different kinds, the currents of the water, the pulling of the tides, the changing speed and direction of the winds. If he is conscious of all these forces, he can seek to align his craft with them all in such a way as to achieve the greatest feeling of satisfaction and personal power. A conscious or "lucid" sailor knows he cannot control the forces of nature nor would he even think in those terms. Instead, he concentrates fully on moving *with* the elements, feeling, thinking, living and acting in harmony with them. Out of this awareness, this empowerment through surrender of the ego, he learns how to be in charge of his craft. He maintains a constant vigilance toward the changings of these forces around him so that he and his craft can shift when the larger forces shift. In a way, the conscious sailor becomes one with his craft, and his craft becomes an extension of his own consciousness. As the sailor masters this art of attunement, flexibility and instant realignment with nature, he becomes both a more powerful and a more sensitive helmsman. Essentially, the lucid dreamer is like this helmsman. His greatest satisfactions will come from those lucid dreams in which he was most alert in caring for himself, as all of the elements and energies within the dreamscape were moving and surging around him.

In lucid dreams, the symbols and characters in the dreamscape always retain a life of their own. They can change, shift or simply vanish altogether in an instant. Like his counterpart, the lucid sailor, the lucid dreamer will experience his greatest pleasures and satisfactions not only from his moments of greatest alertness and mental clarity, but also from his moments of fullest surrender of the self, and from feeling his deepest harmony and oneness with the Tao, the cosmos and with the forces of the unconscious. In summary: In a fully lucid dream the dreamer is in such a state of inner enlightenment where he is so fully in charge of his inner world that he would not be seriously tempted to control the outer world around him as a means of caring for himself.

Having concluded this section on the "negative definition" of the lucid dream, let us now turn our attention to those qualities and characteristics that describe the lucid dream in positive terms.

SECTION II: What the Lucid Dream Is

The lucid dream is an altered state of consciousness occurring within the normal dream. Since normal dreaming can be spoken of as an altered state of consciousness, it would be accurate, then, to describe the lucid dream as an "altered state within an altered state." Many of the qualities of normal dreams, such as flying, telepathy, levitation, symbolization, etc., are readily found within lucid dreams. In addition, there appears to be a certain set of qualities and characteristics that are unique to the lucid state, and I will attempt to itemize the most prominent of these in the pages that follow.

In the lucid state, the dreamer is experiencing two or more levels of awareness occurring simultaneously. (On one occasion I became conscious on as many as six levels at once within a lucid dream that occurred during my experiment.)* Theoretically, I am currently speculating that this expansion of human awareness could extend to many levels at once, perhaps up to infinity. In a typical lucid dream, as soon as the dreamer becomes lucid, he often feels his consciousness "rise" to the second level (lucidity), from which vantage point he now responds to the normal dream which is usually still in progress. There is usually a definite "energy shift," a "rise in consciousness," a feeling of "expansion" or "awakening" accompanied by a strong mental clarity that frequently occurs at this point. In many instances, the whole quality of the dream changes markedly at the onset of lucidity, and the change is usually quite noticeable to the dreamer, both immediately within the dream and afterward when the dreamer recalls the dream in the waking state. From this second (lucid) level of awareness, the dreamer will often automatically respond to the ongoing dream scenario in new and expansive ways. He or she may simply observe the dreamscape, but observe it with a most intense *clarity,* similar to, but usually much more vivid than, the clarity sometimes experienced in a deep trance state in hypnosis. He may actively intervene in the sequence of events in the dream, in order to "play" with the elements of the dream, or in order to create a positive outcome for a scenario that is ambiguous or potentially negative. Or, the dreamer may experience a full "surrender of the ego" in the lucid dream, knowing that he has absolutely nothing to fear, since he knows

---

* See in chapter eight "The Majestic Mountain" and the commentary following it as an example of multilevel awareness experienced in a lucid dream state. Also see in chapter three "The Gift of the Magi" as an example of simultaneous trilevel awareness in a lucid dream.

with full certitude that the images he sees are a dream. There are many other aspects of consciousness that develop from this "second level" of awareness which cannot be fully itemized here. They are mentioned and described in further detail throughout the text.

Sometimes, at the moment in which the dreamer becomes lucid, the "rise" in his consciousness and energy will be felt as a very powerful jolt, causing the dreamer to awaken immediately from the dream. With continued practice, however, the dreamer can eventually learn how to sustain this extra energy burst that arrives with the onset of lucidity and can learn to retain lucidity and progress toward a satisfactory completion of the dream. Over a period of time, then, it appears that the lucid dream state becomes some sort of psychic laboratory in which a person learns how to tolerate, integrate, experience, channel and use higher and higher levels of consciousness or spiritual energies.

Some lucid dreams are mystical or "peak" experiences by their very nature. From my own experiment with lucidity, I have had a number of lucid dreams that I can only classify in this category. Speaking for myself, I would have to say that the most memorable and empowering of my lucid dreams were of a specific spiritual nature, in their themes, symbolism and overall context.* Some of these symbols were explicitly Christian and some were more reminiscent of Eastern religions. In both cases it was not the symbols that were most important to me, but rather the Light that each conveyed. In these lucid dreams, I was fully clear that the symbols were the vehicles for the Light and that the Light itself was the highest value, the value beyond all vehicles and the value beyond all values. It is important to remember that lucid dreaming was originally used by certain ancient Tibetan Buddhist meditation masters as a special technique for the training of their disciples. Hence, in its earliest human origin, as far as can

---

* See "The Gift of the Magi" in chapter three and "The Arrival of the Serpent Power" in chapter six as two examples of lucid dreams in this category.

presently be determined, lucid dreaming emerges from a spiritual context. In the Buddhist tradition the development of lucidity in the dream state was referred to as "the yoga of the dream state" and "the dawning of the clear light."*

On the other hand, most lucid dreams are not overtly spiritual or mystical in their content or symbols. Many contain symbols that are generally comparable to those of normal dreams. Not all lucid dreams are especially exhilarating or inspirational either. Some can feel quite ordinary or even routinely dull from time to time, even though the dreamer may be fully lucid. Thus, there seems to be a wide spectrum to lucid dreaming and its scope will vary tremendously, according to the beliefs, expectations and personalities of the dreamers, and according to the various changes and mental rhythms that will invariably occur within the life of any one dreamer over an extended period of time.

The lucid dream is often marked by high degrees of intense pleasure and heightened sensual acuity that distinguish it from ordinary dreaming. The dreamer often feels an elevation of pleasurable emotions in the lucid dream, so that its impact may easily remain in his conscious awareness for days, weeks, months or even years afterwards. In particular, lucid dreamers often report experiences of ecstasy, frequently sexual ecstasy, that feels very fulfilling. Sometimes, lucid dreams are very rich in their presentation of sensory delights in the form of vivid colors ("more vivid than the real world"), beautiful imagery, celestial music that is indescribably beautiful, a delicate sense of inner balance, and feelings of highly refined energies moving through the body. In such instances the dreamer is often at a loss for words upon returning to the waking state, and he or she may have great difficulty in describing the beauty of the dream experience, which may seem, upon awakening, to have taken place in some distant heavenly realm or lost paradise.

---

* Evans-Wentz, *Tibetan Yoga and Secret Doctrines*, pp. 215-242.

The lucid dream is characterized by an extraordinary degree of creativity, imagination and mental freedom. Although these qualities can easily appear in a normal dream, they seem to occur with a higher quality and frequency in the lucid dream. In the lucid state, the dreamer is more apt to approach a problem or dilemma with an attitude of possessing a high number of options. While confronting a difficult challenge, he or she is more likely to sense that the mind could almost be infinite, incredibly rich and varied in creating a solution to the problem, and that it could happen in the twinkling of an eye and with the greatest of ease.

In these instances, the lucid consciousness takes the dreamer beyond two of the most commonplace negative beliefs that plague the human race, namely, (1) that life is a struggle, and (2) that transformation can be achieved only after a long, arduous endeavor. In truth, the lucid dream power opens us up to the possibility that these negative beliefs can be transcended, first of all in the mind and eventually on the physical plane as well. The richness and vastness of this mental creative power are all-encompassing in the lucid consciousness. These riches are everywhere and appear constantly in the lucid state, an ever-beckoning invitation to create and enjoy moment by moment by moment. In the lucid state the dreamer is likely to feel, so to speak, the incessant drumbeat of the cosmos, as it throbs continuously from beat to beat. Each beat is a moment. Each beat is a special "now," and each beat is an eternity. In each second, in each moment, the creative possibilities of the mind are infinite, and the lucid dreamer can sometimes fully grasp this powerful truth, so full of human consequences.

In the lucid dream the dreamer may also easily have a totally different experience of time. Time is often no longer felt as a duration, a limitation or a prison. Rather, in the lucid state, the sequence of temporal moments is often experienced with great conscious acuity, and each moment, coming one after the other, is filled with power and opportunities. Or, on another level, in the lucid state time may be experienced as one great, eternal NOW, in which everything that happens in the lucid dream happens all at once, not in a way that is stressful, but in a way that speaks of totality and fullness, in a way that is uplifting and "full-filling" to the human spirit. This abundance of creativity and mental freedom is common in the lucid state primarily, I believe, because of the complete absence of fear. Thus, a lucid dreamer can experience firsthand the literal truth contained in the New Testament teaching: "Perfect love casts out fear."* After having a number of these kinds of transformation experiences in lucid dreams, one cannot help but speculate and wonder about the kind of world we could create for ourselves on the physical plane, if we were to eliminate and overcome our human fears.

The lucid dream is, above all else, a pathway toward a direct and personal experience of THE LIGHT. The term "lucid"** is, in my opinion, a most appropriate name for this type of dream because of the many beautiful ways in which the light appears and manifests itself in many lucid dreams. Lucid dreams commonly present numerous variations of sunlight, moonlight, starlight, etc. The light can appear anywhere in the lucid dreamscape, in the air, on the earth or under water. It sometimes emanates from objects, from the eyes of birds or animals, and from human faces and figures. Sometimes there is an other-worldly quality to the light and sometimes it looks like ordinary sunlight. Sometimes I have seen it radiate from one source in the dreamscape and sometimes from a myriad of similar and identical objects, such as raindrops, dewdrops, bubbles, or from each and every grape on an entire giant cluster of thousands. More than anything else, the appearance of the light with its endless variations and the countless ways in which it

* I John 4:18.
** "Lucid" is derived from the Latin root *lux*, meaning "light."

works its way in and out, over and under and through the fabric of such a lucid dream, eventually convinces the dreamer of the age-old philosophical/metaphysical premise that the essence of the material universe is light, and that matter and energy and light are, indeed, interchangeable.

In many lucid dreams, this gift of THE LIGHT is the ultimate gift, to which the dreamer feels connected and related in some highly personal way. The lucid dreamer is usually not a cold, neutral observer studying these beams of light, but more of an ardent seeker and a passionate lover who "delights in the light," savoring its beauty and joy in every detail.

I am convinced that the more anyone follows the path of the lucid dream, the more he or she will see that our prime human purpose in this world is to become enlightened, to fill ourselves with the essence of light, and eventually to become ONE with THE LIGHT. Our traditional Judeo-Christian scriptures have prepared the way for this inner synthesis through such teachings as "God is Light," "God is Love," and "God is One." The lucid dream state can carry us into the *experience* of these ancient truths, demonstrating how light and love are one, and how the ultimate grace is to be living in a state of mind where we are steeped in the oneness of love and light.

CHAPTER ELEVEN

Understanding the Benefits of Lucid Dreaming

"If our blindness has been with us for as long as we can remember, it becomes the only truth that we know."

—Merle Shain

"The real voyage of discovery consists not in seeking new landscapes but in having new eyes."
—Marcel Proust

Because of the complexity and newness of the field of lucid dream studies, I thought it would be helpful to provide here a brief outline of the benefits of lucid dreaming. Most students of psychology, parapsychology and spirituality are abound to raise the initial questions: What is the value of lucid dreaming? How could it benefit someone? In this chapter I will briefly describe some of the more evident benefits of lucidity in the dream state based upon my experience and observations thus far. I feel certain that many other benefits of the lucid dream will become better known later, with the further passage of time and with our deepened, collective understanding of this altered state.

First of all, lucid dreaming provides a person with an experiential base for seeing all of the cosmos as "lucid," that is, ultimately composed of energy and light, rather than dense, physical matter. My first emphasis here is on the word "experiential." Once the dreamer has experienced the light, his awareness is affected far more profoundly than if he were merely stimulated by a concept or informed by an idea. The lucid dream experience usually goes far deeper than the intellectual level of the mind. It can open the heart level and touch it deeply. It can also permeate the dreamer on the visceral level and evoke intense energies and sensations. Such an experience can move a person in the roots of his being, not only because a lucid dream might touch him on a deep level, but also because that person will realize afterwards that the lucid dream was his own experience rather than someone else's. The lucid dream experience, therefore, assumes a high value from the fact that it is direct and immediate, not "mediated" through another person or some social institution.

Once a person *knows* that the cosmos is ultimately composed of energy and light, he or she is likely to relate to the material world in a different way. No longer will the lucidly awakened person view things as mere things and objects as simply objects. Nor will he view people, animals, plants and all life forms quite so casually as before. The whole thrust of this new awareness leads a person toward seeing the unity of the whole cosmos and everything in it. In a way, the lucid dream becomes a natural antidote for the limitations of the five senses. Through this vehicle, a person can eventually redefine his physics and his cosmology, drawing upon his own lucid dream imagery and experiences as the basic building blocks for this transformation.

Lucid dreaming provides a person with a basis for cultivating an "energy consciousness" in his own mind. As a person becomes more aware of these basic laws of energy, there are certain positive changes that begin to occur. In interpersonal relationships, for example, a person becomes more aware of the *process* of communication as well as its explicit *content*. This allows a person to discern more quickly and clearly the essence of what is really being communicated. It allows a person to hear more clearly the "meta-messages" in human interactions, so that he can hear the message beyond the literal and spoken message. Lucid dreaming experiences intensify and accelerate the process in which the dreamer refines his consciousness to become more readily attuned to the subtle energies of people and the world around him and increasingly attuned to the subtle realms of his or her own inner life and feelings.

Through lucid dreaming a person can advance toward the further cultivation of intuition. Intuitive awareness can be a powerful and helpful assistant in seeing the world. It is developed, in part, by learning to be conscious of the inner voice, the inner image or the sudden flash that can go through the conscious mind. The lucid dream, because it is often so amazingly clear, allows us to continue to remember and focus on our dream images with high clarity after we have returned to the waking state. As we become increasingly conscious of our own dream imagery, we also become increasingly conscious of all types of imagery, and we learn to use it as one of the most effective communicative devices known to man. Primarily, we learn increasingly how to use inner imagery as a bearer of vital messages from our unconscious mind to our conscious mind. The unconscious is a vast storehouse of knowledge, sensitivity and insight that we carry about with us always as we travel through the world. In stages we can begin to notice how these images and metaphors from our inner depths will spontaneously and continuously come to mind as we interact with people and the world around us. These images often tell us exactly, in a very potent and distilled way, what is transpiring in the moment. To become more intuitive means, for one thing, to have a ready, conscious access to these images, as we realize that the unconscious mind is generating them constantly, non-stop, day and night, whether we are awake or asleep. In essence, the unconscious mind never ceases from its metaphoric outpourings, and its images are always potentially available to enter our conscious mind. Through the cultivation of lucid dreaming, a person becomes immediately and acutely aware of the perpetual generativity of the unconscious and deepens his or her understanding of how to benefit from it directly. In due time, the lucid dreamer will seek to apply this inner outpouring to his relationships in the waking world. This application can be called "building intuition," or moving toward a fuller ownership of the intuitive power.

Through lucid dreaming, a person can transfer the quality of mental lucidity into the waking state. One of the results of lucid dreaming is that the dreamer realizes the higher level of clarity of which he or she is capable. This clarity is in a positive way stunning to the mind, like the impact of a beautiful, clear day immediately after a rainstorm. Naturally the lucid dreamer carries some of the quality of the lucid state over into his or her everyday affairs in the waking state. This carry-over is a completely understandable and normal chain of events. It is not so much the result of a conscious effort as it is the natural human desire to extend and prolong any experience that is truly remarkable and enjoyable. Increased clarity of mind is an obvious asset and benefit to people wherever it can be created.

Through lucid dreaming, a person can learn to sense more quickly and clearly any negative forces that may be approaching and can learn how to get out of harm's way more quickly. As a person learns to read human energy patterns and to determine more clearly the vibrational quality of other people's thoughts, moods, feeling states, body language, etc., he can respond more effectively, more quickly, and above all more creatively. I like to think of this process as "Aikido of the mind" and it follows the basic principles of this Japanese martial art. Aikido is one of the most spiritual of the martial arts, a highly enlightened form of self-defense

225

and conflict resolution. The basic intent of Aikido is to practice total love for oneself *and* one's adversary, so that one can take care of (protect) oneself completely while not inflicting harm or retaliation upon one's adversary at the same time. To create these "win-win" solutions out of potential conflict situations requires a great deal of sensitivity, clarity and mental agility. The lucid state of mind helps to provide this clarity of perception more quickly. In avoiding mental traps and verbal pitfalls in interpersonal conversations, speed of perception is of the essence. The sooner one can spot the trap the more quickly one can respond internally, and therefore, the less energy will be drained in the dialogue and the more lovingly one can respond to the "adversary." The practice of mutual care and love in Aikido is based on something very real, namely, the maintenance of a high level of energy. It is so much easier to love others *in practice* when we ourselves are full of energy. Conversely, in moments when we are tired and drained, it is usually much more difficult to be loving in actual practice. A practical lover, therefore, will be someone who learns to do three things with his own energy: (1) become aware of and remain aware of his own energy level from moment to moment; (2) maintain his own energy at a high level; and (3) prevent others from draining his energy excessively. In the lucid dream state, the dreamer often feels an abundance of energy, clarity and love (total fearlessness) toward his dream adversary and from that abundance can often create loving and imaginative solutions to conflict. With practice and with a deeper understanding of these mental principles, the lucid dreamer can use that same mental acuity to create happier solutions for himself in the waking state as well.

Through lucid dreaming a person will often feel great surges of positive energy upon returning to the waking state. Quite commonly, lucid dreamers report that this uplift of energy will last all the following day or even for several days after the dream. This natural "high" can sometimes last for weeks, months or even years if the intensity and power of the dream are high enough. In my own case, I know that a certain number of my lucid dreams will inspire and elevate me for the rest of my life. The inspirational quality to these dreams has often assisted me to attune myself to the goodness, love and beauty of the physical world whenever and wherever I meet it. In the waking state, I am now more likely to seek out beauty and to appreciate it more keenly whenever I find it.

Through repeated experiences of lucid dreaming, a person is increasingly motivated to develop a "transformational consciousness." This transformational consciousness is characterized by a number of basic beliefs and attitudinal stances toward life. A person who harbors these beliefs is more likely to affirm to himself: (1) I believe that there is a solution for every conflict or problem I have; (2) I believe firmly in my own capacity to grow and change and I fully expect to grow and change as my life unfolds; (3) I believe in discovering my *full range* of options before I make an important decision; (4) I will never doubt or sacrifice my basic self-esteem no matter what pressures the world may put upon me; (5) I believe that I can, in a conflict situation, love myself and my adversary at the same time.

A transformational awareness is one that approaches any situation in life by steadily looking for the "creative response" that is appropriate to the situation. Here I am making a basic distinction between a response and a reaction. A reaction is an instinctual, automatic, unconscious behavior that sometimes can be destructive, such as revenge or vindictiveness, for example. A response, however, is a conscious choice, and if a person can exercise a creative response toward an aggressor, the outcome is more apt to be positive for everyone concerned. In the lucid state, lucidity allows the dreamer to ask: "What is the creative response that this current dream scenario calls for?" The lucid level of awareness assists the dreamer substantially to ask for, seek and find these creative responses as he moves through his dream world. Again, by inference and natural carry-over, the dreamer can at some point begin to exercise this powerful spiritual tool in the waking world as well. When encountering a distressful or negative situation in his waking world, the "lucid person" can mentally step back from his or her environment, can mentally affirm to himself that he will view the situation *as if it were a dream,* and then can ask: "What is the creative response that *this* situation calls for?" This method, consciously employed, is one of the more imaginative and powerful spiritual tools available for promoting lucidity in both the dream state and in the waking state as well. Applying this tool in both states is ideal for the promotion of transformational consciousness.

In the lucid dreaming state a person can see clearly the direct relationship between his own thoughts and his manifestable reality. Many of us already realize in some mysterious way that the thoughts we hold in our minds eventually create the reality or world in which we live. Sooner or later, our thoughts and attitudes manifest themselves to us on the physical plane in some tangible, material form. This ancient principle of cause and effect is one aspect of the law of karma in the Hindu and Buddhist traditions. This principle is also present in the Christian tradition as well, as stated in the New Testament: "As a man sows, so shall he reap."* However, in spite of its universality, it is still difficult for most of us to see this spiritual law of cause and effect in actual operation in our lives, because its workings are usually too subtle to be perceived by our present, normal levels of awareness. In addition, most of us are especially blind because of ego concerns when it comes to applying this powerful law to the particular details of our own lives. It is always easier to see how the law

* Galatians 6:7.

works for somebody else, especially for some famous or tragic figure in history. Also, this karmic law often requires a time span of many years before it is fully carried out on the physical plane, before it passes from cause to effect, from inner thought to tangible reality. This extensive time span can make it very easy for most of us to doubt the efficacy or even the existence of this mental principle.

But in the lucid dream state, a special psychological condition exists which removes the above-mentioned barriers to our perceptions. With lucid consciousness, the dreamer is suffused with both the creative *immediacy* and the creative *power* of his or her mind. In certain lucid dreams the dreamer will be able to hold a thought form in his mind, willing it to appear in the dreamscape, and then witness its immediate appearance in that particular dreamscape. The thought can manifest itself in the dream scenario at once. The spiritual, mental law of cause and effect can operate instantly in the lucid dream, and the power of sowing and reaping can be observed and studied unmistakably. The lucid dream provides a "psycho-spiritual technology," and a "psycho-spiritual laboratory," as it were, in which this karmic law can be practiced and witnessed firsthand by the dreamer himself. Throughout the text of this book, I have presented numerous examples of this process in lucid dreams. The repetition and reoccurrence of these dream experiences have led to a deepening of my own faith in this aspect of the law of karma and a sharpening of my perceptions of its operation in people's lives. Seeing is believing. Experiencing is *knowing* on the deepest level. In the lucid state, the dreamer, using his thought, conscious willing, and visualization can often create, de-create, and re-create the world that lies before him. After lucid dreamers have practiced and experienced this process a number of times, perhaps many hundreds of times, it becomes conceiveable that they will some day, perhaps in the not too distant future, seek out ways to carry over these mental practices into the waking state, into what most people now short-sightedly call "the real world." Clearly, there are many ethical considerations that are important here, and those who wish to study the lucid state seriously must at some point begin also to contemplate the creative and constructive uses for the exercise of this level of personal power.

Certain Hindu yogis and advanced spiritual masters have already claimed the ability to exercise and manifest these creative powers on the physical plane. For example, in his book *The Autobiography of a Yogi* Paramahansa Yogananda recounts an episode from the life of Lahiri Mahasaya, a Hindu yogi, who reportedly was able to visualize into existence a palace in the Himalayas, use it to gratify a residual desire of his ego, then dematerialize it at will after he no longer needed it.* These accounts seem absolutely unbelievable to most Westerners and yet, based on certain experiences in my lucid dreams, I have found myself more open to the possibility that they are true. My own lucid dream experiences have begun to lend more and more credence to Yogananda's account and to other similar claims from the spiritual traditions of the East. At this point, I have come to the conclusion that lucid dreaming can provide a safe training ground for initial and advanced levels of spiritual practice. It is a place where spiritual practitioners can work and play with the laws of mind and spirit that govern the subtle realms. It is a state where we can also learn about and resolve our numerous ego attachments, old karmic desires, and other obstacles that need to be resolved for the furtherance of our own spiritual growth.

Lucid dreaming usually adds to the spontaneity and vitality of our dream experiences. One of the most frequent objections that people raise to lucid dreaming is that lucidity will detract from the spontaneity of

* Yogananda, Paramahansa, *The Autobiography of a Yogi*, p. 314 ff.

dreams. Some are hesitant to tamper with their dream material in any way for fear that this will obstruct or interfere with the spontaneous messages of the unconscious. They fear that lucidity will become another tool for the ego, to repress or minimize the true messages that the unconscious seeks to deliver into the conscious mind. I think that this objection is well considered. Potential lucid dreamers will need to confront and explore this issue thoroughly, primarily through their own personal experiences. Upon doing so, I believe they will probably discover what I myself was pleasantly surprised to discover: that this particular problem was more theoretical than actual and that such anticipated fears were not borne out in actual practice.

At the beginning of my experiment, I also experienced some initial doubts and hesitations about the wisdom of consciously influencing my dream material. However, based on my own experiences, I have found that lucidity does not seem to act as an inhibitor of the unconscious, nor does the lucid level of consciousness generally take on some kind of adversary relationship toward the dreamscape, as if to suppress it, distort it for ego gratification, or manipulate it in any harmful way. Usually in most of my lucid dreams, lucidity is primarily characterized by an expansion of consciousness, one that includes rather than precludes the spontaneity of the unconscious. Take, for example, my lucid dream, "The Magical Rabbit," discussed in chapter two. In this dream, after I succeeded in mentally commanding the dreamscape to produce a rabbit, there was a sudden change of scene in which I saw the eagle floating in the air above me with its outstretched wings. Here the unconscious demonstrated its ability to reassert itself, eliminate the rabbit scene altogether, and suddenly present me with new material. This process has happened to me numerous times in numerous lucid dreams. In short, through repeated experiences, I have learned that lucidity adds to the spontaneity of the dream as it brings its own special form of higher consciousness into the dream. I have also learned that lucidity does not suppress the freedom and creative force of the unconscious, contrary to what some of my original hesitations and concerns about this possible danger might have been.

*Lucid dreaming can provide people with a natural experience of ecstasy.** In this context I refer to the experience as "natural" because it is not induced by drugs or chemicals of any kind. Rather, lucid dreaming seems to be induced primarily by a particular combination of emotional readiness and willingness to enter the lucid state. The ecstasy that I refer to seems to run the whole gamut of human possibilities, from intense sensual delights, indescribable sexual orgasms and pleasures, to peak mystical-spiritual experiences and everything that people can possibly imagine. Numerous examples of these ecstatic dream experiences are described throughout this book and in Patricia Garfield's work, *Pathway to Ecstasy: The Way of the Dream Mandala.*

One of the byproducts coming from my work with lucid dreams has been to deepen my own understanding of the value and role of ecstasy in people's lives. I have come to appreciate more clearly that human beings *need* ecstasy in one form or another. Some may seem to need more of it and others less, but everyone, I think, needs it to some degree. Some will seek it in one form and others in another. Ecstasy comes in many forms. Without ecstasy the human ego, both individually and collectively, soon becomes bound and limited within some ordinary set of experiences that ultimately proves to be too confining and restrictive for our total wellbeing. Human beings seem to need those special

---

* The word *ecstasy* is derived from the ancient Greek *ekstasis*, which means a "standing apart from." To experience ecstasy, therefore, is to stand apart from ordinary human experience at some particular moment in time and to be outside of or momentarily apart from ordinary consciousness. In certain cases, such as mystic trance states, it also implies that the person's consciousness may be somehow separated momentarily from the physical body.

moments when the ego can experience a liberation—a breaking out from the ordinary confines of its "reality." These special moments of breaking out are exhilarating, inspiring, and deeply nourishing to the human spirit. Without them, life could easily become oppressively barren.

The lucid dreaming state has the capacity to provide people with ecstatic and expansive experiences of many different varieties and levels. One general benefit from its cultivation is the opportunity to enter an ecstatic state of consciousness with increasing frequency and intensity. At first, when the seeker begins to touch this inner space, he or she may often awaken from the dream abruptly as soon as lucidity begins. This is usually because the onset of lucidity may bring such a powerful jolt of energy into the dreamer's mind that it may arouse him from sleep and from the dream. But with right intention and continued practice, the patient student can eventually learn how to become accustomed to this initial energy jolt and stay lucid for longer periods within the dream. As one continues with this discipline, one can gradually increase one's capacity for lucid ecstasy; that is, one can tolerate and process internally, longer and more elaborate dreams, as well as tolerate dreams that convey a higher level of energy and intensity. It seems that some kind of psychospiritual "muscle-building" or inner strengthening is a necessary prerequisite for sustained ecstasy in the lucid state, and would probably also be a welcome byproduct that regular lucid dreamers would develop over the years through continued practice of this method of personal growth.

The fullest integration of all of these experiences seems to be the unification of the lucid dream state with the waking state, the state we call normal consciousness. It is only natural that after receiving a taste of lucidity, a person would want to be in that state more and more, and eventually would desire to dwell there permanently. Eventually, a lucid dreamer would probably want to live lucidly and he would open up his mind to that possibility. At that stage a person would seek to advance from "getting high" to "being high" and from "becoming clear" to "being clear." This integrated level of existence would probably have some similarities to and parallels to the altered states of *satori* or *samadhi,* as referred to in the spiritual writings of certain Oriental philosophers and spiritual teachers. I believe that as a spiritually evolving culture we will have a need some day to discuss and evaluate these possibilities when enough people have practiced lucid dreaming and lucid living as a discipline for a sufficient length of time. Time and persevering practice, I believe, will have a great deal to tell us about this some day, and for now we must leave that judgment to the future.

In conclusion, I have to say that the terms lucidity, higher consciousness, enlightenment, clarity, ecstasy, pleasure, exhilaration and joy have all become synonymous for me as I reflect on my entire experiment. In short, that is what my experiment has been about, an increase of joy and en-joyment in my life. As Leon Bloy once said, "Joy is the infallible sign of the presence of God." Since the lucid dream is a joy, then it is, in itself, its own reward and its own benefit, pure and simple.

CHAPTER TWELVE

Expanding the Circle: The Availability of the Lucid Dream

"When we come to the last moment of this lifetime, and we look back across it, the only thing that's going to matter is 'what was the quality of our love?'"

—Richard Bach

Is the lucid dream readily available to the average person? From everything that I have learned by experience, reading and professional dialogue the answer seems to be "generally, yes." Many people have reported receiving occasional spontaneous lucid dreams at various times in their lives without any special desire or intention on their part to become lucid. A fair number of children that I have spoken to also report that they are aware of dreaming while dreaming, and even consider the experience to be so common-place that they often wonder why the phenomenon should merit any special attention. Some adults also express this kind of innocent puzzlement as they report that they are regularly aware of dreaming during their dreams but have never attached any special signifi-cance, importance or value to this inner process. I am reminded here of the early days of the petroleum industry, slightly over a hundred years ago, when numerous people were aware of the existence of petroleum in its crude state. They had certainly noticed from time to time the black, sticky liquid that often seeped from the earth in certain places, but they doubted it had any value or practical use and they certainly did not have the knowledge to work on refining it. Then a man named John D. Rockefeller entered this arena with his own vision of the future of petroleum—and the rest of his story is history.

One of the most common initial questions that dream students ask about lucid dreaming is: Can a person learn to dream lucidly if he or she wishes to do so? According to Dr. Stephen LaBerge, who has conducted extensive lucid dream research in the sleep laboratory at Stanford University, the answer again is "generally, yes." There are numerous methods and techniques available for teaching ordinary dreamers to become lucid dreamers. Many of these methods I have described throughout Part I of this book. According to Dr. LaBerge's findings as well as my own, it seems that a strong, sincere desire to develop lucidity is usually the first motivational requirement for such learning. For readers who wish to review a succinct compendium of methods and techniques for inducing lucidity, I refer you to chapter six in LaBerge's recent book *Lucid Dreaming* and to the appendix in Sparrow's earlier work, *Lucid Dreaming: Dawning of the Clear Light.*

Shortly after I had begun to receive lucid dreams on a regular basis, I decided that I wanted to design a seminar to teach others about the possibilities of the lucid state. I felt so amazed and excited about my experiment that I wanted to share it with others and see how they would respond to the material. I developed a sixteen-hour course and taught it to four different small groups in 1981-1982. About twenty-five people in all completed the course. Most of these students were adults between the ages of 25 and 60 who had studied and worked with me before in various other classes and dream workshops. The results from this short course were mixed. Seven students in these lucid dream classes reported receiving two or more lucid dreams during the

236

eight-week course, while the remaining eighteen students reported little or no changes in their dream life vis-à-vis lucidity. However, three students out of these eighteen subsequently reported receiving their first lucid dream some time *after* completing the course. I did not conduct a systematic survey to follow up on students regarding any other long-range results of the course. The circumstances of this project were not at all uniform, in that each student had his or her own levels of desire and motivation in taking the course, as well as a variation in consistency in doing homework assignments and practicing the basic visualization and self-hypnosis methods for inducing lucid dreams. I have not analyzed any of these preliminary results scientifically because that was not my principal desire or purpose in teaching the class. My principal desire was to deepen my own understanding of my experience, share it with others, and see if others could obtain similar results. Some students did and some did not.

My opinion about this disparity is that it stemmed from differences regarding the *internal readiness* of each individual person who approached the lucid state. I believe now that this readiness is not always known to the conscious mind. For some, it remains mostly within the realm of the unconscious and is difficult to discern with any degree of certitude. If a person is somehow not ready to enter the lucid state, then the passage probably will not happen. On the other hand, if a person is ready for this type of dream expansion, then it could easily happen and may even happen spontaneously without any inducements or specific training. The important initial question remains then: How is a person to know if he or she is ready to cultivate lucid dreaming?

The best answer that I can provide so far is to relate my own experience. My own sense of internal readiness, I believe, came in two stages. In stage one, I became theoretically informed about lucid dreaming from the reading I had done and from discussion of the topic with other professionals and students who were also interested in dreams. I felt intrigued with the possibilities of the lucid dream and had occasionally received one spontaneously. These occasional, spontaneous eruptions of the psyche were so beautiful and satisfying to me that I gradually became open to receiving more of them. In stage two, I began to feel a strange, difficult-to-define sense of internal readiness come over me. I have described this change in attitude in detail in chapters two and nine of this book. I believe now that this subtle change was the voice of the unconscious, gradually seeping into my awareness at a certain point in time and telling me in essence: "The time is now."

Even though I cannot say much more about this sense of internal readiness, I still believe that it is beneficial for people to know about, study and choose to induce lucid dreaming as a conscious exercise, because it appears that some conscious anticipatory spadework can be done successfully in advance of the seeker's internal readiness. I base this conclusion mostly on my own experience and on the reports of those students who received their first lucid dreams some time *after* they had taken the course. In essence, it appears that in the cultivation of lucid dreaming, we can prepare our conscious minds in advance, and then with an open and willing attitude we need to wait for the response of the unconscious, whenever and however it arrives. The unconscious, I believe, will have the final word about this whole process.

Of the seven students who reported having lucid dreams during the eight-week class, one was already a regular lucid dreamer before beginning the class. With the assistance from the class, however, she raised the frequency of her lucid dreams and enhanced their quality as well. All of these students remarked that their lucid dreams were definitely qualitatively different from their normal, ordinary dreams. In general, they described their lucid dreams as more enjoyable and pleasurable, and more exciting and satisfying than ordinary dreams. Quite commonly,

238

these dreams were described as more vivid than waking consciousness or "more real than real life." Oftentimes, upon awakening from a lucid dream, these new lucid dreamers would be filled with strong feelings of personal power and high energy that would carry over into the day with beneficial effects. Some reported lucid dreams in which sexual pleasure and orgasm were so intense and so satisfying that it was greater than any level of sexual satisfaction they had ever achieved in the waking state during lovemaking. These reports lend credence to the many powerful, orgasmic lucid dreams recounted by Patricia Garfield in her book, *Pathway to Ecstasy*. Almost all of the students reported experiences of flying and/or bodily levitation in their lucid dreams, often beginning with the onset of lucidity. These dreams of flying and levitation were also quite pleasurable and rewarding.

One of the most interesting phenomena surrounding dream inductions is the so-called "first-night effect." A certain number of people experience it when they begin to use self-hypnosis or other suggestion techniques to influence the content or quality of their dreams. The first-night effect is an instant response to the power of suggestion, in which the unconscious mind of the dreamer will produce the type of dream suggested on the very first night after the suggestion is given. The following ordinary dream is an interesting example of this first-night effect. The dreamer, Angela, is a woman in her mid-forties who participated in one of my lucid dream classes several years ago. Before taking the class, she had had an occasional lucid dream from time to time. At the time that she began the class, she seemed to be quite interested in expanding this aspect of her dreamlife.

This dream, "Golden Elixir," occurred during the night after the first class meeting. At the end of this first meeting, I had led the class through an exercise of deep relaxation and visualization, using Castaneda's induction technique of seeing one's hands in one's dream as the cue for stimulating the lucid dream.

GOLDEN ELIXIR
October 15, 1981

I am in the perfumerie of an elegant store. I am trying to decide on a new fragrance for me. There are two bottles on the glass counter, a smaller, rather nondescript bottle and a larger crystal bottle containing a golden liquid. The saleswoman leaves while I make my decision. I first pick up the smaller bottle and sniff the contents. I am disappointed by the bland and watery substance and cannot imagine why I even considered it. The bottle slips out of my hand onto the hard tile floor. Fortunately, no damage has been done; neither has the saleswoman noticed my gaffe. Carefully, I replace the smaller bottle on its glass shelf. The crystal bottle is what I want! I am attracted by its beauty and want to possess it. But as soon as I pick it up, it jumps out of my hand and dashes to the floor. I am horrified as pieces of crystal fly left and right. "What have I done?" I think in dismay. Gently and with great remorse, I pick up the bottle. It lies in the palm of my hand. Now despite the accident it looks strangely whole. The golden liquid has been exposed yet is not leaking out. It remains intact!

I know there is no way I can sneak out of the store without confessing my crime to the saleswoman. She, however, seems unconcerned by the whole business. "Don't worry," she says, "as long as none of this golden essence has escaped, nothing is lost. Besides, this is magical crystal and it heals itself very easily." She places the crystal bottle on the glass shelf next to the smaller bottle. By now the whole store is full of the heavenly fragrance of the golden elixir. A wistful longing remains with me as I gaze at the bottle. "I wish I could afford that bottle of perfume," I murmur by way of reply, "but $75 is just too much money."

When Angela reported this dream to the class at our second meeting, she seemed a bit uncertain about its importance or its message. Fortunately, I saw its importance at once as a pre-lucid dream, because in the dream she looked at the broken yet intact crystal bottle as it lay *in the palm of her hand.* In this dream Angela definitely saw her hand, but did not become lucid upon doing so. Quite simply, she missed her cue. When I pointed this out to her, her eyes lit up quite brightly and the rest of the class reacted with merriment. The suggestion technique had worked for her on the first night, and in this case the dreamer now needed to realize that she had missed her cue. The next step in the process would be for her to see her hands in a future dream and to recognize the cue in the dream state.

As we continued to open up the dream symbolism, it became clear to Angela that she was serious about approaching the lucid state. She acknowledged that the golden elixir was an apt symbol for the special beauty that could pervade her entire life, just as the heavenly fragrance of the perfume pervaded the entire store in her dream. As she put the pieces of her dream together, Angela saw that like everyone else who has ever considered approaching the light, she too must confront and resolve her feelings of ambivalence and inner resistances to the journey. Her "accident" in the dream was, of course, no accident. Rather, it was a meaningful event. In her dream, the crystal bottle, the container of the precious golden elixir, simply jumped right out of her hand. Angela, like anyone else on a conscious spiritual journey, will inevitably at times experience the elusiveness of grace as it slips right through her fingers. Like everyone else, she will make mistakes and unconscious blunders along the way. These "mistakes" and "accidents" are an inevitable and necessary part of her journey, and everyone's journey; they cannot be altogether avoided. This journey, according to the dream, is marked with miracles. In the end, the bottle was somehow miraculously restored to wholeness and remained intact. Also forgiveness, the greatest miracle of all, was abundantly available in this dream so that the dreamer only had to open herself up to forgiveness in order to receive it.

The dream ends on a perfect note, one that clearly

outlines the classic ambivalence that each seeker must resolve as he or she contemplates entry into the lucid state: wistful longing versus resistance about paying the high price. *"Can* I afford it?" is not the question. *"Will* I afford it?" is the clearest focus on this question as we begin to wonder what basic changes the lucid state may bring to our lives and whether each of us is willing to pay this price. These were some of the reflections and observations that we all shared with Angela as we explored her dream. She was quite receptive and took in these items of group feedback in a reflective and open spirit.

Eight nights later, shortly after the second class, Angela had a lucid dream which she aptly entitled "In Training."

IN TRAINING
October 23, 1981

I am watching football players on the field. They are wearing bright blue and yellow uniforms and are standing in formation down the line. The head man is juggling the ball back and forth in his hands. He is obviously eager to go, because he hops from one foot to the other marking time. At some given signal he is off, running down the line, and I watch him run around the perimeter of the field. Now he is approaching me and I am fascinated by the way he so cleverly plays with the ball. His hands seem to move like lightning! All of a sudden I realize I am dreaming; this is a dream and I am dreaming it! I become very excited and capture the football, thinking that now I can perform a similar juggling feat. But my excitement is making the ball less distinct and I get the feeling that I am not going to be able to hold on to it . . . or have much time, for that matter, to experience this new power. I look up at the ceiling and decide I must try a flying feat while I have the opportunity. I have no idea how to do this but I jump up off the floor and, to my amazement, find myself floating toward the ceiling. The shock of actually succeeding leaves me immobilized. The ceiling is very white and the brightness hurts my eyes. Disorientation and nausea hit me and I close my eyes tightly. At this point I awaken, feeling quite frightened.

I found this to be a rewarding follow-up dream for Angela, considering the overall context of her dream-world and her intention to become lucid. In this dream her attention was powerfully and repeatedly drawn *to the hands* of the chief football player. His unusual manual dexterity was fascinating to her. At the point where his hands appeared to be moving like lightning, she suddenly realized she was dreaming—using the football player's hands as her cue to become lucid.

Upon attaining lucidity, Angela became empowered, filled with excitement, and began to take charge in the dream. Her lucid dream realization was a classic one: "This is a dream, and *I* am dreaming it." Her sense of "I" was important, because it took her consciousness to a higher level of individual, creative power than had previously existed in the dream. At this point, she began to exercise her power in various ways in the lucid dream, by capturing the football and trying the juggling feat for herself. However, as many lucid dreamers experience in the beginning of their development, she then became flooded with her own excitement and power, and began to lose her clear perception of the dreamscape. Because of this emotional flooding, the football became less distinct in her field of vision and she began losing her balance in the lucid state. The emotional flooding within this lucid dream also created a sense of time pressure for Angela, and she soon felt compelled to fly instead of juggling the football. She felt she had to make a choice. Her flying then proved to be successful, which brought on still another exhilarating emotion, the shock of success, followed by immobilization. At the end, the powerful flood of Angela's emotions, including the disorientation and nausea, caused her to tighten up and to contract her dream body. The strong fear that she felt upon awakening is not uncommon under these circumstances. This fear was an essential and even a healthy part of her learning process because the lucid state invites us to identify and confront every one of our fears consciously. As Angela plunged into the experience of her own power in this lucid dream, she entered the floodstream of inner emotions as well. The dream clearly demonstrated the typical exciting and challenging prospects that are commonly found upon entering the lucid state.

I felt pleased with Angela's lucid dream experiment and she felt pleased with herself as well. For her, it was a promising beginning. Her lucid dream "training" had begun in earnest.

Another interesting example of a lucid dream came from a friend and colleague named George. George is an ordained Presbyterian minister, the pastor of a local church in Marin County. Over the years, we had both been participants in a small group of professionals, ministers, psychotherapists and educators, who met regularly to discuss our own dreams. From the beginning of our relationship, George and I shared a particular interest in lucid dreaming and in the spiritual dimension of dreamwork. We both made a regular practice of using our dreams in meditation and supporting our clients and parishioners in doing the same. In addition, George had one special, particular desire, vis-à-vis lucid dreaming; he strongly wished to meet Jesus in one of his lucid dreams and have a prolonged serious conversation with Him.

On the day after Thanksgiving, 1984, George and I met for a long and stimulating interview, updating our views and experiences on lucid dreaming. He told me of a long dream that he had had approximately one year earlier, the most beautiful and exciting lucid dream that he had ever had. Here is his account of the dream:

> I am going into a large, old mansion. It is intricate, multistoried and has many, many rooms. It is filled with beautiful furniture and is very elegant. I enter and as I walk down the hallway I see a mirror on the wall and an

unknown lady standing beside the mirror. As I look in the mirror I remember something that Stephen LaBerge and I had once talked about and suddenly I become lucid.* I say to myself, "Ah! A lucid dream!" I look into the mirror and it's fuzzy, though I can tell that the image is really me. What I really want to do is to examine myself very closely and look deeply inside myself, into my own eyes. The more I try to do this, however, the more foggy the mirror becomes, and so I try to clean the mirror with my mind by thinking to myself, "I want that mirror to be clear."** However, the harder I try, the more foggy the mirror becomes. Finally I say to myself, "Well, forget this!"

Now I look at the lady standing beside the mirror and I think to myself, "I don't want her to be here; I want Linda† to be here." And with that thought, the woman becomes Linda.

Now I say to Linda, "This is a lucid dream, and I want to go outside through the wall." So I go over to the wall and I put my hand against it to see if I can go through it and indeed I can. I step through the wall and turn around to wait for Linda to get through, and she can't get through. So I reach back through the wall, get hold of Linda's hand and pull her through.

Now we are walking uphill on a sidewalk in a typical San Francisco residential neighborhood. We are going up the left-hand side of the street and Linda starts to skip like a child in a very playful, light-hearted manner, saying over and over with lots of excitement, "We're lucid! We're lucid! We're lucid!" Her joy makes me feel very good.

Now we see an auditorium up ahead on the right side of the street and we decide to go inside. As we start to climb the outside steps I say to Linda, "Wait a minute. This is a lucid dream. We don't have to walk up these stairs. We can just fly!" With that, we fly up the steps

* In a prior waking-life conversation, George had once discussed with Dr. LaBerge his unfulfilled desire to meet and converse with Jesus in a lucid dream. LaBerge had suggested to George that he begin first by looking at himself in a mirror to become lucid, and that later in a subsequent dream he could create the desired encounter with Jesus.
** George had experienced the creative power of manifesting his thoughts in several prior lucid dreams. In these dreams he had been able to create the dreamscape by simply thinking or visualizing it into existence.
† Linda was the woman in his life at the time, whom he married about one year later.

into the auditorium. Inside, the auditorium is sparsely filled and there is a play going on. We are walking up a staircase now to find a seat to watch the show. A man comes out of his seat and deliberately and aggressively stands in our way. I say to myself, "This is a lucid dream and no harm can come from this, so I'm going to kick this guy in the nuts." With that I kick him in the testicles and he folds up with great, shrieking convulsions.* We proceed to walk up to the top of the stairs. Once we arrive at the top of the stairs, we decide not to stay for the show after all and we walk outside.

Now we are in a business section with many shops along the street. All the shops are closed. We are walking on the right side of the street and we look into one of the shops, an art gallery. There are paintings on the walls and I see a special piece of sculpture sitting close to the floor on a little pedestal. It has a small decorative fence all around it. I say to Linda that I am going to go inside to examine the sculpture. I walk right through the window and study the sculpture very closely and then I remember, "Ah! What I really want to do in lucidity is to have a conversation with Jesus." I sit down and begin to meditate, using the same techniques I use in my regular meditation. I begin to have some of the same experiences I have had in deep meditation, that is, remembering past lives** and remembering past lives with Linda. Then I remember Linda and I say to myself, "Wait a minute! I wonder if Linda has been able to get through the window." So I open my eyes from the meditation and I look back. Sure enough, Linda has not been able to get through. So I stand up and walk to the window. I reach through and try to pull Linda through the glass. At this point I lose the lucidity and return to an ordinary dream. A few moments pass and I wake up.

I had a delightful time interviewing George about this dream, mostly because he displayed so much energy

---

* George added a comment here, that in ordinary waking life he would be extremely diplomatic if anyone confronted him in such a rude way. But in the dream he acted differently and released his own aggression instantly to counter the aggressor in the dream.

** George added here that it was more of a feeling than a remembering, very much like stepping through a large paper hoop, leaving an old reality behind and breaking through into a new reality on the other side.

and enthusiasm for it and for the many rich and varied experiences that it conveyed. I asked George how he had used this dream in his waking life and his first reply was that he had not interpreted it at all. I was not surprised because like so many lucid dreams, this one too seemed to propel the dreamer beyond the level of interpretation. George said that the dream has served, above all, to whet his appetite for more lucid dreams simply because it was such a marvelous experience. It was a wonderful display of so many of his greatest treasures in life: the woman he loves was present, his creative thought power was operating, and his resolve to meet and talk with Jesus was a part of the dream. The overall tone and spirit of the dream were delightfully playful.

George told me that he has had about a dozen lucid dreams over the past few years. After having worked with his dreams for many years, he has now developed a tendency to write down only his lucid dreams because they are of a much higher quality than his ordinary dreams. At this point, he can easily discern the difference in beauty and pleasure between the two types of dreams, and he naturally gravitates toward those that bring him the greatest pleasure and joy. He said that for him dreamwork has become a lot like eating out at a smorgasbord. Whenever he goes to a smorgasbord, he always passes up the display of breads because he can eat bread at home anytime. But when standing before all that exotic and enticing food, he picks out only the most savory delicacies and enjoys them tremendously. The lucid dream has become, for him, something like the nectar of the gods, the divine food, that the human soul naturally seeks and deeply craves.

George reported that he has frequently had the experience of sitting down to meditate in a lucid dream. This was not surprising to me, because meditation has been such an important part of his daily life for almost fifteen years. This combination of spiritual disciplines, he said, has been extremely valuable to him in the long

247

run. In his experience, these two disciplines naturally flow into one another, expanding and nourishing each other. His meditations have enriched his lucid dreams and his lucid dreaming has definitely enriched his meditations in the waking state. In essence, George assured me that the prime benefit of lucid dreaming, for him, has been the deepening of the quality and richness of many of his meditation sessions. As an example, George related another short lucid dream, one that occurred at about the same time as the previous dream.

> I have been dreaming for a while and then I become aware that I am dreaming. I remember that I want to see Jesus and so I sit down and begin to meditate. I concentrate on the top of my head, at the crown chakra. Suddenly, instead of Jesus coming to me, it now feels as if I am being taken to Him. I have the feeling of incredible speed, as if I am being shot out of the universe at such a remarkable rate that it is impossible to describe. As I contining shooting through the galaxy, this sensation of speed becomes so great that I awaken and come out of the dream.

When George awoke from this dream it was about 4:00 a.m. As he lay in his bed, he felt the exact same sensation of energy in his physical body as he had felt in the lucid dream. He was amazed to discover this type of "energy transfer" from his dream body to his physical body. (Patricia Garfield has reported similar experiences in *Pathway to Ecstasy,* and I have had numerous similar experiences of my own.) This type of energy transfer can occur from normal dreaming as well, but when it orginates from a lucid dream it is often quite intense. George reported further that immediately after this dream, he conducted a brief experiment with these sensations as he lay motionless in his bed. He closed his eyes and felt again the original sensation of shooting through the universe at the same incredible rate of speed. Then he opened his eyes a few moments later, and felt as if the whole universe were bearing down on him with incredible speed. For several minutes he experimented with these sensations, alternating back and forth between opening and closing his eyes, while lying physically still. Each time he alternated between opening and closing his eyes, he felt the direction and movement of the energy change. The energy itself felt like a large, cone-shaped field over his head, falling directly onto his head like a giant waterfall. He was in awe of this whole experience, which only lasted about three to four minutes. He said that he is still not sure what to make of this experience, although he assured me that it was quite remarkable and memorable.

George said that he has learned a number of lessons from these two lucid dreams. One lesson was that there are times when it is morally and spiritually appropriate to use force. In the lucid state, he felt no guilt or hesitation about kicking his adversary in the groin, because he knew that no harm would come from it. In the waking state afterwards, however, he often felt guilty about kicking that man in the dream. Through reflection, George came to resolve this dilemma by realizing that the lucid dream state is often something like the state of grace, as spoken of in traditional Christian terms. When a person is in the lucid state, he or she possesses such an extraordinary degree of clarity (love combined with the absence of fear) that moral dilemmas and problems are often quickly resolved. They are resolved with an extraordinary sense of inner peace and harmony that is difficult to attain in the normal, waking state. However, upon returning to the waking state, it sometimes feels as if the dreamer has "fallen from grace," suffering the usual mental strains of guilt, fear, confusion, anxiety, etc., that are a part of everyday life. In this fallen state, the dreamer can usually still remember that former state of grace, the lucid state, and although he or she can remember so much of what it was like, the dreamer unfortunately cannot always return to that state by an act of the will or conscious choice.

These concepts led George to another important lesson gleaned from his own experiments with lucid dreaming and meditation. A spiritual master, George has come to believe, is someone who can attune his consciousness to any level or frequency that exists on the entire spectrum of consciousness, and can do it at will any time he wishes or needs to do so. A spiritual master flows with the living Tao (the Holy Spirit, in Christian terms) at all times. He can be aggressive when it is appropriate; he can be gentle and peaceful when it is appropriate. He is always in tune with the cosmos, and takes his cue instantly from the movements and energies of the situation in which he exists at the moment because he senses how the universe, and God through the universe, is flowing all around him, every moment. Freedom, love, correct attunement and flexibility, then, are the essence of a spiritual master's consciousness. A spiritual novice, on the other hand, has only begun to experiment with this spectrum of consciousness and is still quite limited with his range, spontaneity and flexibility. A novice is likely to be imprisoned by the rules of his spiritual tradition. A master will respect the rules of his tradition, but also knows exactly when to break them. I listened with a lot of appreciation as George brought together these concepts that have become so vital to his spiritual evolution.

In exploring this issue, George shared some new parts of his own life journey with me. He said that he used to be an absolute fundamentalist about pacifism and nonviolence, believing that a moral person is one who always turns the other cheek. At some point in his life, he realized that this view was actually quite rigid, just as rigid as those who hold the opposite view of "shoot first and ask questions later." Now through his meditation practice and lucid dreamwork, he has become committed to living each moment in its own special uniqueness, staying open-minded to all its possibilities,

250

and asking God, "What is appropriate behavior (or the Will of God) in *this particular circumstance?*" He believes now that a full and genuine spiritual life can only flow out of attunement to the voice of God as manifested in the Tao of each moment. In his lucid dream, George somehow experienced a moment of liberation from social convention and moved in complete unison with his own aggressive energy and with the full realization that in a lucid dream no harm could come from such a choice.

George seems fully committed, perhaps captivated and enchanted, toward further explorations of his lucid dreams. I wished him well as our interview ended, and I know that I will stay in contact with his journey. I cannot wait to discover what will happen when he eventually does encounter Jesus in the lucid state and finally has that long-awaited dialogue.

Still another interesting area of lucid dreaming and one that is full of psychospiritual possibilities, is the sexual lucid dream. Some lucid dreamers seem to report a relatively high percentage of explicit sexual dreams, whereas others report very few or none at all. An interesting example of a therapeutic, sexual, lucid dream came from a woman who was a member of one of my dream therapy groups. At the time that this dream occurred, Sharon,* a married woman, was in her early forties. She frequently had lucid dreams that were very rewarding, including numerous sexual dreams and flying dreams. At the time this dream occurred, she was experiencing some sexual frustration in her marriage, due in part to a physical problem on her husband's part and her own tendency to express her frustration through an attitude of *subtle* demanding.

One day, in the group session, the issue of sexuality was raised by another woman in the group, Marcia,* who was also having with her husband the same type of problem as Sharon had described earlier. I supported

* A fictitious name.

Marcia through some intense Gestalt therapy work, in which she used guided fantasy and dialogue to identify the issues and feelings on both sides of her conflict. In the process it emerged that Marcia and her husband Rob* were both very demanding about Rob's ability to maintain his erection during intercourse. Over the years they had established a pattern in their lovemaking in which Marcia's demanding attitude was compounded by Rob's own self-demanding attitude, which usually turned their sexual contacts into high pressure situations, often ending in impotence for Rob and frustration for Marcia. Eventually, over a period of time, they had become locked into this pattern and often simply avoided sexual contacts with each other altogether rather than risk the likelihood of impotence, which would be experienced as another round of "failure" on his part and "feeling rejected" on her part. In this particular piece of Gestalt work Marcia made a major breakthrough for herself, in allowing herself to see very clearly the negative impact of her demanding attitude. She released a lot of tears and sadness about it, and then created an affirmation of transformation** for herself. In this case Marcia's affirmation turned out to be: "I can be satisfied even if you don't have an erection." She reinforced this affirmation in the group session and agreed to take it home with her and say it over and over to herself during the week to solidify this new realization from within. Marcia had been so open and creatively vulnerable that day that everyone in the group felt deeply moved by her work and highly appreciative toward her.

Out of this context, an important lucid dream came to Sharon, arriving on the night immediately after that particular group therapy session.

---

* A fictitious name.

** The "affirmation of transformation" is a specific psychotherapeutic tool. It is usually a short positive statement, tailored specifically to the needs of the client, which emerges from a given therapy session. Idealy, it sums up succinctly the desirable, a positive change sought by the client.

THE GIANT BLUE PENIS

I see an image of a world map. The continents are painted in color on a glass-like surface with a light in back of the glass. The whole map is translucent, in an oblong shape. I realize that it is not a current world map; some of the land masses seem different or somewhat distorted. I gaze steadily at this image, coming very close as I examine it carefully. Now I realize I am dreaming.

Suddenly I am feeling extremely sexual. I know that I have to seek sexual satisfaction before I can do anything else. I am fully lucid, floating on my back in an amorphous sky. Then a great blue penis appears! It is about three feet long and one foot thick. It comes "out of the blue" with no body attached to it. I take it inside of me and shortly come to a tremendous orgasm. I experience a tremendous rush and flood of feelings going through my whole body. The power of all the feelings that surge through me is intensified beyond real life and beyond all belief. I realize I have never had such a powerful orgasm before. The immensity of the sexual feelings are so great that I awaken. After a while I fall back asleep hoping to re-enter the dream but am unable to do so.

When Sharon related this powerful lucid dream to us at the next group session, she clearly impressed upon us how astonished and amazed she felt over the intensity of the sexual experience. It was, without any doubt in her mind, the most powerful sexual experience she had ever had anywhere, before or since, in any other dream or in any waking life experience. Sharon frequently enjoys deep and powerful orgasms in her lucid dreams, but this experience with the giant blue penis elevated her into a realm she had never known before. As the group members responded to the dream, we began to see that it was not only a special gift to Sharon but also a perfect sequel to the Gestalt therapy work done by Marcia the week before. This dream was a double gift! In the dream, Sharon demonstrated the qualities that both she and Marcia needed to cultivate in themselves, relaxation and letting go, symbolized by Sharon

253

floating on her back in the amorphous sky. The dream spoke of the great potential for pleasure and satisfaction that comes from the state of deep, trustful relaxation and surrender.

This dream also demonstrated an interesting and exciting facet of the unconscious mind, working within the context of group therapy. In this dream, Sharon's unconscious picked up on the work begun by Marcia in the group and carried it to a completion for Sharon. Apparently, Marcia's Gestalt work had struck a deep respondent chord in /Sharon, since their internal dynamics and relationship dynamics with their respective husbands were so much alike. It was intriguing and rewarding to observe this type of gift exchange or energy exchange in a group where the level of intimacy and trust were deeply established. Marcia's work was a gift to Sharon, and Sharon's dream was the return gift to Marcia. This lucid dream taught them both to relax, trust and surrender. By letting go, not just in dreams but in waking life too, experiences heretofore unbelievable to them had become possible.

When I later interviewed Sharon about her dreamlife, she assured me that the rewards of her nocturnal journeys have been immense. In particular, she enjoys lucid dreams because they allow her to experience the nonjudgmental state of mind very clearly, creating what feels to her like a "full objectivity of consciousness." This objectivity is not a dull or inanimate state of mind. On the contrary, it is fully vibrant and very pleasurable. Her lucid dreams have given her experiences that she has never had in any other state of mind. For example, one of her greatest dream gifts is the feeling of *utter fearlessness* which she often experiences in the lucid state. By most external criteria, Sharon would appear to many people as a normal middle-class lady, leading a rather calm and satisfying life and not having much to fear in her life anyway. Yet, through her lucid dream adventures, she claims it is particularly rewarding for her to know what *utter fearlessness* feels like. In the lucid state, it is easy for her to have this experience because, when lucid, she sees that all the parts of her dream are in some way different parts of herself. When lucid, it is easy for her to be both the doer and the observer of her actions at the same time. These qualities, in addition to the gift of deep sexual fulfillment, are but a few of the benefits that have made the lucid dream such an important part of her life. "Above all," she says, "the lucid dream is a gift from God. When it comes, don't ask too many questions. Just accept it."

As a final illustration, I would like to relate a lucid dream reported by a student named Julia.* Julia is a happily married woman in her mid-fifties, has three adult children, and has repeatedly described her life as "blessed" and "very fortunate." She grew up in a socially prominent and prosperous family in Atlanta and had a very happy childhood, feeling close to her family and emotionally secure with the many signs of love and support that she received from them. She has had excellent and often vivid recall of her dreams throughout her life, including lucid dreams from early childhood. During the lucid dream class and shortly thereafter she received a number of uplifting and inspiring lucid dreams. One of them went as follows:

A LUCID DREAM
September 21, 1982

It is a warm, rainy night in Monroe, Georgia. I am standing alone on an asphalt road in front of my grandparents' house beneath the glow of a streetlight. I am barefoot and feeling the warm, wet street and the mist on my face. I notice the way the needles of the pine trees have drops of water on them that sparkle like diamonds in the halo of light. There is no one else around. Now my brother George comes driving by in an open convertible. He looks *very happy*. He passes by. I wave, and he turns the car around and drives by again. I

---

* Prior references to Julia are made in this book in chapters five and seven.

see that on the front of the car where the hood ornament should be is a life-sized bust of Daddy. Now George turns the car around and drives by again. Again I laugh and wave. This time he drives out of sight and I am alone. For the pure joy of it, I start splashing through the puddles on the street and all at once I say—*aloud, "I'm dreaming."* I have a *rush* of excitment and say to myself that, this being the case, I can do *anything.* I decide to fly and before that thought is complete I am floating up just over the tops of the pines. I look up and see the dark night sky with MILLIONS of stars shining. I think, "I can be among the stars," and in an instant I feel myself transported into the heavens with the millions of stars all around me. I feel a little afraid and I *hear,* as well as sense the words: "God will take care of me." I wake up and know something important just happened to me. I want to keep this awareness and the certainty I feel from this dream forever.

Immediately after recording this dream in her journal, Julia wrote as an initial commentary: "The writing of the dream is very pale compared to the way it felt." This is a common response from lucid dreamers when they feel the inadequacy of words to convey the beauty and power of a dream. When I interviewed her, two years after she had the dream, she said she could still remember it quite vividly and was still moved by its freshness, inspiration and emotional impact. In her own words she said, "This is a dream of *ultimate comfort.* I always felt that Daddy would take care of me as a child. I always felt very secure with him. In fact, I felt almost *invincible* because of his repeated reassurances that he would not let anyone harm me. And, as you *think* you are, then, to some extent, you *are.*"

Julia is a most fortunate person in that she felt she had received unconditional love as a child from both of her parents. This dream, which was filled with the familiar sights, sounds and sensations of her native Georgia, portrayed her father in the life-sized bust on the front hood of the convertible driven by her brother George. Though her father has been deceased for some years, in a very real way he lives on and is still very much alive in Julia's mind and spirit. According to

Julia, his loving influence continues to occupy a most prominent place in her awareness and in her brother's awareness, suggested by the fact that, in the dream, her father's bust stood in a prominent place on the front hood of the convertible. That unconditional love and total reassurance that she felt from her father as a child have never been altered or even diminished with the passage of the years. Once given and once deeply felt by Julia as a child it has only been solidified and strengthened through time. This lucid dream serves as a good reminder to parents of the importance of conveying to one's children that they are deeply loved. Once such a conviction is established in the mind of a child, it will last for a lifetime and continue to pay emotional dividends long after the parents are gone. Julia stated in our interview that, as a child, she knew that her parent's love was not only unconditional, it was also fully abundant. There was plenty to go around and it would never run out, even though there were three other children in her family.

Her older brother George, who appeared in this dream, has always played a very special and even unique role in Julia's life. She told me that over the years they have come to regard each other as "psychic twins," having enjoyed and maintained a special bond of closeness that is very rare between brother and sister. Even today, they live within a twenty-minute drive from each other's homes, they work together professionally and usually speak to each other on the telephone every day. They are deeply bonded to one another and always have been, for well over fifty years. It was perfectly natural, she said, for her brother George to appear in the dream, very happy and driving the open convertible. In their teenage years, George had a similar convertible and it was a fantastic plaything for them and all their friends. Drag-racing and driving all over town and into the countryside were among their favorite pastimes. For her, the convertible symbolized fun, play, excitement, change, flexibility and openness, all positive values that have been an important part of her life since childhood. Her parents had strongly instilled in her the importance of these values and, in particular, the value of knowing how to play. Her brother George accepted this philosophy as thoroughly as she. A philosophy of play has been steeped into his soul as deeply as into her own. Though they both see themselves as highly responsible individuals as adults Julia and George have never forgotten how to play through the years and have always made time for play no matter what. They have often consciously reminded each other of the importance of play and reinforced that value in each other, especially in times of stress, when life was pressing heavily upon one or the other.

Julia, who has had vivid dreams all her life, summed up this lucid dream when she said in our interview: "This *is* my life." This dream simply and clearly expressed to her the way she is and the way her life has always been. It gave her an inspirational cross-section of herself, a succinct summation of her own history, her own way of being in this world. Her life has always been "among the stars." In childhood, she was raised in a socially prominent family, where the governor of Georgia and numerous other leading public figures were frequent guests for dinner in her parents' home. In her youth, she was fortunate enough to attend the best private schools available and was an outstanding student in all respects. When the civil rights movement began in the Deep South in the 1950s, she and many of her closest relatives and friends marched in numerous demonstrations to express their convictions publicly, putting their bodies on the line. Today, she is deeply involved in the human potential movement in California and counts many of the leaders and creative innovators in this field among her close, personal friends. She will probably always be among the stars, placed there by what seems to be the creative force of her own destiny and the nurturant love of her close family ties throughout her life. Not that her life has been devoid of personal suffering. Julia has had her share of personal pain and grief as most people have. But her basic security and unconditional love for herself have equipped her to meet such challenges firmly and transform them into opportunities for personal expansion.

258

Certain lucid dreams have the power and intensity to sum up a person's life in a way that is unforgettable. For Julia, I think, this is a dream of that caliber. I suspect she will remember it for the rest of her life. If this were my lucid dream, it is precisely the kind that I would like to remember on my deathbed as I was preparing to depart from this world. Such a dream is a wonderful gift with many levels and dimensions, because it presents to the dreamer the incomparable beauty and uniqueness of his or her own journey and says: *"Look! This* is who you are. This *is* your life."

In conclusion, the longer I reflect upon the lucid dream, both as a psychospiritual phenomenon and as a vast inner realm in its own right, the more I return to the word *transcendence.* I acknowledge that I still have a great deal to learn about transcendence. Most of us do. Because the lucid dream takes us so far beyond our ordinary, mental limitations and so far beyond the dimensions of reality as we commonly know it, I believe that it has a great deal to teach us about transcendence. In my present view, this is its chief and overriding value. This is what makes it a frontier of human consciousness, for within the lucid dream state there is a very wide range of human possibilities for transcendence. Some of these possibilities are more evident and some are very subtle. All, I believe, are important. For without the actual experience of transcendence, mankind eventually becomes hopelessly earthbound, mired in our everyday struggles for survival, practically heedless of that precious spark of divinity that each one carries in his or her own breast. Without the actual experience of transcendence, it becomes so easy for us to forget what matters most: remembering God, discovering the higher self, and caring intelligently about every person we meet who also is on a journey toward full realization.

I also strongly believe that for any human civilization to achieve its fullest vitality, it is mandatory that the *inner life* of its people, both psychological and spiritual, be advanced to the highest degree possible. In order for this fullest advancement to occur, a society must guard and exercise its spiritual and intellectual freedom with a total passion. This implies that it must also encourage and nurture in practical ways each person's own individual experiences of transcendence. Many nation-states on our planet today have a political and social climate in which this highest degree of psychospiritual advancement can be nourished. Many still do not. Nevertheless, I firmly believe that the cultivation of the individual experience of transcendence is still of the utmost psychological and spiritual significance, for without one's own actual experiences of transcendence, each individual person becomes totally dependent on the claims of others, such as charismatic religious leaders, prophets, gurus or inspiring teachers, listening to their dreams, gleaning something from their visions, hoping to ignite oneself by borrowing from their spark or aliveness. Therefore, I steadily find myself becoming more convinced that transcendence and the direct personal experience of the Light are both the basic right as well as the basic inherent potential of every spiritual pilgrim.

To be a human person and to be living a human life is to be embarked on a temporary journey, which we all somehow sense is aimed at some inevitable and higher purpose. In this spirit, therefore, I offer this book as a way of encouraging others to see for themselves, through the lens of the lucid dream, the beauty of creation and the grandeur of our own humanity as a most vital part of that creation. There are a few dangers, to be sure, along this particular path. These I have described as candidly as I can in this text, based on my own personal experience. For me, the rewards have far outweighed the personal risks.

To those of my readers who have appreciated this book, I express my own appreciation and gratitude in return. For those of you who remain skeptical or uncertain about lucid dreaming, I welcome your skepticism and only ask that you refrain from drawing any permanent or final conclusions about a field of human endeavor that is still in its infancy. Perhaps you may even consider rereading this material at some future date as additional knowledge and research on lucid dreaming become available. Time can also sometimes work wonders on one's perspective, and it is my fond desire that this volume be of genuine assistance to those who wish to explore this new frontier of the human spirit today, tomorrow and tomorrow's morrow. To those of you who are ready to begin or deepen your own journey in the exploration of the lucid dream state, I offer my very best wishes, my strongest support and my genuine admiration.

PART III

Epilogue

THE LAND OF THE MIDNIGHT SUN

There is a land within the dream
Where the sun flows on like a bubbling stream
Of Light, that never ends. It bends
Its rolling rays of sparklets and circlets
Its dazzling daze of bubblets and droplets
That pass in a mindful, mindful flow.
They fall in radiant rivulets, to be
On the outstretched arms of a stalwart tree,
Eager to embrace these drops of golden dew
And hold them all, yes, not a few
In the hollow of its hungry heart . . . to glow
Within, forever . . .

This is the land of the Midnight Sun
Its light, so bright, has never begun
To strike the slightest likeness
To the normal noonday brightness.
This is a land beyond compare,
Where spangling visions sparkle there
In the ether of the innersoul.

The music there with gentle strains
So sweet and pure it falls, it rains

Author's note:

   References made throughout this poem are to those images and
themes from my own lucid dreams that have inspired me the most
throughout my experiment.

Into the caverns of the human heart
And pours through the pores of a thirsty skin.
It pervades the All; it has no kin
Even to the loveliest, sweetest sound,
That springs from earthen joys, unbound.
This is sound celestial.
This is rhapsody so rapturous
It fills the soul's voice-well within
As if vast choirs before the throne of God
Were singing in the chambers of the heart,
Causing their winged whisperings
From within the inmost ear to start.

"Beautiful dreamer, wake unto me
Starlight and dewdrops are waiting for thee."
So literally true it is, my friend,
This land of the Midnight Sun can send
The sights and sounds of ecstasy
That sail on a sea of bliss
That swim in an ocean of sheerest sheen.
Its likeness has never been seen
Or heard in the everyday land of nod.
We are asleep! We are asleep! I've trod
By fortune, though invited all along,
Onto a panto-plain of silken song,
To feast on starfood.

Starlight and dewdrops . . . and ever so much
Bathed in light my innersoul and touched
Its place of peace. As a favored guest
In the bosom of the All did it rest
For a priceless, timeless moment,
From an eternity of wanderings.

So much, so much to tell and bend
Our frozen words to form half-penned
A vision of lights with you.
No need to wait, no time for tarrying,
The guardian of grace is carrying
Us all, so close, each night to stand
By the golden gateway to a luminous land.

I saw an eagle there with wings outstretched,
Full far above me floating.
The gleaming rays danced through the haze,
As the pure sun seeped through vibrant feathers,
And freed my eyes from lifelong tethers,
I saw how fair the light can be,
And in those rays I knew that we
Were brothers, twain, yet one within,
Upswift my spirit soared with him.

Circles of grapes and circles of lights
Carefully cast, kaleidoscope sights,
I saw such symmetry in motion . . .
They fired me . . . inspired me . . .
To grant *pure* imagery . . . devotion.

I saw what IS, I felt the ALL
Its thusness perfect, just in being;
No reasons, whys or wherefores needed
Just purest joy, from simple seeing.

The doors are cleansed in lucid dreaming
And a vista of vision now comes streaming
Upward through the spine,
With energy soft and subtly fine.
This surging sluice of cosmic juice
Came flowing all throughout
My body, with jingles and jangles
In my forehead, 'round and about
Across my chest both in and out,
So electric, these sparks and spangles,
Where a shower of stardust falls to meet
The strokings of a tiny angel's feet
Dancing upon the eye between the eyes,
And bidding it to open . . . wise.

And open it may to riches where
No earthly coffer could compare
Though fables mute through countless tellings run,
Superb over all is the Midnight Sun.

I found the Child! Aglow with Light

His eyes transcending day and night,
A soul of ages, with a face
That knows of total peace. A trace
Of Silence-Deep, all wordfull
Yet wordless just the same.
Such a radiant orb shone through Him
A thousand blazing suns renew Him
And radiate through His tender frame
Superlative became His name.

I sobbed and sobbed, I thrilled and throbbed
This wondermoment in the making,
My thoughts raced on, the whole trip long
I saw in sum. With trembling dire and shaking,
I approached my journey's end to find—
How endings in the Magi's mind
Are beginnings of another kind.

The wheel of life has spokes of light
And magi watch its subtle turnings;
In midnight light, the Child so bright,
With mother's telepathy so quiet
They filled my deepest yearnings.

My mind raced on, and on it raced
With speed, but led me nowhere.
In a bursting heart with thankful throbs
In full surrender on a sea of sobs
I found the courage of a somewhere.

There I stood and there I knelt
And watched all hesitations melt
As I gave my gift, of purest gold,
To a Light so pure, it gained a hold
Upon my heart and never did let go.
The Babe while basking in His glow
Was one with the purest light I know
And I longed to linger there and slow
My vision down, forever. From seeing,
Knowing, a tidal wave of being
Washed through my every cell, and quell

Its sweep I could-not, would-not
So suffused was I with one desire only
To bask as-one with the basking Babe
And remain forever in that light
Of quiet peace and simple sight.

My friend, in readiness are we
For Light that calls us to this spot?
For those who ask the Babe "Why me?"
His answer comes "Why not?"

In time I watched this vision fade
Until it dimmed before me;
Its imprint sealed upon me stayed,
A living signet to restore me.
And when, at last, its glow was spent,
With a conscious, lucid choice I went
Out . . . out from that marvelous dream
And returned to the more familiar stream,
(Oh God!) this everyday land of nod.

Blinking blindly I now wandered,
Bearing a burning glow I wondered
Deeply on this treasure find
As I turned it over in a raptured mind
A million times in a thousand days
THE LIGHT! THE BABE! THE LIGHT! THE RAYS!
I knew that I would treasure them . . .
Forever.

The lucid streams of the Midnight Sun
Through countless labyrinthine caverns run
A river-story bending;
Who loves this land, its light transcending
Worlds, shall know a thousand pearls,
And the gentle string of light that curls
Them all, each one, somehow, so whole,
Each dream, the timed unfolding of a soul.

Yet another day and another time
The Midnight Sun in a stalwart climb
Arose within, unleashed its rhyme

In symbols basic and sublime.
I saw a wildebeest in black
With a naked savage on its back
In thundering force came their attack
Upon me. Headlong they charged
And across some serenghetti barged
Against my solitary stand.
From a high plateau I took a stance
With a panoramic sweeping glance
Around me. Then a jolt of light
Flooded me full that lucid night,
At once I knew that I was dreaming,
And a flashing flood of light came streaming
Into every corner of my soul.
Of-a-sudden I felt completely whole
Without the slightest trace of fear,
And calmly beckoned those beasts come near
As perfect light and love were here,
Within me. Both arms bristling with power
I waited and watched that moment-hour.

Time stood still on that granite hill,
Where I lived for a moment, from moment to moment,
Each thudding and thumping of hooves did foment
With a perfect rhythm and poise, the noise
In flesh and ears. Beyond all fears
From the thumpety-thump of the animal's feet
An incessant cosmic drummer's beat
I heard. I stood and watched it all.
Each beat a Now, in sum, the Tao,
I waited to watch it flow and flower,
So easily can our beasts be thrown
When the rodeo sage within is known.

Headlong they charged till the beasts as one
In the very last step of their mindless run
Ground to a halt at my feet.
Steady and straight six eyes did meet
As we looked and looked and looked.
The beast's great eyes burned bleary and red,

All but buried in its shaggy head
While the savage just sat surmising.
A cloud of dust came gently rising
From the restless pawing of hooves, a token
Of a tenuous, tentative truce, unspoken.

No need to throw them to the ground,
A vigorous rule of soul refound:
From the power of full intention
Comes a path beyond contention,
Its way is simple, and profound.

Still another time and another place
The Midnight Sun turned its face
Upon me with a swirling might
And swept me away in a flood of light
And mingled the messages of night
With mystic misconceptions.

I wrestled with two serpents there
Two giants on the brown earth bare
And barren; face down I lay
Never to forget the day
And night on which the match took place.
Two sets of glowing eyes, above my face
Each hovering, held me in its coil.
They gripped me on the naked soil
As I sensed some masterplan designed,
And after thrashing I resigned
To trust them totally. Light green
Luminescence, wordless in its being
Seeping from those serpents' eyes;
I trust them now, so deep, so wise
Inviting my surrender

Warm blooded were they both, I found,
And much to my surprise, unbound
Inside, I turned from fear to love them;
In mystery, a full embrace
They gave to me and I to them
Each luminescent eye a gem

Of light, relentless on its beam
So ultra strange all this did seem
For this was not an ordinary dream.

With a sudden jolt I came awake
And felt my singing body shake,
And wondered if I would lose my mind.
And beyond my years I came to find
Those rumbling ruminations ending,
Four super-neutral eyes befriending
Me to depths not touched before.
In yielding full before that morn
A spark of inner light was born
And grew, until the day I *knew*—
They! They! brought the serpent power through.

The treasured rays of the Midnight Sun
Through countless caverns on will run
A river-story unending . . .
The stream flows on, and on and on
Till this river of rainlight floods the dawn,
And opens the day with a sated burst
Enough to slake that hunger-thirst,
Which grows within our yearning.

Shall I call it "Luminescence"?
Those ethereal droplets that sparkle so—
So fine and rare?
Finer than the finest mist
That kissed
The greenest leaves of grass.
Still more! More cosmic sparklets
That shimmer and burst into a . . .
Into a million spangles.

Oh yes, I turn aside and churn
And yes, I yearn inside and burn
And yes, for the light, I shall return
To the land of the Midnight Sun.

Life calls to Light, a beacon gleaming,
To live one day, beyond all seeming

To flow down the river of onward dreaming
And sail with the sun, to our sea of streaming
.....LIGHT.....

And yes, for the Light, I shall return
To the land of the Midnight Sun.

Bibliography

Bach, Richard. *Illusions: The Adventures of a Reluctant Messiah.* New York: Delacorte Press/Eleanor Friede, 1977.

Bach, Richard. *The Bridge Across Forever.* New York: William Morrow Co., 1984.

Bettleheim, Bruno. *The Uses of Enchantment: The Meaning and Importance of Fairy Tales.* New York: Vintage Books, 1977.

Blake, William. "Auguries of Innocence." *The Portable Blake,* edited by Alfred Kazin. New York: The Viking Press, Inc., 1946.

Blake, William. "The Marriage of Heaven and Hell." *The Portable Blake,* edited by Alfred Kazin. New York: The Viking Press, Inc., 1946.

Capra, Fritjof. *The Tao of Physics.* 2nd ed. Boulder, Colo.: Shambhala Publications, Inc., 1975.

Castaneda, Carlos. *Journey to Ixtlan: The Lessons of Don Juan.* New York: Simon and Schuster, 1973.

Castaneda, Carlos. *The Teachings of Don Juan: A Yaqui Way of Knowledge.* New York: Ballantine Books, Inc., 1969.

Cather, Willa. *Death Comes for the Archbishop.* New York: Alfred A. Knopf, Inc., 1927.

Coffey, Reginald, O.P. *The Man from Rocca Sicca.* Milwaukee: Bruce Publishing Co., 1944.

Evans-Wentz, W.Y. *Tibetan Yoga and Secret Doctrines.* London: Oxford University Press, 1935.

Drucker, Peter. *The Practice of Management.* New York: Harper & Row, 1954.

Eliot, T.S. *Four Quartets.* London: Faber & Faber, 1959.

Faraday, Ann. *Dream Power.* New York: Berkley Medallion Books, 1973.

Faraday, Ann. *The Dream Game.* New York: Harper & Row, 1976.

Freud, Sigmund. *The Interpretation of Dreams.* New York: Avon Books, 1965.

Garfield, Patricia. *Creative Dreaming.* New York: Ballantine Books, published by arrangement with Simon & Schuster, 1976.

Garfield, Patricia. *Pathway to Ecstasy: The Way of the Dream Mandala.* New York: Holt, Rinehart and Winston, 1979.

Garfield, Patricia. *Your Child's Dreams.* New York: Ballantine Books, 1984.

Goldbrunner, Josef, S.J. *Holiness Is Wholeness.* Notre Dame, Indiana: University of Notre Dame Press, 1965.

Green, Celia. *Lucid Dreaming.* London: Hamish Hamilton, 1968.

Grimm, The Brothers. *Grimm's Fairy Tales.* New York: Avenel Books, 1981.

The Holy Bible, Revised Standard Version. New York: Thomas Nelson and Sons, 1946-1952.

Jung, Carl G. *Man and His Symbols.* London: Aldus Books Ltd., 1964.

Jung, C.G. *Memories, Dreams, Reflections,* edited by Aniela Jaffe. New York: Random House, 1961.

Krishna, Gopi. *Kundalini: The Evolutionary Energy in Man.* Boulder, Colo.: Shambhala Publications, Inc., 1971.

LaBerge, Stephen. *Lucid Dreaming.* Los Angeles: J.P. Tarcher & Co., 1985.

Luthman, Shirley. *Collection 1979.* San Rafael, Calif.: Mehetabel & Co., 1979.

Perls, Frederick S. *Gestalt Therapy Verbatim,* edited by John O. Stevens. Lafayette, Calif.: Real People Press, 1969.

Perls, Frederick S. *The Gestalt Approach: Eyewitness to Therapy.* Palo Alto, California: Science and Behavior Books, 1973.

Sanella, Lee. *Kundalini—Psychosis or Transcendence?* San Francisco: H.S. Dakin Co., 1976.

Sparrow, Gregory Scott. *Lucid Dreaming: Dawning of the Clear Light.* Virginia Beach: A.R.E. Press, 1976.

Suzuki, Shunryu. *Zen Mind, Beginner's Mind.* New York: John Weatherhill, Inc., 1970.

Tart, Charles. *Altered States of Consciousness,* edited by Charles T. Tart. Garden City, N.Y.: Anchor Books, Doubleday & Co., Inc., 1969.

Tholey, P., and Krist, H. *Klarträumen.* Frankfurt/M: Fachbuchhandlung für Psychologie, in press.

Wilbur, Ken. *The Spectrum of Consciousness.* Wheaton, Illinois: Theosophical Publication House, 1977.

Yogananda, Paramahansa. *The Autobiography of a Yogi.* Los Angeles: Self-Realization Fellowship, 1971.

THE WORK OF EDGAR CAYCE TODAY

The Association for Research and Enlightenment, Inc. (A.R.E.®), is a membership organization founded by Edgar Cayce in 1931.

- 14,256 Cayce readings, the largest body of documented psychic information anywhere in the world, are housed in the A.R.E. Library/Conference Center in Virginia Beach, Virginia. These readings have been indexed under 10,000 different topics and are open to the public.

- An attractive package of membership benefits is available for modest yearly dues. Benefits include: a bi-monthly magazine; lessons for home study; a lending library through the mail, which offers collections of the actual readings as well as one of the world's best parapsychological book collections, names of doctors or health care professionals in your area.

- As an organization on the leading edge in exciting new fields, A.R.E. presents a selection of publications and seminars by prominent authorities in the fields covered, exploring such areas as parapsychology, dreams, meditation, world religions, holistic health, reincarnation and life after death, and personal growth.

- The unique path to personal growth outlined in the Cayce readings is developed through a worldwide program of study groups. These informal groups meet weekly in private homes.

- A.R.E. maintains a visitors' center where a bookstore, exhibits, classes, a movie, and audiovisual presentations introduce inquirers to concepts from the Cayce readings.

- A.R.E. conducts research into the helpfulness of both the medical and nonmedical readings, often giving members the opportunity to participate in the studies.

For more information and a color brochure, write or phone:

A.R.E., Dept. C., P.O. Box 595
Virginia Beach, VA 23451, (804) 428-3588